Doing CHAT in the Wild

Practice of Research Method

Series Editor

Wolff-Michael Roth (*University of Victoria, Canada*)

VOLUME 7

The titles published in this series are listed at *brill.com/prmd*

Doing CHAT in the Wild

From-the-Field Challenges of a Non-Dualist Methodology

Edited by

Edited by Patricia Dionne and Alfredo Jornet

BRILL

LEIDEN | BOSTON

Cover illustration: Photograph by Alfredo Jornet

All chapters in this book have undergone peer review.

Library of Congress Cataloging-in-Publication Data

Names: Dionne, Patricia, editor. | Jornet, Alfredo, editor.
Title: Doing CHAT in the wild : from-the-field challenges of a non-dualist methodology / edited by Patricia Dionne and Alfredo Jornet.
Description: Leiden ; Boston : Brill, 2023. | Series: Practice of research method, 2542-8853 ; volume 7 | Includes bibliographical references.
Identifiers: LCCN 2023015689 (print) | LCCN 2023015690 (ebook) | ISBN 9789004548657 (paperback) | ISBN 9789004388758 (hardback) | ISBN 9789004548664 (ebook)
Subjects: LCSH: Culture--Research--Methodology. | Sociology--Methodology.
Classification: LCC HM623 .D65 2023 (print) | LCC HM623 (ebook) | DDC 306.072/1--dc23/eng/20230414
LC record available at https://lccn.loc.gov/2023015689
LC ebook record available at https://lccn.loc.gov/2023015690

Typeface for the Latin, Greek, and Cyrillic scripts: "Brill". See and download: brill.com/brill-typeface.

ISSN 2542-8853
ISBN 978-90-04-54865-7 (paperback)
ISBN 978-90-04-38875-8 (hardback)
ISBN 978-90-04-54866-4 (e-book)

Copyright 2023 by Koninklijke Brill NV, Leiden, The Netherlands.
Koninklijke Brill NV incorporates the imprints Brill, Brill Nijhoff, Brill Hotei, Brill Schöningh, Brill Fink, Brill mentis, Vandenhoeck & Ruprecht, Böhlau, V&R unipress and Wageningen Academic.
All rights reserved. No part of this publication may be reproduced, translated, stored in a retrieval system, or transmitted in any form or by any means, electronic, mechanical, photocopying, recording or otherwise, without prior written permission from the publisher. Requests for re-use and/or translations must be addressed to Koninklijke Brill NV via brill.com or copyright.com.

This book is printed on acid-free paper and produced in a sustainable manner.

Printed by Printforce, United Kingdom

Contents

Preface   VII
List of Figures and Tables   IX
Notes on Contributors   XI

1   From-the-Field Challenges of a Non-Dualist Methodology   1
    Patricia Dionne and Alfredo Jornet

2   Knowledge Production as a Process of Making Mis/takes, at the Edge of Uncertainty: Research as an Activist, Risky, and Personal Quest   15
    Anna Stetsenko

3   Agency and Activity of Students from Non-Dominant Groups: Methodological and Ethical Issues   46
    Isabelle Rioux and Patricia Dionne

4   THE CONSTANT or Person-as-Place, and Research-Life: Sustaining Collaboration between University-Based and Field-Based Co-Researchers   71
    Beth Ferholt and Chris Schuck

5   Dialogical Epistemology as a Resource of CHAT Methodology in the Close Interaction of Science and Society   102
    Ritva Engeström

6   Dialectical Analysis of Learning and Development through Career Counselling Groups: The Challenge of Emotions   127
    Patricia Dionne

7   Decision-Forming Processes Leading to Peer Mentorship   150
    Sylvie Barma, Marie-Caroline Vincent and Samantha Voyer

8   Problematizing Questions about Development in Adulthood and Freedom in Developmental Intervention: The Relevance of the Concept of Zone of Proximal Development   193
    Frédéric Saussez and Philip Dupuis-Laflamme

9   Studying with/out an Object: Participant Observation in CHAT   221
    Alfredo Jornet

10 A Reflection on CHAT's History and Direction: Interview with Michael
    Cole   244
    Patricia Dionne and Alfredo Jornet

Preface

Since the publication of the first English translations of Vygotsky's works in the 60's and the 70's, Cultural-Historical Activity Theory (CHAT) has continuously increased in popularity, having today become a major framework informing fieldwork in a multitude of settings of human practice across the world. Although the precise intellectual foundations are continuously debated, few scholars and practitioners question the premise that a foundational trait of CHAT is its pursuit of a non-dualist ontology and epistemology. CHAT inquiry ought to investigate human matters of praxis in terms of the way singular persons, the members of practice, are *internally* connected to collective society, that is, to practice itself. This premise poses a major departure from all other classical frameworks and methods, where connections between persons and their societal 'contexts' tend to be treated as two different, self-contained factors or elements that need to be externally connected. This clash between CHAT and classical approaches has been and continues being discussed in the literature, with a number of volumes having been published that address the challenges and implications with respect to theory and methodology. But precisely where this clash takes place most notoriously is not in the abstract discussions in textbooks and journal articles but in the real, everyday work of scholars and practitioners who stand to the practical task of implementing CHAT in actual practice. This concrete lived world of methodological practice, however, remains largely invisible and under-documented in the research literature. What are the concrete challenges faced in the pursuit of a non-dualist approach in actual inquiry? What are the 'real life' stakes and implications involved in confronting deeply ingrained and long-standing beliefs and attitudes concerning the dualism between person and society, and between a 'subjective' soul and an objective "body"? How do these otherwise theoretical and abstract problems exist in and as practical matters of living inquiry and method? And what further lines of inquiry and method do they open?

The present volume addresses these questions by bringing together contributions that tackle otherwise abstract problems of methodology from the perspective of everyday experience. This volume, therefore, addresses methodology in its most fundamental sense, as *praxis* of method, where the emphasis is on the actual lived research praxis and the gap between that practice and the theoretical discussions that inform it. It contributes to an expanding body of literature with a set of first-hand accounts of what it takes, from a methodological point of view, to mobilize—to actually bring to life—a CHAT methodology, and which prospects and possibilities such mobilization does bring about. A central topic throughout the book is the problem of the relation of the self and society, which concerns the emergence and development of consciousness, both as a feature of the individuals who contribute to and develop through collective activity, and as a feature of that very collective activity. This implies not only the need to address research participation in terms of dynamic subject-environment units, but also the need to address our own self, as researchers, in terms of a collective process of consciousness development. The book thus brings up issues of subjective and social transformation as inherent part of research praxis, and of the role and mission of research in developing new hybrid forms of transformative practice. A further, related issue is the irreducible connection between the affective, the intellectual, and the material dimensions of consciousness, with particular attention to the role of affects in methodological praxis. The aim is to not only provide deep, concrete, and new insights on the target topics, but also to appeal to both more and less experienced researchers who, despite being well versed on CHAT theoretical issues, often struggle with the challenge of bringing CHAT to life in their research.

The volume is divided in two types of contributions: CHAT living praxis and epistemological problems of method. The chapters in epistemological problems of method review the premises of CHAT and provide historical context to the problems CHAT epistemology and methodology. The chapters in the CHAT living praxis—the most extensive part of the book—bring in the testimony, struggles, challenges and propositions that emerge actual research settings, including work, education and counseling. A concluding chapter, in the form of a commentary, rounds up the volume and provides a greater sense of coherence.

Figures and Tables

Figures

5.1 Activity system model (Engeström, 1987/2015, p. 63). 105
7.1 The geographic expansion of *Building site 7*, a 'collaborative action' research project (2010–2017). 155
7.2 *Building site 7* (2009–2017): an overview of the DWR and the iterative research interventions (qualitative and quantitative) between teacher professional development workshops (gray) and research activities (white). 165
7.3 The first professional training day begins in Simon's classroom in front of his peers. The main researcher participates the entire day and intervenes to support Simon. Jane and Francis are present to help with the hands-on activities happening in the afternoon (2011). 168
7.4 Two years later, a new workshop for Simon: the colorimeter. Jane and the leading researcher are also participating (2013). 168
7.5 Intervening in a science and technology classroom outside the Quebec region: Jane, Francis, the research leader and a ST teacher welcoming us in his classroom with students to learn how to optimize the use of and ipad when teaching electromagnetism. 169
7.6 Testing a prototype in robotics with a ST teacher who had attended the professional workshops in 2011. He eventually became a mentor himself and is preparing a workhop at AESTQ for peers. Philip (joins the team of *Building site 7* in 2017), Francis and the main researcher (2017). 169
7.7 Discursive manifestations of contradictions (Engeström & Sannino, 2011, p. 375). 172
7.8 Expressions of transformative agency over seven years for Simon. 178
7.9 Trend in the recurrence of discursive manifestations of contradictions. 178
7.10 Students working on their robot. 179
7.11 Expressions of transformative agency over seven years for Jane. 183
7.12 Trend in the recurrence of discursive manifestations of contradiction. 183
10.1 Model of the structure of learning activity, inspired by Engeström and Hedegaard (1985, p. 189). 246

Tables

7.1 Ethnographic data analyzed and used to prepare the sessions with teachers (2010–2017).   163
7.2 Professional development teacher training workshops: 170 peers from 15 school districts (2010–2017).   167
7.3 Speaking turns analyzed.   170
7.4 Discursive manifestations of contradictions: analytical criteria (Engeström & Sannino, 2011).   173

Notes on Contributors

Sylvie Barma
is Full Professor at Laval University, Faculty of Education and focuses on teachers who question and redefine their praxis. Her work focuses on CHAT theoretical and methodological approaches especially Expansive Learning and the Change Laboratory method. She has been a visiting professor at the University of Helsinki, University of Sao Paulo, University of Stockholm, University of Ioannina and University Côte-d'Azur. She is co-founder of the ISCAR STEAM international research group aiming to support professional development of educators and researchers and to enrich science education policies with a strong sociocultural perspective.

Patricia Dionne
is Professor in Career Counseling at Université de Sherbrooke. She adopts a CHAT perspective and clinic of activity methods to study the work of counselors and group intervention with adults in vulnerable or transitional situations. Immigrant and unemployed populations are central in her work. She focuses on emotions and group activity, the conceptual instruments used, and the learning and development that occur as a result of participation in these groups. In close collaboration with educational and work practices settings, she has contributed to the development and evaluation of group career counseling programs in emancipatory guidance aimed at promoting the empowerment of youth and adults.

Philip Dupuis-Laflamme
began a Master's degree in Education under the supervision of Frédéric Saussez at the Université de Sherbrooke after completing a Bachelor's degree with Honours in Psychology at Bishops University. His research project is a replication of the Sakharov-Vygotsky experiment on the development of conceptual thinking. He is interested in the influence of students' social environment on their intellectual and cognitive development, from the perspective of Vygotsky's cultural-historical psychology. Currently embracing his role as a father, Mr. Laflamme also works as a consultant and organizer for private companies and political organizations.

Ritva Engeström
is Adjunct Professor in Sociology of Education at the University of Helsinki, Finland. Through her academic carrier she has been active in the Center for

Research on Activity, Development, and Learning (CRADLE), which works on CHAT, particularly concerning social transformations. Her research is carried out mainly in developmental projects in multidisciplinary and inter-organizational arena in the fields of education, health care and social work. The research interests, explicated in her publications, center on the theoretical and methodological questions on activity, interaction, dialogue, interpretive methods, and collaboration between academic researchers and practitioners.

Beth Ferholt
is Associate Professor in the Department of Early Childhood and Art Education at Brooklyn College, City University of New York, and an affiliated faculty member in the Ph.D. Program in Urban Education at The Graduate Center, CUNY and Preschool Education Research Group at the School of Communication and Education, Jönköping University. She studies playworlds: a form of adult-child joint play and a way of being, in which play is combined with art or science. Her research focuses on play, imagination, creativity, perezhivanie, care, early childhood education and care, and methods for the study of all of these.

Alfredo Jornet
is a Ramon y Cajal researcher at the Institute of Educational Research, University of Girona. He has been visiting researcher at the University of Victoria, British Columbia (Canada) and full professor at the Department of Teacher Education and School Research, University of Oslo, Norway. His research focuses on cultural, technological, and affective aspects of learning across formal and informal settings, with an emphasis on creativity, pedagogical innovations, and social change. Methodologically, he has been using design-based and participatory ethnography methods in diverse contexts such as arts-based education and science learning in and out classrooms. Recently, he works on promoting and investigating open-schooling pedagogical innovations as a means to address the needs of school and societal transformation in the current context of environmental crisis and threat to democracy.

Isabelle Rioux
is a lecturer, research professional and doctoral candidate in Education at University of Sherbrooke. She worked for several years as a popular literacy trainer and as guidance counselor. Her research interests include formal and non-formal adult education and literacy of non-dominant populations. She is member of the Centre d'études et de recherches sur les transitions et l'apprentissage (CERTA).

NOTES ON CONTRIBUTORS   XIII

Frédéric Saussez
is Full Professor of Educational Foundations at the University of Sherbrooke. Intrigued by the enigma of human activity in the human and social sciences, he specializes in theories of activity. More specifically, the analysis of labor activity is his main research object. He places it within the Vygotskian framework of the historical psychology of cultural development. He is particularly interested in the process of meaning making and in the conditions for the development of the power to act in researchs/interventions based on the analysis by the participants of their own activity. He founded the Vygotsky/Activity Analysis Group dedicated to develop with professors and graduate students a critical reading of Vygotsky and a critical use of activity analysis in education. He is also interested in the epistemological and social foundations of educational research and in the transformation of the relationship between educational research, practice and policy in a context of new public governance.

Chris Schuck
is an MA student in the Applied Social Psychology program at University of Guelph, where he works with Jeff Yen. He is interested in the relationship between systematic inquiry and lived life, how the personal shows up in research and practice, and implications of these for our understanding of the "psychological" and the questions that we find compelling.

Anna Stetsenko
is Professor in Psychology and Urban Education at The City University of New York, The Graduate Center. Her research is situated at the intersection of human development, philosophy, and education, with a focus on agency and social transformation. Rooted in Marxism and Vygotsky's project, she advances this project to bring out its political-critical edge and activist agenda, while drawing connections to scholarship of resistance including topics of decolonizing knowledge. She has proposed the Transformative Activist Stance—an approach that captures ethically-politically non-neutral nature of knowing-being-doing, including science and research, culminating in a proposal for pedagogy of daring.

Marie-Caroline Vincent
has a bachelor's degree in education (mathematics) from Laval University that she completed in 2010, before starting her graduate studies in psychopedagogy. Her research interests included learning difficulties of mathematics in a context of problem solving in science. She completed her Master's degree in 2014 with Professor Sylvie Barma and continued working with her on multiple

projects until 2018, including being a course lecturer for science didactic and geometry didactic at Laval University.

Samantha Voyer
taught high school science and technology for a decade. With a particular interest in adolescent health, she completed a Master's degree at Laval University with Professor Barma focusing on the renewal of pedagogical practices when teachers wish to address a socially charged issue with their students. One of the concrete results was to see a shift in the power and status of the participants (principals, teachers from different fields and special educators) as they agreed to exchange, collaborate, and model promising interventions for the well-being of youth concerned with a sensitive health issue. Samantha has joined the Centre de transfert pour la réussite éducative du Québec as an innovation and knowledge transfer consultant.

CHAPTER 1

From-the-Field Challenges of a Non-Dualist Methodology

Patricia Dionne and Alfredo Jornet

Abstract

Cultural-Historical Activity Theory (CHAT) is today one of the most often cited sources in research concerned with the social and cultural dimensions of human thinking and praxis, whether this concerns cultural psychology studies, workplace studies, or studies in education. Although CHAT's ontological and epistemological premises are still highly debated—and indeed a wave of revisionist projects have emerged during the last years that question many of the often taken-for-granted propositions (e.g., Roth & Jornet, 2017; Yatniski & van der Veer, 2015)—the framework's aim to achieve a non-dualist, developmental methodology is hardly contested. Whereas these premises are well discussed in the theoretical literature, the practical implications of such a methodology are seldom the object of journal and textbook's publications (cf. Engeström & Sannino, 2010; Postholm, 2015). What are the concrete challenges faced in the pursuit of a non-dualist approach in actual inquiry? What are the 'real life' stakes and implications involved in confronting deeply ingrained and long-standing beliefs and attitudes concerning the dualism between person and society, and between a 'subjective' soul and an objective 'body'? How do these otherwise theoretical and abstract problems exist in and as practical matters of living inquiry and method? And what further lines of inquiry and method do they open? The chapters in this volume address these questions by tackling them from different perspectives and actual research settings. This introductory chapter presents the general problematic and provides an overview of each of the contributions and their connection.

Keywords

Cultural-Historical Activity Theory (CHAT) – non-dualist methodology – development – transformative praxis of method

∙∙∙

Since the publication of the first English translations of Vygotsky's works in the 60's and the 70's, Cultural-Historical Activity Theory (CHAT) has continuously increased in popularity, having today become a major framework informing fieldwork in a multitude of settings of human practice across the world. Although CHAT's ontological and epistemological premises are still highly debated—and indeed a wave of revisionist projects have emerged during the last years that question many of the often taken-for-granted propositions (e.g. Roth & Jornet, 2017; Yasnitsky & Van der Veer, 2014)—the framework's aim to achieve a non-dualist, developmental methodology is hardly contested.

The use of the CHAT term itself is contested. On the one hand—and this is the use that we make in this book—the term is used to refer to a broad set of approaches that have in common a lineage stemming from the Soviet psychology school started by Lev S. Vygotsky and his collaborators and students, including Aleksander R. Luria and Aleksei N. Leontiev. Vygotsky himself never settled on a particular name or acronym for his developing theory, although he considered the terms cultural, historical, and instrumental (Cole et al., 2005). Often, Vygotsky's theory is referred to as Cultural-Historical psychology, while Leontiev's later development, where the notion of activity became central, is called Activity Theory. According to Cole (this volume), CHAT was an acronym aimed to unify diverging but related schools stemming from the common premises of tool mediation and of activity as core concepts. But the notion of CHAT is also used to refer a very specific approach put forth by Yrjö Engeström in his seminal thesis of 1987, and that has been evolved in what is referred as various generations of activity theory (Engeström & Glăveanu, 2012).

Nomenclature issues aside, from a broad perspective, all CHAT inquiries have in common that they investigate human matters of praxis in terms of the way singular persons, the members of practice, are internally connected to collective society, that is, to activity itself. Vygotsky argues that systematic knowledge and concepts have a liberating power, which constitutes instruments of awareness and freedom, instruments of development of the capacity to act voluntarily in and on the world (Saussez, 2017). Those premises pose a major departure from all other classical frameworks and methods, where connections between persons and their societal 'contexts' are treated as two different, self-contained factors or elements that need to be externally connected. Thus, to mark this historical departure, Vygotsky's work has been termed as "organic psychology," "non-classical psychology" and even as "post-non-classical psychology" (Asmolov, 1998; Chernorizov et al., 2015; Vassilieva, 2010). This departure from classical approaches to the mind stems from the fact that,

> Unlike the natural sciences, where knowledge and procedures are "applied" to study and describe an object that exists independently of

them, in psychology such knowledge and procedures become constitutive with regards to the very laws that regulate the operation of its object—the living human being. ... The knowledge that is acquired in the process of a psychological inquiry becomes incorporated into the very object it studies. (Vassilieva, 2010, p. 144)

In developing a non-classical paradigm, "the overarching goal of Vygotsky ... is to find a unity of the objective and subjective without reductionism" (Robbins, 2003, p. 304). Thus, overcoming the classical dualism between objectivity and subjectivity is at the core of any Vygotskian approach. The dualism is problematic because it prevents from a truly materialist approach to psychological inquiry, which otherwise becomes trapped in idealist versus empiricist positions (Vygotsky, 1997).

This clash between CHAT and classical approaches has been and continues to be discussed in the literature (e.g. Dionne & Jornet, 2019; Kozulin et al., 2003; Stetsenko, 2016), with a number of volumes having been published that address the challenges and implications with respect to theory and methodology. But precisely where this clash takes place most notoriously, where it exists as a real and objective clash, is not within textbooks but in the real, everyday work of scholars and practitioners who stand to the practical task of implementing CHAT research in the field. This concrete, lived world of methodological practice however remains largely unaddressed in the literature. It is with regards to this field of research practice that we have titled this volume as research "in the wild." Textbooks often focus on methodological challenges belonging to specific approaches, but less often on the actual challenges researchers face when moving across very different research paradigms. What are the concrete challenges faced in the pursuit of a non-dualist approach in actual inquiry? What are the 'real life' stakes and implications involved in confronting deeply ingrained and long-standing beliefs and attitudes concerning the dualism between person and society, and between a 'subjective' soul and an objective 'body'? How do these otherwise theoretical and abstract problems exist in and as practical matters of living inquiry and method? How do we transmit to graduate students the "ropes of the job" to do enter in the CHAT's field. In our view, those questions need more attention, and dialogue across long-established researchers, emergent researchers, and graduate students, who have specific methodological and epistemological challenges in their relation to CHAT practice.

The present volume addresses these questions by bringing together contributions aimed at considering otherwise abstract problems of methodology, from the perspective of everyday experience. This volume, therefore, addresses methodology in its most fundamental sense, as *praxis* of method, where the emphasis is on the actual lived research praxis. It contributes to an expanding body of literature with a set of first-hand accounts of what it takes, from a methodological point of view, to mobilize, to actually bring to life, a CHAT epistemology, and which prospects and possibilities such mobilization can bring about. This specific angle on methodology can serve researchers and graduate students who have an interest in mobilizing the conceptual framework of the CHAT's perspective particularly in their relation to their actual inquiries and practices. To address this specific view of the method as praxis, we sought to bring together researchers with varying experience, and using a variety of methodological approaches (e.g. Change laboratory, Transformative Activist stance practice, Clinic of activity, Social Design Experiments) within a cultural-historical perspective, and who worked in different countries and various research fields. This introductory chapter presents the general problematic and provides an overview of each of the contributions and their connection.

A central topic throughout the book is the problem of the relation of the self and society, which concerns the emergence and development of consciousness, both as a feature of the individuals who contribute to and develop through collective activity, and as a feature of that very collective activity. This implies not only the need to address research participation in terms of dynamic subject-environment units, but also the need to address our own self, as researchers, in terms of a collective process of consciousness development. Here, the central category of *activity* is understood as genetically connected to human psyche, and it is assumed that "the activity of the human individual represents a system included in the system of relationships of society" (Leontiev, 1978). According to this author, activity implies an active and progressively conscious relation of the subject to the world and society.

In considering the question of the individual subject in cultural-historical theory—this *riddle of the self* (Mikhailov, 1980) that continues to challenge CHAT researchers—the notion of consciousness is central. In concluding his masterpiece, Myšlenie i reč [Thinking and Speech], Vygotsky identified the problem of consciousness as one "broader, more profound, and still more extraordinary than the problem of thinking" (Vygotsky, 1987, p. 285), a problem that his prior research had barely touched at its "threshold" (p. 285) and which should constitute the center of future investigation. For Vygotsky, thus, Thinking and Speech is preliminary; a step towards the study of the relation between word and the motivating sphere of consciousness. It is in this sphere, which "includes our inclinations and needs, our interests and impulses, and our affect and emotion" that "thought has its origins" (p. 282). Vygotsky's untimely death, however, left the psychologist's project unfinished, leaving us with only a few works and lectures written during this last period directly addressing this yet-to-be theory. The methodological implication has to do with the often discussed distance that exists between the life experience of the researcher and the "objective" field of (transformative) practice that is being investigated. As Elias (1993) formulates it, scientists seek to solve human problems by a detour of conceptual distance. But this detour does not exclude that scientists are involved in the social realities they seek to describe and that they are driven by values that influence their relationship to their research objects.

The book thus brings up issues of subjective and social transformation as inherent part of research praxis, and of the role and mission of research in developing new hybrid forms of transformative practice. At a time in which social and environmental crises are becoming more acute across the world, the significance and potential of transformative research paradigms is undeniable, with CHAT perspectives offering a unique potential to help researching not just what there is to learn about the social world, but also and at the same time, what could become. In this regard, issues of freedom and social justice are indeed a central concern of the cultural-historical perspective from the outset, as scholars reflecting on Vygotsky's revolutionary roots and significance have made it clear, acknowledging that, from a cultural-historical perspective, "the distinctly human quality of our species is its capacity to practice revolutionary activity" (Newman & Holzman, 1993, p. 44). Concerns of social change and social justice are addressed throughout the chapters and in relation to specific methodological questions. The book, thus, serves as an unvaluable tool for the student and the scholar interested in exploring scholarship and scientific practice as activist projects of social, political and personal transformation.

A further, related issue is the affective, the intellectual, and the material dimensions of consciousness as irreducibly connected to each other, which demands attention to the role of affects in methodological praxis. The subjectivity of individuals who contribute to and develop through collective activity is an important issue to consider in cultural-historical activity theory (Engeström, 2009). Yet, precisely characterizing the differences and relationship between the individual and the collective planes of activity remains an unresolved problem within cultural-historical theory (Davydov, 2005). Vygotsky sees in the social sphere of life the genetical origins of individual consciousness. It is in addressing this problem that a concern grew to find a concrete unit—as in unit analysis (Vygotsky, 1987)—that should embrace the whole person, including her intellect, affects and relations with the environment. One important category that Vygotsky began sketching and which has received much attention during the recent years is perezhivanie, which is a unit of analysis that denotes the unity/identity of person and environment, and where the affective, the intellectual, and the material dimensions of consciousness unfold in irreducible relation (Roth & Jornet, 2016). In spite of this, the affective component receives the least attention from CHAT contemporary researchers (Levykh, 2008). Even when models are proposed to integrate the practical, affective, and intellectual dimensions, the complexity and the challenges of this integration and its implications for research practice are often left unaddressed.

In addressing these issues, the aim of this book is to provide deep and concrete insight on the target topics, but also to appeal to more and less experienced researchers who, despite being well versed on CHAT theoretical issues, still have to struggle and address the task of bringing CHAT to life in their research. As it is made clear across the chapters, CHAT is not a self-contained approach that can be readily applied, but rather a transformative activity that engages scholarship and fields of practice in hybrid and transformative relationships.

1 The Structure and Chapters in This Book

The volume is divided in two types of contributions that intertwine: CHAT living praxis, and epistemological problems of method. The chapters in epistemological problems of method review the premises of CHAT and provide historical context to the problems CHAT epistemology and methodology, specifically in conceiving the non-dualist relation of self and society development, historically. The chapters in the CHAT living praxis, the most extensive part of the book, bring in the testimony, struggles, challenges and propositions that emerge in and through conducting research in a number of settings, including work, education, and counseling. To make clear what the contributions to questions of praxis of method are, following each chapter, we include a section briefly summarizing the most important take-home aspects having to do with non-dualist, dialectical methodology.

In her chapter, Anna Stetsenko, discusses methodology in terms of its status and role with regards to the production of knowledge, more specifically concerning the researcher's role in the production ok knowledge. In her argument, she points out the limitations of many qualitative inquiry methodologies (including postmodernist approaches) in taking account of the role of creativity and innovation in knowledge generation. From her point of view, this difficulty to consider the creative role of research leads to a situation in which the researcher methodological choices are de facto limited to choosing from among the pre-existing established research canons. At the heart of her argument is the premise that researchers cannot remain indifferent—as classical approaches have it—but need to engage with their objects of research as they matter for them, and within the concrete sociohistorical and political contexts that make up the researcher's scholarly activity. Based on her transformative agency stance (TAS) approach, she describes methodology as the enactment of human agency through a process of co-authoring community practices.

In her emphasis on research as creative process, Stetsenko emphasizes the importance of uncertainty and the open-ended nature of the research process, and the importance of the researcher grappling with issues of research "on their own terms and from their own positions, interests, set of values, commitments and sociohistorical and political contexts," and emphasizing the importance of making mistakes and developing knowledge from and through them. She further discusses the current division of labor between research and practice and argues for challenging that division as a means to achieve a more democratic research and methodology. In line with the revolutionary roots of CHAT mentioned above, her conclusion is that research method is not about understanding what there *is*, but about what needs to change, what has to be done next, and what can be accomplished, taking on a responsibility and risk for moving forward in collective transformative activities.

Isabelle Rioux and Patricia Dionne discuss methodological propositions within CHAT considering the agency of students from non-dominant groups in their educational activities. They point out that, in other frameworks, these students are usually considered as passive actors who receive knowledge or information. They highlight the importance of acknowledging the power relations and inequality in the classroom in research generally, and when working with non-dominant groups more particularly. They propose considering, in research on students' activity, (1) how students' agency is conceptualized, and (2) the research design and methods used/adapted to examine this activity. Four methodological approaches within CHAT scholarship are discussed: Social Design Experiments (SDE) (Gutiérrez & Jurow, 2016), Transformative Activist Stance (Stetsenko, 2016), The Change Laboratory (Engeström, 1987/2015), and The Clinic of Activity (Clot, 2017). The review exhibits how, as methodologies with transformative aims, SDE and TAS methods have a tradition to address non-dominant individuals and groups specifically as a means to achieve greater justice and social equity. They further discuss how these approaches seek to stimulate the agency of individuals or groups, on the collective as well as on the individual levels, to contribute to emerging social transformation. The findings of several of the studies reviewed illustrate how students who initially positioned themselves as "victims" or members of minority groups can take prominent roles as agents if they are given—through the research—the opportunity to develop tools and positionings from which to affect the school's structure and transform their own identity. The authors raise the ethical question of the role of research to contribute to creating the conditions that stimulate student's agency and power to act, especially when they belong to non-dominant groups.

Beth Ferholt and Chris Schuck present a very personal and inspiring account of how research participations involve processes of mutual transformation in researchers and participants. More specifically, they describe what they refer to as a research-life process, where scholarly work becomes shaped and altered as suggestions "'from the field' fundamentally challenge conventional social scientific inquiry and concurrent ways of thinking and being." Beth and Chris[1] describe this process through an intimate account of a research collaboration with an early childhood educator, Michael, whose inputs and challenges leads to dilemmas that challenge the researchers' and the collaboration's assumptions. Their account puts emphasis on how those encounters impact the actual lived research praxis and their life experience as the researchers strive to (1) integrate Michael's suggestions in the research process, and (2) integrate a second researcher's suggestions into a research analysis.

Focusing on playworld significant events linked with issues of inclusion, the authors discuss the role of Beth as the "constant"—as he refers to it—in Michael's playworld activity. This view of the researcher as a "constant" or invariable point of reference that helps Michael reflect back on his own actions and activity in the playworld is offered to Beth, the researcher, whom then gains access to a new way of conceiving her own research from the perspective of the participant. The authors explore this transformational and reflexive interaction with the field further, as Beth puts on trial this notion of the "constant" in the writing of this chapter with a research colleague, Chris, who in turn has been a constant in Beth's life since the teenage years. Circling back, the authors further discuss how the inclusion of Chris as constant bears analogies with and helps illuminate the process of inclusion of one specific child in the playworld with Michael. Through the chapter, the authors show how, in the very praxis of method, life and science generate something new in their engagement with each other through and as research-life process. The authors conclude by discussing how this reflexive process, under certain methodological conditions, contributes highlighting developmental and affective dimensions that would otherwise go unnoticed.

In her chapter, Ritva Engeström discusses some important methodological challenges that characterize empirical studies taking a CHAT perspective generally, and in developmental work research (DWR) more particularly. Ritva Engeström anchors her methodological and practical stance on the model of the activity system (Engeström, 1987/2015) as the unit of analysis, and raises foundational dilemmas that emerge from the conceptualization of *object-oriented activity* with regards to the relation between individual and society. This is certainly a central question to anyone encountering CHAT research coming from classical psychological perspectives, which tend to assume a primacy of individuals, and where CHAT offers an alternative way of conceptualizing the relation between collective activity and the emergence of consciousness and mental processes.

Ritva Engeström proposes to focus on the role of semiotic mediation in processes of objectification and subjectification, which she illustrates drawing on several empirical studies using the change laboratory method in health care organizations in Finland and in education. More specifically, she draws on the notion of *dialogicality* to understand the cultural dynamic of semiotic mediation, and presents examples where concepts and words change in their social meaning through the agency of individuals and their different voices through the research process. Her chapter concludes pointing out that "the new constitution of subjectivity" is produced when subjects experience and perform agency in activity as they part take in society and the construction—with the help multivoiced semiotic mediation—of a meaningful collective activity. Her concluding reflections elaborate on the methodological challenge of constructing, in collaborative activity, the process of subjectification of an historical subject,[2] a process that involves engaging with a pluralism of meaning systems, including political and ideological aspects of culture that influence the production of scientific knowledge.

Vygotsky's notion of the *motivating sphere of consciousness* is the focus in Patricia Dionne's contribution, where she discusses how this notion sets affects and emotions—often neglected in methodological discussions—in a dialectical relationship with concrete material collective activity. Her empirical context is a career counseling group with long-term unemployment women, where she illustrates how, from a CHAT perspective, one of the methodological foci from a CHAT perspective concerns considering the dialectical movement that takes between cultural-historical development and the affective, subjective development of individuals who gain consciousness through their participation in collective activity. In the research setting described by the author the meaning of emotions has often become an object of learning. Facing long-term unemployment, some participants may interpret this social situation as a personal responsibility (Blustein, 2006). This can cause sadness, anger, and shame that can hinder actions toward social and professional integration (SPI) (Dionne, 2015). The present analysis puts emphasis on a methodology that permits tracing the discursive manifestations of systematic cultural instruments that the participants learn and/or develop (collectively) as means to attributing meaning to and managing emotions. The author demonstrates how those systematic instruments serve two complementary purposes: as concepts of analysis, and as tools for development in praxis. She discusses how empathic support becomes a social condition to stimulate learning and development in a career counselling group. The results show that the systematic instruments, transmitted and learned in the collective activity, contribute to more control and to a greater consciousness of the relationship to self, to others and to the world, which further promotes actions of the actors toward their SPI. The results show that the progressive mastery of emotions seems to create a movement from an initial sense of powerlessness to an engagement and a progressive power to act, thus tapping into how CHAT scholarship informs issues of freedom and social justice.

Developmental intervention, where research involves intentional, normative actions aimed at transforming activities to generate new knowledge, is a staple of CHAT scholarship. In their chapter, Frédéric Saussez and Philip Dupuis-Laflamme address this issue by discussing the relevance of a widely used Vygotskian concept, the *zone of proximal development*, in problematizing questions about developmental interventions and freedom in adulthood. The authors advance the idea that *The Ethics* of Spinoza provides Vygotsky with a normative orientation, according to which the purpose of developmental researcher intervention is the creation of conditions to stimulate the power to act and to nurture a person's progress on a path to freedom. In their discussion, the authors present the concept of development in adulthood in terms of the necessity for the adult to construct a form of continuity across different microworlds which, however, differ greatly in terms of the language instruments, norms, and social relationships they involve. Precisely those differences bear the possibility of confronting the person with many contradictions, a confrontation that bears the possibility for learning and development, with specific aspects related to adulthood. Indeed, the authors discuss the use of the concept of the zone of proximal development (ZPD) and the methodological challenge of tracing, in developmental research, the dialectical relation between learning and development.

Grounding the discussion in the francophone methodological tradition of ergonomic analysis and the so-called *clinic of activity,* Saussez and Dupuis-Laflamme discuss the above questions of contradictions and development as they are mobilized through intervention research. They argue that analyses of activity need to rely "on the production and recording of traces of actual, concrete material activity as it occurred in its living environment, in order to reconstruct its modes of operation," which are co-analyzed with a researcher and peer through *self confrontation*, where social management of conflicts and contradictions is orchestrated in relation to the socio-historical needs and situation of an extended collective of co-workers. From this approach, research-intervention involves the collective constitution of socially normed activity designed to develop the participants' power to act. This methodology can, in some conditions, generate a zone of proximal development and stimulate individuals to explore ways of understanding/signifying their work and their biographical and social experience.

Another example of development work research (DWR), this time in the context of education, is presented the chapter by Sylvie Barma, Marie-Caroline Vincent and Samantha Voyer. Their empirical case concerns the implementation of a major reform of science and technology education in high schools in Quebec, Canada, where peer mentoring among teachers was embedded in the implementation. The authors draw from experiences in the field, notably in training workshops co-created by the mentors, to discuss and illustrate the relevance of emotional experiences in the decision-making process that leads to teacher professional development. Here, the relevance of contradictions for developmental processes is further taken up. The authors use the principle of double stimulation to analyze how a prototype created to prepare a workshop became a way to resolve identified challenges in science and technology teaching. In their analysis, the authors trace moments where teachers feel emotions such as fear and powerlessness as part of their efforts to implement the new curriculum and during the research process. They also trace the discursive manifestations of transformative agency, of transformative actions in their teaching activity and while they create new curricular artefacts that are used to resolve the contradictions. The dialectical analysis illustrates how the emotional experiences and the actions of resisting or imagining the future become central to the teachers' working through the contradictions. The expansive resolution of conflicts of motives gives new meaning to their teaching activity, leading to a new involvement of the broader school district when the workshops moved from one school to another. Here, the involvement of communities beyond the initial research partnership appears to be key in the expansion of the activity beyond individual practitioners—an aspect that sets a stark contrast with more traditional methodologies and which illustrates CHAT fluid nature and expansive potential as method.

Also dealing with affective dimensions in the resolution of socio-historical contradictions in teacher development, the chapter by Alfredo Jornet discusses a specific and widespread research method in the social sciences, *participant observation*, from a CHAT perspective. Jornet takes the question of "observation" as starting point and problematizes the demands of an "objectivity" that is supposedlyy opposed to "subjectivity" and that characterize issues of validity and reliability in most traditional approaches in psychology and education. Elaborating on how CHAT presents, in the notion of object-oriented activity, a non-dualist alternative to this dichotomic way of thinking, Jornet goes on to illustrate cultural-historical premises as they become embodied in a first-person account of a one-year-long participant ethnography at a young, small but growing primary arts-based primary school. Drawing from video recordings, field notes, and other ethnographic materials, the author analyzes and describes the change by means of which the participant researcher becomes a legitimate member (teacher assistant) at the school as a process in which the school practice, as object, changes and develops. Here, the researcher's subjectivity, and the objectivity of the phenomenon being investigated, are intrinsically connected and change along. In concluding, Jornet discusses how coming to observe a research object, through CHAT informed participant observation, is directly tied to the researcher's (as participant) personal investment and commitment in pursuing the object as meaningful through instrumental—social, political, and material—activities. By emphasizing personal commitment as a condition for the observation of a research object, by way of a very common method as it is applied within a CHAT framework, the chapter further illustrates not only the unity of objective and subjective aspects, but also the politically and value laden nature of research activity.

The book concludes with an interview with one of the most charismatic and influential voices in CHAT scholarship, Professor Michael Cole, who was a most central actor involved in the internationalization of CHAT scholarship beyond Soviet borders. In conversation with the book editors, Cole discusses the origins of the notion of CHAT as a means to unite and set into dialogue otherwise distinct lines of thought within Soviet psychology and across later uptakes in the West. Cole further shares with the readers first-person accounts of his own methodological quandaries and gained insights, starting from his pioneering explorations in cross-cultural studies, passing by the establishment and historical development of the 5th Dimension research intervention project—an after-school intervention project that continues to grow and develop into new forms of research activity and networks today. Cole insights provide historical and intellectual context to the chapters, and provides specific insights addressing both early career and more experienced scholars.

Acknowledgments

We want to acknowledge the exceptional contributions and intellectual engagement of all contributors of the book and we would like to extend our sincere thanks to Audrey Dupuis, Professor at the Université de Moncton, Canada, for her support in finalizing the manuscript.

Notes

1   They used their first name in their chapter.
2   She includes researchers as historical subjects.

References

Asmolov, A. G. (1998). *Vygotsky today: On the verge of non-classical psychology.* Nova Science Publishers.

Blustein, D. L. (2006). *The psychology of working: A new perspective for career development, counseling, and public policy.* Lawrence Erlbaum.

Chernorizov, A. M., Asmolov, A. G., & Schechter, E. D. (2015). From physiological psychology to psychological physiology: Postnonclassical approach to ethnocultural phenomena. *Psychology in Russia: State of the Art, 8*(4), 4–22. doi:10.11621/pir.2015.0401

Clot, Y. (2017). *Travail et pouvoir d'agir* (2nd ed.). Presses Universitaires de France.

Cole, M., Levitin, K., & Luria, A. (2005). *The autobiography of Alexander Luria: A dialogue with the making of mind.* Routledge.

Davydov, V. V. (2005). The content and unsolved problems of activity theory. In Y. Engeström, R. Miettinen, & R.-L. Punamäki (Eds.), *Perspectives on activity theory* (pp. 39–51). Cambridge University Press.

Dionne, P. (2015). *Le groupe d'insertion sociale et professionnelle : apprentissages et développement au cœur de l'activité collective des personnes en situation de chômage de longue durée* [Doctoral dissertation]. Université de Sherbrooke.

Dionne, P., & Jornet, A. (2019). Conceiving work as (an) activity: Epistemological underpinnings from a cultural-historical perspective. In P. F. Bendassolli (Ed.), *Culture, work and psychology: Invitations to dialogue* (pp. 37–57). Information Age Publishing.

Elias, N. (1993). *Engagement et distanciation.* Presses Universitaires de France.

Engeström, R. (2009). Who is acting in an activity system? In A. Sannino, H. Daniels, & K. D. Gutiérrez (Eds.), *Learning and expanding with activity theory* (pp. 257–273). Cambridge University Press.

Engeström, Y. (2015). *Learning by expanding: An activity theoretical approach to developmental research* (2nd ed.). Cambridge University Press. (Original work published 1987)

Engeström, Y., & Glăveanu, V. (2012). On third generation activity theory: Interview with Yrjö Engeström. *Europe's Journal of Psychology, 8*(4), 515–518.

Gutiérrez, K. D., & Jurow, A. S. (2016). Social design experiments: Toward equity by design. *Journal of the Learning Sciences, 25*(4), 565–598. http://dx.doi.org/10.1080/10508406.2016.1204548

Kozulin, A., Gindis, B., Ageyev, V. S., & Miller, S. M. (2003). *Vygotsky educational theory in cultural context*. Cambridge University Press.

Levykh, M. (2008). The affective establishment and maintenance of Vygotsky's zone of proximal development. *Educational Theory, 58*(1), 83–101. doi:10.1111/j.1741-5446.2007.00277.x

Mikhailov, F. T. (1980). *The riddle of the self*. Progress Publishers.

Newman, F., & Holzman, L. (1993). *Lev Vygotsky. Revolutionary scientist*. Routledge.

Robbins, D. (2003). Vygotsky's non-classical dialectical metapsychology. *Journal for the Theory of Social Behaviour, 33*(3), 303–312.

Roth, W.-M., & Jornet, A. (2016). Perezhivanie in the light of the later Vygotsky's Spinozist turn. *Mind, Culture, and Activity, 23*(4), 315–324. doi:10.1080/10749039.2016.1186197

Roth, W.-M., & Jornet, A. (2017). *Understanding educational psychology. A late Vygotskian, Spinozist approach*. Springer.

Saussez, F. (2017). La zone de développement la plus proche : une contribution de Vygotski à l'approche par l'activité ? In J.-M. Barbier & M. Durand (Eds.), *Encyclopédie d'analyse des activités* (pp. 911–920). Presses Universitaires de France.

Stetsenko, A. (2016). *The transformative mind: Expanding Vygotsky's approach to development and education*. Cambridge University Press.

Vassilieva, J. (2010). Russian psychology at the turn of the 21st century and post-Soviet reforms in the humanities disciplines. *History of Psychology, 13*, 138–159.

Vygotsky, L. S. (1987). *The collected works of L. S. Vygotsky: Vol. 1. Problems of general psychology*. Springer.

Vygotsky, L. S. (1997). *The collected works of L.S. Vygotsky: Vol. 3. Problems of the theory and history of psychology*. Plenum Press.

Yasnitsky, R., & Van der Veer, R. (2014). Introduction. In R. Yasnitsky, R. Van der Veer, & M. Ferrari (Eds.), *The Cambridge handbook of cultural-historical psychology* (pp. 1–8). Cambridge University Press.

CHAPTER 2

Knowledge Production as a Process of Making Mis/takes, at the Edge of Uncertainty

Research as an Activist, Risky, and Personal Quest

Anna Stetsenko

Abstract

The hallmark of methodologies that are consistent with cultural-historical theory, in my view, is that they are considered alongside a broad, overarching set of issues about ontology, epistemology, and ethics. This includes assumptions about science, research, knowledge, and above all, about ourselves and our role and place in the world and in the production of knowledge. In my take on these matters, termed the *transformative activist stance*, knowledge production is a part of human becoming understood to be about people *contributing* to shared community practices, from a position of non-neutral struggles to transcend these practices and overcome their constraints. My suggestion is for a novel transformative onto-epistemology, coupled with the socio-political ethos of equality and social justice, to challenge the ideology of adaptation and control so prevalent in science and research. Highlighting instead that science and research are fundamentally open-ended and uncertain—made up of successive mis/takes rather than any universal solutions and also, always ethically-politically non-neutral—opens ways to develop new methodologies fit for the world in need of radical changes. The resulting transformative methodology encompasses (a) a duly historicized account of processes in question; (b) an ethical-political stance achieved within a critical inquiry into socially constructed forms of knowledge and their history, and (c) a practical intervention in the course of social life—all seen as interrelated and presupposing each other. At stake, centrally, is a strong rebuttal of science normativity, especially in its focus on a presumed research objectivity cum neutrality. This approach builds upon and resonates with works that emphasize the need to decolonize knowledge and overcome its hegemonic and racist roots and entailments.

Keywords

transformative activist stance – decolonizing knowledge – onto-epistemology – socio-political ethos – science normativity – debunking objectivity

> As they become known to and accepted by us, our feelings and the honest exploration of them become sanctuaries and spawning grounds for the most radical and daring of ideas.
> AUDRE LORDE (*Sister outsider: Essays and speeches*, 1984)

⋯

> A claim to objective knowledge is an absolute demand for obedience.
> MENDEZ, CODDOU, AND MATURANA (*The bringing forth of pathology*, 1988)

∴

Methodology is a multiply complexified topic due to its inherently problematic character, especially in terms of its philosophical and conceptual ambiguity, and its convoluted history. This complexity, however, is typically ignored or only hinted at in the presently influential accounts such as, and especially, textbooks on the methodology of research. In discussing methodology, the arguments typically focus on particular topics such as qualitative versus quantitative approaches, specifics and advantages (versus disadvantages) of various techniques, and similar partial aspects that actually belong to a set of issues of a much broader nature and import. As important as these particular topics are, they are but parts of what is, I believe, a much broader, overarching set of issues and questions, outside of which any of its partial aspects inevitably remains addressed only partially and, therefore, superficially. This overarching set is about how we understand what methodology is—in terms of its status and role as regards our core beliefs, theories, and assumptions about science, research, knowledge, and above all, about ourselves and our role and place in the world generally, and in the production of knowledge more specifically.

These broad issues presently are very far from being resolved, even though they undergird all specific inquiries and research methodologies, shaping every step in our decisions as to what to study, how to approach what we study, how to validate knowledge and devise appropriate inquiry techniques, and ultimately, how to draw conclusions and make sense of what we study, such as in terms of meaning, "objectivity," truth, and validity of our findings. Addressing this broad set of questions and their multiple corollaries inevitably leads into the domains of epistemology and ontology and, therefore, philosophy—a much-dreaded destination which often evokes assumptions of abstract, empty speculations and inconsequential, idle conjectures that are presumably detached from substantial and tangible specifics of conducting research.

Yet, rather than dismissing discussions of methodology in light of its embedding within broad philosophical questions and, thus, taking a skeptical stance on discourses of "method" as such (as some do, see e.g., Brinkmann, 2014), I believe we have to "face the music," stay with the trouble, and make the best we can in formulating our position on these difficult philosophical issues. Because of space constraints, I will not be able to address all of these complicated questions in sufficient detail (for an extended discussion, see Stetsenko, 2010, 2014, 2015, 2016a, 2016b). Instead, I intend to address what I think is one core issue that cuts across and bears relevance to all of these questions.

In particular, my argument is that broad philosophical issues (including as they underpin methodology) have to be grappled with by all researchers on their own terms and from their own positions, interests, sets of values, and above all, commitments to the future. All these emerge from, and are defined within, specific sociohistorical and political contexts—even while inevitably drawing on, yet also at the same time, also challenging, previous traditions, accounts, ideas, and modes of thinking. That is, all researchers have to come up with their own answers to these complex and utmost complicated questions, though most certainly not in isolation from others, and not in a sociopolitical and cultural-historical vacuum.

This argument is predicated on a particular view on what is knowledge production, including in research and science. Knowledge production, I suggest, is an open-ended, continuous, never-ending, deeply personal, and profoundly risky process, always at the edge of uncertainty and novelty. In it, nothing is handed down "ready-made" and instead, everything is about overcoming, interrogating, transgressing, challenging, and disrupting the taken for granted. The process of knowledge production is about a constant struggle and striving for matters stretching far beyond the limits of what is traditionally taken as knowledge, that is, beyond "the rational" and the ivory tower of academia and, moreover, of much more relevance than merely epistemic issues. This process evolves through way stations (that is, relatively stable stopping points) on the long and protracted—indeed, endless—and also quite treacherous journeys and quests for our own answers that, too, cannot be taken for granted. In these ever-unfolding and deeply personal quests for our own answers, we not only never arrive at any "final destination"; we only ever achieve what essentially are unstable, open-ended, and inevitably temporary solutions in need of being corrected and rectified again and again, in new cycles of inquiry that produce ever new solutions, again in need of correction, revision, and rectification, every step of the way. All of this is to say that knowledge production consists of constantly making and refuting mis/takes, coming up with our own answers and updating them in the ever new rounds of coming up with new answers which are, again, none else but mis/takes in need of further elaborations and refutations.

This is about understanding knowledge production, including science, as being a forever unstable and unfinished flow of activities and quests, where everything is always on the move. Importantly, knowledge production processes are quests and, essentially, struggles not only for knowledge but, simultaneously, for our own becoming as members of communities and agents of the world-in-the-making. Ultimately, since every researcher, each and everyone of us, is understood to be an agent of history—and of the world-in-the-making, all our quests for knowledge are ultimately about our quests for a world we want to see come into existence. This is what makes these quests always so personal and responsible, getting to the very core of who are and who we are becoming in the world that we continuously co-create with others. It is therefore that so much is at stake in knowledge production, including courage and responsibility.

A related point is that science is a social practice that is realized and sustained, first and foremost, by rank-and-file scholars, whereby activities and contributions by members of inquiry communities make a difference and matter in realizing science, that is, in making it real. Predicated on this idea, a push for a more democratic and empowering-liberatory research and methodology, including for participants and researchers themselves, especially those excluded and marginalized—people of color, ethnic minorities, women, scholars working in the global South—has to include a challenge to an established division of labor within sciences and research. Namely, we need to overcome the situation where we have, on the one hand, the elitist approaches to philosophy and other broad questions in science and research (under the purview of the so called "big philosophy" hero-figures, typically white men) and, on the other hand, the rank-and-file researchers (especially from non-dominant groups, and typically women), who are supposed to merely implement these pre-established approaches, answers, and methodologies.

Overall, the gist of this chapter builds upon and resonates with works that emphasize the need to decolonize knowledge and unearth its hegemonic and racist roots and entailments—such as summed by Gloria Anzaldúa in her call to "move beyond confining parameters of what qualifies as knowledge" (1990, p. 230). This is important so that we can all move past the stifling canons and prescriptions—typically, eurocentric and racist—that still dominate science and research (e.g., Tuck & Yang, 2014). As Cornel West (1999) has formulated, "the initial structure of modern discourse in the West 'secretes' the idea of white supremacy, [which is] a particular logical consequence of the quest for truth and knowledge in the modern West" (p. 91). In West's (1999) powerful words,

> The creative fusion of scientific investigation, Cartesian epistemology, and classical ideals produced forms of rationality, scientificity, and objectivity which, *though efficacious in the quest for truth and knowledge*, prohibited the intelligibility and legitimacy of the idea of black equality in beauty, culture, and intellectual capacity. (p. 91, emphasis added)

In building upon these ideas, I suggest additionally (as the next step in the same line of arguments) to problematize and relativize West's (1999) statement, as just quoted—namely, that classical forms of rationality, scientificity, and objectivity are efficacious in the quest for truth and knowledge. My point, to be elaborated in this chapter, is that such forms of knowledge production are actually deeply flawed and ultimately not efficacious—in addition to them being hegemonic and racist. In particular, whatever success we attribute to science (and, of course, this cannot be ignored), an argument can be made that this success has been achieved in spite of, not due to, a rigid imposition of rationality, scientificity, and objectivity.

This suggestion, which is admittedly quite radical, is critically important in my view, because many even among critical scholars in social sciences still remain deferential to the natural sciences model and often tacitly accept its supposed superiority, even while developing alternative approaches (as in crypto-positivism, see Kincheloe & Tobin, 2009). In this deference, there is sometimes a residual subordination of qualitative, sociocultural, and critical approaches to those prevalent in natural sciences. This is about a rather uncritical acceptance of the natural sciences' ideals, which are typically in fact mythologies (!), of certainty and reliability of the so-called hard facts and "neutral" (sometimes dubbed "naked") evidence. This is exemplified, among other things, in the belief in the incontrovertible authority of mathematics that proclaims that numbers are the ultimate test of objectivity, in a naive disregard of how contingent, open-ended, malleable, and uncertain the very endeavor of science, including mathematics and any science without exception, is.

A strong rebuttal of these normativities, especially in their focus on presumed research objectivity cum neutrality, is much needed as part of the struggle to decolonize knowledge and strip it of its dark, centuries-old legacies geared to serving the privileged and the powerful. In making this step, I solidarize with the works of scholars such as Audre Lorde (discussed in the next section) and also the words by Mendez et al. (1988) that "[a] claim to objective knowledge is an absolute demand for obedience" (p. 170).

To reiterate, sciences elaborated on principles and normativities of objectivity and neutrality are much more flawed than is commonly believed—though I will make distinctions between my position and those views that completely strip science of any efficacy and legitimacy. In fact, these principles are counterproductive and stifling for advancing sciences in their core mission of serving and meeting the needs of all people including the need for equality, social justice, and well-being for all.

1 Science as a Search for Our Own Answers: Innovative Disruption or Disruptive Innovation

Paradoxically, it is an utmost unusual idea by today's canons and standards all across sciences and education that all researchers cannot just count on, nor take for granted, what has been already established and instead, have to come up with their own answers to all the complex questions in science and research, including those about methodology. Most textbook introductions and handbooks on science and methodology of research offer relatively little advice and suggestions (if at all) for the compelling task to innovate and promote creativity and, thus, to encourage taking risks so that we not only learn from mistakes but also make one's own mistakes, in the first place, as a natural and inherent part of knowledge production process. These introductions also typically do not engage broad topics such as what is science, how it is "made," and how to understand knowledge and knowledge production (and if this is done, then almost invariably in the form of a boiler platter standard claims to objectivity and neutrality[1]). Instead, the textbooks and handbooks typically provide descriptions of various types of established methodologies and de facto invite researchers to join in with the approved canon to thus follow suit with what has been previously accomplished and is presently taken for granted. This is the case even with the works that purport to break with established positivist and empiricist models of science and strive to develop new approaches, concepts, and research lenses such as in what is known under the broad label of "qualitative methodology." Even in these progressive works, it is highly uncommon to encounter an invitation for researchers to be innovative and creative in breaking the canons, moving past the established models, including and especially at the level of broad philosophical ideas and notions of methodology, while striving to develop new philosophies, strategies, ideas, and approaches.

For example, a highly influential work by Creswell (2007) makes explicit a number of assumptions, worldviews, and paradigms that are available in qualitative research, representing beliefs brought to qualitative projects. The author does state that researchers need to choose their stance on these beliefs and thus, does invite individual choice. However, the genre of presentation that clusters extant views and approaches in an established typology—along with a lack of explicit statements on the role of creativity and innovation in moving past the canons and paradigms—strongly suggests that individual choice is actually quite limited to choosing from among the options that are already in place. The readers are supposed to examine these established views and approaches and come to a "correct" interpretation of their meaning to then pick a side within what is a defined and preestablished set of choices.

By way of another illustration, the methodology within the so-called grounded theory approaches are seemingly all about how both method and content emerge in the course of research, rather than them being preconceived before empirical inquiries begin. Yet here, too, the core point is that qualitative researchers have to aspire to achieve their goals by following the established guidelines. For example, Charmaz (2008) reflects on the reception of the key works within this approach (e.g., by its founders Glazer and Strauss) and how these works have become canonized. She writes that these classical works "did not simply offer guidelines; they *prescribed* procedures as a path to qualitative success," with this approach becoming "something of an *orthodoxy*"(!) and even "something of a *bible*(!!) for novices" (ibid., pp. 399–400, emphasis added).

These stunning characterizations require close scrutiny and critique. How more extreme could the gap be between what is supposed to be an unorthodox approach focused on novelty and emergence, on one hand, and this approach itself being accepted as an orthodoxy, and even "a bible," on the other? (Note that by using this example, I am not implying that grounded theory methodologies are somehow more troubled than others; it is just that they illustrate the point I am making with particular clarity).

Perhaps it is specifically the genre of textbooks and handbooks that makes their descriptions of methodology (even qualitative and postmodernist ones), non-flexible, authoritative, nearly universalistic, and as if set in stone. Indeed, many textbooks in sciences across the board are notorious for their unreliability due to extensive distortions and omissions (including that they avoid addressing complex problems and ambiguities always present in science). Such distortions and omissions in many textbooks has been well documented (e.g., Steuer & Ham, 2008). As Morawski (1992) wrote, introductory textbooks often reflect a distorted and commercialized view of the discipline with reputation for "deception and inaccuracies, made for the sake of clarity, simplicity, or profit" (p. 162), which often turns them into "the object of derision" (Weiten & Wight, 1992, p. 487). Many leading scholars in natural sciences have also claimed that science textbooks act as purveyors of outdated myths about science and knowledge (Gould, 1988). Jarrett (2008) further argues that the foundation of psychology as depicted in textbooks can be described to be more sand than rock, with many myths being employed to reinforce empirical legitimacy of this discipline. Remarkably, this distorted coverage has not only persisted but increased over the past 30 years (Griggs, 2015).

The ethos of fitting in, conforming with, and adapting to what is already in place and taken for granted (while in effect fundamentally flawed)—all in following with the status quo—can be described as an overarching adaptationist ethos (Stetsenko, 2008, 2016a) prevalent in eurocentric models of science. Unfortunately, this ethos has penetrated and colored even non-dominant, critical approaches to methodology. An alternative ethos of breaking the rules, daring to innovate, creating novelty, and generally moving beyond what is "given" is still not highlighted among the guiding principles even in qualitative and postmodernist research (with few exceptions). According to this alternative ethos of innovative disruption or disruptive innovation, as I intend to emphasize in this chapter, all researchers need to discover their methodology themselves while working creatively and critically with the sources and, importantly, based in a realization that the "buck stops with them"—because no previously advanced solution can be taken for granted as if established universally, once and for all.

The common tacit strategy of following with the status quo and normativity in science and research in fact belies a deeply seated philosophy that prioritizes the social over the individual, tradition over innovation, compliance over daring, and the past over the present and future. This common strategy is also emblematic of a hierarchical view of science and methodology—fundamentally, of taking them as an established canon that needs to be emulated and conformed with, rather than constantly challenged, interrogated, and transcended. Ultimately, this strategy reflects a hegemonic, patriarchal, and coercive view of science where rank-and-file members of community practices have no authority and, essentially, make no difference and do not matter.

There are many reasons for this lack of emphasis on creativity, innovation, and daring—including on each and every researcher inventing their own methodologies. The deepest reasons have to do with the workings of capitalism, and the structures of power and control that accompany and reinforce it, with its instrumentalist drive for profit at any cost. This drive is dehumanizing all social practices and interactivities while alienating and disempowering those engaged in productive processes, including sciences, especially at the bottom of academic hierarchies.

In the context of the present chapter, what is directly relevant is that the related regime and ideology of adaptation position and prescribe people to be powerless, mindless, and isolated, like mechanical cogs in the wheels of capitalist production. The dominance of individualist, cognitivist theories, coupled with biological reductionism, is a powerful illustration to this trend. Such theories have been debunked, again and again, by many scholars on the spectrum of approaches from postmodernism and feminist epistemologies to sociocultural and activity theories. There is no need to dwell on this critique here other than to say that I fully share many of its critical points (for elaborations, see Stetsenko, 2016a). On the opposite polar extreme, there is an emphasis on collectivities, social discourses, and community practices, which are rendered authoritative and authoritarian over and above individuals, including individual scholars—as in pragmatism and many postmodernist approaches including sociocultural scholarship. In these approaches, locating science and knowledge production exclusively within the workings of a scientific community renders these processes completely external to the individual. In doing so, the notions of the individual, agency, and personhood are regrettably left under the purview of outdated approaches such as cognitivism and mentalism (and more recently, also brainism, see Arievitch, 2017).

This vacillation in research and theorizing from one polar extreme to the other on the spectrum of views about the social and the individual does not leave space for conceptualizing individuals, as each "an ensemble of social relations" (as Marx famously put it), and individual agency non-individualistically—as having to do with agentive contributions to collective practices and, therefore, itself also social through and through (beyond the dichotomy that pits the individual against the social).

Against this background, an invitation for researchers to develop their own answers and approaches might seem to be out of sync. Indeed, in the individualist-cognitivist model, there is no place for agency at all. Yet the postmodernist and sociocultural theories, in debunking the mythology of isolated individuals, have not been careful enough, I believe, to not throw the proverbial baby (i.e., the person, agency, human subjectivity, creativity etc.) with the bathwater of pernicious individualism and solipsism. Fully and completely reducing the individual to the social, and the personal to the collective, in fact tacitly affirms the dualistic view that the person cannot find her due—and non-individualistic place—within accounts of social processes and practices (cf. Stetsenko, 2005, 2012, 2013a, 2013b; Stetsenko & Arievitch, 2004). Ultimately, this conceptual move is akin to an erroneous position that the individual indeed can only be understood as isolated and solipsistic (!), which leaves much space for the old-fashioned notions and approaches to sneak right back into even sociocultural and critical theories. This is in fact what happens again and again and needs to be addressed especially because this division, as all other Cartesian dichotomies, is conducive to hierarchical hegemonies and racism. I will return to this point in the final section of this chapter.

2   Agency in Science and Methodology: Risk-taking and Mis-taking

The invitation and even the demand for researchers to find their own answers, that is, for creativity and innovation at all levels of research, including matters of methodology, are in line with an unorthodox view of what science and knowledge production are. This relates to broad questions (to reiterate, typically skipped in presentations of methodology), although in my view they should be treated with utmost attention. I suggest that what needs to be emphasized, including and especially in science textbooks, is that science and research, in all of their aspects and dimensions including methodologies, are inherently open-ended, indeterminate, forever un-finalized and contested, and as such, resisting any final definition or canonization, just as the world, wherein science is immersed, is too. Rather than following with established and seemingly unalterable norms and canons—which in actuality have been and continue to be refuted again and again, throughout the history and even daily in the everyday conduct of science—it is important to continuously re-discover and creatively re-invent, anew, all aspects of research (including methodologies), in each and every new study or approach, based in original and authentic answers by each researcher.

This is because, to emphasize again, contrary to common perceptions, science and research are primarily and fundamentally open-ended and uncertain through and through—comprised, as they are, of constantly questioning, critiquing, exploring, confronting, deconstructing, falsifying, refashioning, reimagining, refuting, and interrogating knowledge and related practices of its production. These processes are as far as it gets from anything that is canonical or set in stone, once and for all, being instead inherently an unending adventure at the edge of uncertainty (cf. Bronowski, 1976), a continuous pursuit that is chiefly about contestation and dissensus (see Stetsenko, 2017; Vianna & Stetsenko, 2014, 2017). This is a strong epistemic stance according to which contestability is a form of a new quasi-rule where processes of questioning, interrogating and moving beyond the status quo are the very fabric of knowing. That is, science and research need to be normally defined through conflict and contestation and, I would emphasize, contestations, contradictions and dissensus need to be highlighted as the very practices that science and research/knowledge are made of.

This view of science is not fully unexpected though it is often disregarded within traditional orthodoxies and "white coat images" of science (cf. Erickson

& Gutrierrez, 2002). In fact, many among major advances in sciences since the early 20th century (e.g., in quantum physics) have been about shifting away from naïve positivism and beliefs in objectivity of "raw facts" and "pristine reality" purged from human subjectivity, including processes of constructing knowledge as a social and profoundly human endeavor. The naïveté and political expedience of objectivist methodology has been exposed and critiqued by many critical, sociocultural scholars, and even by physicists and other natural scientists too. In the words of Jacob Bronowski,

> One aim of the physical sciences has been to give an actual picture of the material world. One achievement of physics in the twentieth century has been to show that such an aim is unattainable. There is no absolute knowledge and those who claim it, whether they are scientists or dogmatists, open the door to tragedy. (quoted in Critchley, 2014, pp. 387–388)

When social scholars look up to natural sciences in efforts to emulate their supposedly superior ability to objectively understand the world as "it is," they actually miss an important, indeed critical, part of the story about science as a risky adventure, always at the edge of uncertainty and novelty creation. It is common to present claims about uncertainty and provisional nature of knowledge as an exotic postmodernist or postpositivist position attributable to few outsiders distanced from "true" sciences. Along these lines, it has been claimed that "social scientists can never be certain that their techniques will allow them to see objective reality" (Gray et al., 2007, p. 7), apparently implying that it is the prerogative and privilege of natural sciences to see objective reality. Yet such a view fundamentally disregards radical developments in the philosophy of science, science studies, history of science through the past century. Importantly, this view also disregards developments in natural sciences themselves that have moved past traditional epistemologies that still insist that we get to know, or should be able to know, the world "as it is" (that is, the world as purged of ourselves).

It is highly significant that all major recent break-through advances in sciences across the board, including physics and biology, emphasize volatility, uncertainty, complexity, and ambiguity of the world. In biology, Gould (1996) has drawn attention to the fact that "webs and chains of historical events are so intricate, so imbued with random and chaotic elements, so unrepeatable in encompassing such a multitude of unique (and uniquely interacting) objects, that standard models of simple prediction and replication do not apply" (p. 85). Similarly, Prigogine stated that "the more we know about our universe, the more difficult it becomes to believe in determinism" (1997, p. 155). And no less an authority than Niels Bohr accepted the radical premise that "[i]t is wrong to think that the task of physics is to find out how nature is" (quoted in Newton, 2009, p. 40), independently of our questions, instruments, and methodologies. Importantly, this claim did not imply the impossibility of physics but instead, laid grounds for its most significant advances.

Karl Popper (even though his views were mired in sociobiological pseudo-theory) has consistently stated that "all scientific knowledge is hypothetical or conjectural; the central process in knowledge building consists of conjecture and refutation" and "the growth of knowledge, especially of scientific knowledge, consists in learning from our mistakes" (1994, p. 93). He was quite insistent in repeating the latter point again and again:

> What can be called the method of science consists in learning from our mistakes systematically: first, by taking risks, by daring to make mistakes—that is, by boldly proposing new theories; and secondly, be searching systematically for the mistakes we have made—that is, by the critical discussion and the critical examination of our theories. (Popper, 1994, p. 93)

Yet these unorthodox positions have been generally perceived along the lines of a trivial point that we all inevitably make mistakes and can learn from them. No one would ever object to such a triviality. Indeed, no one would ever contest the fact that scientists are human and all humans make mistakes. However, the common view persists (both among lay persons and scientists alike) that by following the "true" scientific method, and adhering to canons of science, scientists somehow are able to overcome mistakes so as to arrive at objective facts and data that are universal, value-free, neutral, and true once and for all.

A much more radical interpretation, which I am suggesting, is that there is nothing to knowledge construction and science but mistakes and the ongoing pursuit to overcome and rectify them. Knowledge building is all about making mistakes, completely and fully, across the board, through and through, all-around, every step of the way, with no exception, front and center, from start to finish. Scientists are truly primarily in the business of making mistakes, which are followed by attempts to find better solutions that inevitably bring about new mistakes, which then again need to be interrogated and overturned in new and unending cycles of discovery and knowledge production.

This might sound unusual and there is a dose of a metaphoric exaggeration in making such a claim, for rhetorical purposes, to shake the "solid," yet deeply faulty foundation of "normative" doctrines about science and its canons. The gist of this claim actually echoes views that can be found, for example, in Dewey's (e.g., 1929) influential works. Central to Dewey's position, as is well known, was the notion of inquiry. This notion can be understood simply as a banality that the pursuit of knowledge is based in asking questions and seeking answers. Yet Dewey was much more radical in that he insisted that no knowledge—and no concepts, ideas, facts etc.—can be posited to exist outside of inquiry at all! The radical connotation of pragmatism is that inquiry is the very process of which knowledge consists and outside of which no knowledge (in whatever form) exists.

Knowledge is made up of inquiry and as such, is itself an open-ended, never-ending process that cannot be said to ever reach anything like a final destination, firm conclusion, full and certain, universal, valid once and for all, answer. There is nothing static or final about knowledge and no part of it—such as facts, notions, concepts and ideas—can ever be universalized, reified (frozen in time), essentialized, or taken for granted by assuming their independent status outside of the ongoing and never-ending process of knowledge production (inquiry), with no finality and no absolute certainty at any point (for important critiques of Dewey's uncertain political stance coloring his overall approach, including his failure to publicly oppose racial inequalities, see Margonis, 2009).

It is highly instructive to pause and consider how someone no less than Albert Einstein, in all the glory and esteem of an iconic scholar, himself made an inordinate number of mistakes, ironically, perhaps more than most scholars(!). And yet this does not take away from his exceptional achievements and enormous contributions to physics and science at large. Consider this quote (Wright, 2004):

> Albert Einstein got it wrong. Not once, not twice, but countless times. He made subtle blunders, he made outright goofs, his oversights were glaring. Error infiltrated every aspect of his thinking. He was wrong about the universe, wrong about its contents, wrong about the workings of atoms. Yet Einstein's mistakes could be compelling and instructive, and some were even essential to the progress of modern physics.

Indeed, as is now established in physics, a century after his discoveries, "almost all of Einstein's seminal works contain mistakes" and his "exploratory paths were often torturous, with many erratic twists and turns" (Ohanian, 2008, p. xix). Of course, Einstein's mistakes were important and highly fruitful in that they challenged himself and other scientists to pursue new questions and problems. Einstein also made important and groundbreaking discoveries of enormous significance that could be held, at this moment, as "true." However, the point I am making is that even those breakthroughs that are holding up until now, too, are in need of further interrogations, critiques, revisions, and upgrades and they, too, are likely to be overturned in the future by new discoveries; these breakthroughs, too, are not "final truths" and are more akin to "mistakes," if even to be revealed as such only in the future. Indeed, this is precisely the pattern that repeats itself again and again throughout the history of sciences in all of its branches and fields.

Seeing science as made up of mis/takes—up-takes, re-takes and problems, rather than solutions and final answers, I believe, is not only accurate but also inherently empowering and decolonizing. This view affords to squash the many myths that put some persons (typically white males in the so called "great men" tradition) high on pedestals—as ostensibly exceptional, extraordinary individuals "out of this world," presumed to possess almost divine qualities and perhaps even mystical access to some transcendental truths hidden from the rest of us, especially those on the margins. These myths erect barriers between those "great men" and the so called "ordinary people," while diminishing incentives for innovating, creating, and daring.

This is an elitist, colonizing, and disempowering approach that masks the fallibility and fragility of sciences on the one hand, and denigrates accomplishments that all humans can be credited with in their seemingly—only seemingly!—common and ordinary lives, on the other (Stetsenko, 2019a, 2018a). Indeed, revealing mistakes that all scientists make, all the time and across the board, is humbling and in a way reassuring for those who are embarking on similar quests. This is reassuring, I believe, more broadly, for all of us, no matter our occupations and pursuits, since everyone merits participating as an equal in what is going all in the world. As Ohanian (the author of the book about Einstein's mistakes and a physicist himself) notes, the experience of exploring Einstein's mistakes

> occasionally brought him [Einstein] down from the Olympian heights of his great discoveries to my own level, where I could imagine talking to him as a colleague, and maybe bluntly say, in the give-and-take of a friendly discussion among colleagues, "Albert, now that is really stupid!" (2008, p. XII)

Importantly, I believe we need to emphasize that knowledge is made up of the whole inquiry process, which cannot and should not be compartmentalized into separate components or steps. Instead, a description of knowledge production has to encompass—in describing any of its seemingly separate "elements"—all steps belonging to one dynamic and systemic totality. Any fact, data, and any methodology, for that matter, have to be described as contingent and non-independent facets within the whole process of inquiry. This process starts with needs, desires, and emotions, proceeds to formulating problems and searching for answers and their verification, which is then followed, inevitably and necessarily, by their critique and disconfirmation, whereupon new problems arise, thus leading to new cycles of inquiry and all its necessary steps, over and over again, with no stopping in-between (unless we mean temporary way stations), and no absolute certainty available at any point along the way.

3   Navigating "Knowledge Is Power" versus "the Limits of Knowledge" Premises

The critical, reflective, and humble outlook on science and scientific method is an indispensable condition (complementary to many others) for decolonizing knowledge. This is a difficult task since so many myths, biases and seemingly incontrovertible canons are involved in the mythologies of science. Many groundbreaking works have been written about decolonizing knowledge and I am humbly joining them from my own positioning as a scholar straddling diverse cultural traditions due to a personal history of dislocation and uprooting (see Stetsenko, 2016a).

As Gould (1996) wrote decades ago, "scientists must give up the twin myths and canons of objectivity and of knowledge as inexorable march toward truth that can be established once and for all" (p. 55). These canons are the pillars that support exclusionary practices and stay in the way of implementing democratic, anti-racist, and egalitarian models of science, research, and methodology where all participants matter and make a difference and where the voices of marginalized are prioritized.

Yet debunking traditional models of science has to be done without falling into the opposite extreme position of uncommitted relativism and the denial of science and knowledge as such, so that no knowledge claims are taken to be preferable (or advantageous, more reasonable, adequate etc.) over any others. On the one hand, it is important to reject quaint epistemologies according to which the purpose of science is to describe, reveal, and explain the world "as it is." On the other hand, however, the challenges to traditional models of science, in my view, have to avoid dismissing the value of knowledge and science all together. Giving credit to science and acknowledging its success does not need to go hand in hand with accepting "facts of science" as some sort of "higher" truths produced by elite authorities that can be neither questioned nor contested. It is of utmost importance to advance critiques of science and its methods in the spirit that is alternative to a stance of groveling before sciences' supposed superiority, on the one hand, and to outright dismissals of science that throw out the baby of knowledge with the bathwater of objectivism, hierarchy, and normativity, on the other.

A reverential attitude towards science, especially physics and more recently neurosciences and genetics, is partly (only in small part) understandable given how much has been achieved in applications of scientific discoveries and advances. Indeed, after only four hundred years of modern science, its record is remarkable and scientific knowledge, as Gleiser (2010) puts it, is now stretching "all the way from the inner confines of atomic nuclei to galaxies billions of light-years away" (p. XVI). Yet mistakes, blunders, wrongdoings and outright crimes perpetrated by sciences are no less enormous, egregious, shameful, and astonishingly costly especially in terms of their harm to communities of color and the oppressed, as well as our common humanity and our ecosystem.

It should be sufficient to mention the heinous history and discriminatory research on rankable intelligence, taken as a unitary biological property (against any sound theory) and the use of genetics in racist research and related practices of sterilization of those deemed "deviant." Gould (1996) has exposed this outrageous line of research (still alive and well today!) to consist in invariably finding that "oppressed and disadvantaged groups—races, classes, or sexes—are innately inferior and deserve their status" (p. 21). The intelligence construct itself, no less that the procedures for its measurement, has been consistently debunked and exposed for its deeply flawed, indeed toxic, premises and implications. So, too, have been the biologically reductionist approaches to explaining human development and knowledge. Yet these approaches are proliferating in debates over the meaning of race and genetics, despite clear indications from epigenetics and dynamic systems theories that "to describe a behavior pattern as innate (or genetically determined) is in fact a statement of ignorance about how that trait actually develops" (Lickliter & Honeycutt, 2013, p. 185, emphasis added). This is not surprising since, as Cooper (2005) sums up in stark and uncompromising terms,

> For the last four centuries Western science has been obsessed with the need to justify White privilege and in so doing has provided crucial support for racist ideas in society at large. To use the rhetoric of science to sell the idea that historical inequity should be embraced as biological inevitability is an insult to those who value a common humanity. (p. 75)

These debates have enormous, and far from merely academic, consequences. Indeed, the application of eugenics, for example, was associated with no less than a campaign of ethnic cleansing in the United States, leading to some 60,000 Americans being sterilized (for a gripping account of this history, see Black, 2012).

To chart a different path into the future, it is important to draw on oppositional voices of resistance in philosophy, social sciences, education, and other fields, especially in the works of Black and Latina feminist philosophers and scholars. Insights by Patricia Hill Collins (e.g., 1991), Audre Lorde (e.g., 1984), Gloria E. Anzaldúa (e.g., 1990, 2015; cf. Moraga & Anzaldúa, 1981), Chela Sandoval (e.g., 2000), among others, are as yet to be learned by many of us still hypnotized by fake promises and a false sense of safety associated with what is taken to be "exact" sciences, "true facts," infallible ideas, established canons, objective data, and absolute certainty. According to Chela Sandoval (as conveyed by Phillips, 2002, p. 254), "Black and other 'U.S. Third World' women, in particular, actually pioneered the prototypical methods of postmodern activism." In this research tradition, people of color and others on the margins of dominant power structures collectively developed progressive methods linked to political activism. Much of this scholarship, as conveyed by Phillips (2002), in building on works by Hill Collins (2000), among others, has developed "culturally situated alternatives to traditional scientific positivism" (p. 579). They have rejected the dichotomy between scholarship and activism while eschewing empty promises of objectivism. Significantly, such an approach does not shy away from elaborating "authoritative metanarrative claims" (Nayak, 2014, p. XIII)—in the face of patriarchy and racism that deny the legitimacy to black women's and other marginalized voices—while accepting that there are no absolute, universal grounds for such claims outside of historically situated struggles. Instead of adhering to existing canons, this work is guided by the dialogical and dialectical relationship between practice and scholarship, while highlighting the necessity of activist positioning (Hill Collins, 2000, p. 30; cf. Phillips, 2002).

Addressing the role in science and research of individual agency, subjectivity (especially in terms of pain and suffering of those who are marginalized) and responsibility—which are never just individual but social at once too (as in the notion of collectividual, see Stetsenko, 2012, 2013a, 2013b)—is, in my view, of prime importance in such activist approaches. In Audre Lorde's (1984, p. 37) powerful formulation,

> As they become known to and accepted by us, our feelings and the honest exploration of them become sanctuaries and spawning grounds for the most radical and daring of ideas. ... This is not idle fantasy, but the true meaning of "it feels right to me." We can train ourselves to respect our feelings, and to discipline (transpose) them into a language that matches those feelings so they can be shared.

To say that the principle "it feels right to me" is an important guide to methodology of research and to the whole conduct of science might indeed sound like "idle fantasy," to reiterate Lorde's expression. Yet, I whole-heartedly support Lorde's powerful idea and in taking up from her, suggest that "it feels right to me" needs to be taken as a paramount methodological principle. This is not about understanding methodology and science to be about doing whatever one wants. Instead, this is about methodology and science being fully our responsibility—responsibility of each and everyone of us, and not as isolated, atomic individuals (which is an impossible abstraction anyway), but as active and agentive members of human communities and active agents of history-in-the-making, that is, as "ensembles of social relations" (as Marx famously formulated). The task, in other words, is to understand individuals non-individualistically (cf. Arievitch, 2017), as not only such ensembles but also, and more critically, as fully activist agents and conductors of such ensembles, who fully matter in their workings and dynamics, every step of the way and in all instances. Persons in this approach can be seen to be in charge of, and fully responsible for, the world insofar as, and the extent of, us joining the activist struggles and collaborative activities (including as these are manifested in political life) that are currently taking place in the world. This is the gist of the transformative activist stance (Stetsenko, 2016a), according to which

> every person matters because the world is evoked, real-ized, invented, and created by each and every one of us, in each and every event of our being-knowing-doing—by us as social actors and agents of communal practices and collective history, who only come about within the matrices of these practices through realizing and co-authoring them in joint struggles and strivings. This position is a departure from the canonical interpretations of Marxism that traditionally eschew the level of individual processes such as agency, mind, and consciousness. (p. 7)

Science and research and all knowledge production processes, in this view and contra dominant individualist-cognitivist approaches, are human endeavors in which we are wholly at stake, in the fullness of our very being and becoming, and in which much is at stake for us and for the whole world, too. I believe this is consonant with Hannah Arendt's (2018) argument (in her building off from Marx) about the importance of each and every person seizing the means of exercising responsibility for the world. This is about each and every one carrying out the work of discerning the course and the momentum of collective world-historical struggles as these are en-countered (and taken up) by us in our particular place and time, while joining these struggles on one or the other

KNOWLEDGE PRODUCTION AS A PROCESS OF MAKING MIS/TAKES 33

side, from our own unique stands/stances—all in striving to make activist and passionate contributions to these struggles.

Returning to the role of mis/takes in knowledge production, we always have to acknowledge that we, including and perhaps especially as scholars, might be mistaken (cf. Critchley, 2014). Moreover, I would expand on this idea so as to suggest that we have to acknowledge that we not only might be mistaken but that, in fact, we always are mistaken, especially if we consider solutions and ideas not just in their present meanings and entailments, but also in their status beyond the current moment. Critchley (2014, p. 390) has summed up Bronowski' views on the importance of uncertainty in the following way:

> Pursuing knowledge means accepting uncertainty. The more we know, the less certain we are ... The play of tolerance opposes the principle of monstrous certainty that is endemic to fascism and, sadly, not just fascism but all the various faces of fundamentalism. When we think we have certainty, when we aspire to the knowledge of the gods, then Auschwitz can happen and can repeat itself. Arguably, it has repeated itself in the genocidal certainties of past decades.

The more we know, the less certain we are, indeed! Yet our confidence and lack of humility play tricks with us, as when (and if) we announce incontrovertible facts, timeless laws, and universal truths, which in effect are but transient and inevitably faulty steps toward the new, and ever-shifting, horizons of knowledge. For example, witness the irony of how excessively confident pronouncements can quickly turn out to be faulty (truly quickly, because a refutation—in this case, self-refutation—encroaches on the "statement of truth" without any delay, literally in the next sentence). This is about the following remarkable quote from Turkheimer (2011):

> *First Law of Behavior Genetics* ... and of a simple fact of human—one might say biological—existence: we are not free to become whatever we want, unconstrained by genetic or other familial constraints. *Or rather, we are free to become what we want, but doing so will take more effort for some traits than for others* ... and an almost unimaginable amount of effort for the most ingrained. (p. 827, emphasis added)

What kind of a First Law (with capital letters, which adds much irony) and what kind of "a simple fact of human ... existence" are these, if the very next sentence contains their de facto full and blunt refutation? Stating that "we are not free to become whatever we want" to then immediately say that "we are free to become what we want" (separated only by an offhand "or rather") is a striking example of how tricky such seemingly incontrovertible statements can be and how important it is to avoid anything bearing the name of a "First Law," especially in human sciences. In contrast, it is refreshing to find honest and humble appraisals of science and knowledge, such as when Reich (2018) insists that

> from the errors of thinking that the sun revolves around the earth [and many, many others]—from all of these errors and more, we should take cautionary lesson not to trust our gut instincts or the stereotyped expectations we find around us. *If we can be confident of anything, it is that whatever* [we currently believe in] *is most likely wrong.* (p. 264, emphasis added)

Note that none of the points discussed so far in this chapter implies that knowledge is impossible, unreliable, or unattainable. This is absolutely not the intended implication here because drawing attention to knowledge production being provisional, un-finalizable, and uncertain does not suggest that we cannot know or cannot achieve anything in the process of inquiry and knowledge production, along the way. Knowledge and its "products"—such as conjectures and hypotheses, assumptions and positions, claims and theories—however unstable, provisional, fallible and even mis/taken, can and do nonetheless work, albeit only in a certain sense and under a number of provisions. That is, they do work for given problems, at a given time, within given circumstances and confines, in view of given goals and as defined by given investigative projects they belong to, that is, under given contingencies, restrictions, and specifications. Moreover, if these specifications are accounted for and taken into consideration (especially as regards practical-social projects that the knowledge production process serves to advance), then knowledge claims can be compared, argued for or against, validated, adjudicated, contested, and—temporarily (!)—accepted.

My argument is that the workings of knowledge involve so many contingencies that they are best described as temporary waystations and horizons of possibility, rather than as fixed and rigid solutions, or facts (let alone as "first laws"). I think that the metaphor of knowledge production as a continuous and fluid mountain stream that never ends (paraphrasing Thelen's, 2005, metaphor of development) can be apt. This is playing off of the notions of instability, flow, fluidity, liquidity (e.g., Bauman, 2000, Fuchs, 2011; Hardt & Negri, 2000; cf. Sutherland, 2013). Their popularity has to do, as Tomlinson (2007) argues, with attempts to grasp the social ontology of recent modernity [and thus] ... to comprehend, variously: *the permeable, protean nature* of social space; the *intrinsic mobility* both of agents and of social processes and relations (as in the flows around a network); and the phenomenology of modern social existence. This latter, not only in terms of the common experience of mobility and deterritorialization, but also in terms of the *constant dissolution of fixity* in value, and of a different "texture" of life. (p. 75, emphasis added)

In using such metaphors, it can be claimed that knowledge production is like a mountain stream that is moving all the time in an unending and dynamic flow of continuous changes. Like a stream, this process has no programs or instructions dictating its course and dynamics in advance, in fixed and predetermined ways. Like a stream, knowledge production reflects (or embodies) the history of the past in the present and carries this past into the future, with this future itself being co-embedded within, and intermingled with, the present and the past. Like a stream, knowledge production, too, is nonlinear so that no rigid prediction for the next stages is ever possible. It, too, has to be understood in its totality, as a whole system, all parts of which are mutually co-embedded, co-acting, co-implicated, intertwined, and interdependent—all in the course of fluid and continuous re-arrangements, re-constitutions, and re-assemblages.

Within such a dynamic, situated, and nonlinear understanding, it is possible to address (again, relying on Thelen's, 2005, apt metaphors) how knowledge production also, like a mountain stream—albeit being fluid and constantly changing—has patterns and eddies, milestones and plateaus, and even relatively stable contours and moments which are giving rise to something best described perhaps as a relative, dynamic stability. At such moments, knowledge can be regarded as being relatively reliable and somewhat predictive and thus, even warranted, if only momentarily. Yet again, all of this has to be formulated while centrally keeping in mind the ongoing quest and the unending flow of unfolding knowledge-practices, wherein nothing is fixed or stable forever, in a decontextualized, abstracted, neutral, and universalistic way, that is, as if "set in stone." Even in cases of relative stability, this stability does not mean immutability and finality, nor absolute certainty, since stability itself is dynamic throughout, comprised as it is of many shifting parts and dimensions that can rearrange and in fact do rearrange themselves all the time, depending on context, timing, goals, commitments, pursuits of particular projects and so on. Like any moving process, knowledge too is assembled and maintained "softly," on line and in response to context (cf. Thelen, 2005). So is methodology in need of being assembled softly, each time in novel and flexible, creative ways that defy canons and taken for granted assumptions—in a personal and passionate quest for answers, where our responsibility and indeed our very lives are on the line.

4 Democratizing Science and Research as an Empowering-Liberatory, Decolonizing Practice

Importantly, in the approach suggested herein—building off of many scholars, especially those in the resistance tradition—knowledge and science are not about elitist endeavors conducted in the "ivory tower" by exceptional individuals supposedly standing on pedestals at some putatively unreachable Olympian heights (as science is still typically portrayed in the so called "great men" tradition). Instead, knowledge and science are but parts and parcels of collaborative projects carried out in the real world of activist struggles and strivings for answers—and de facto also new questions—emerging within the ever-unfolding dynamics of history and society, in which each and every participant makes a difference and matters through individually unique contributions.

A related point is that science can and needs to be seen as a social practice that is de facto realized and sustained not only, and not so much, by "great men," but—first and foremost!—by the so-called rank-and-file scholars and "common" people, including in their everyday lives, whereby activities and contributions by all members of communities make a difference and matter, if only on a small scale (especially given that whether the scale is "small" or not often cannot be determined with any certainty at any given time; this is a fluid and dynamic scale and its composition forever remains open-ended).

Indeed, broad questions of ontology, epistemology, and methodology are typically supposed to be the province of a "big philosophy," to be addressed by a select coterie of elite, high-ranking professionals. These professionals are apparently assigned with a special role of providing us with answers and instructions of how to work in the footsteps of traditions and paradigms established by "giants" (typically, white men) no less than those like Kant, Hegel, or Marx (and their modern-day incarnates taken to be, or self-declared to be, "the leading authorities"). Most researchers and educators are, unfortunately, trained to not count themselves among such elites and thus, they typically tend to stay away from formulating their own answers to many cosmic philosophical questions they encounter and, often, do not dare to interrogate these on one's own terms. This trend is paralleled by the so called "theory into practice" approaches that, too, are autocratic and hegemonic since they favor hierarchies and attribute authority to those deemed "on top," as in charge to prescribe solutions to those who are considered to be at "subordinate" levels (i.e. especially teachers and students; cf. Fenstermacher & Richardson, 1994).

In other words, the rank-and-file researchers typically consider themselves to be engaged in putatively less significant, allegedly "minor" topics such as, for example, exploring new applications for established concepts, while following with broad theories and philosophies developed for them. Both this supposedly "natural" hierarchy of topics and this hegemonic distribution of labor and tasks need to be resolutely challenged.

A push for a decolonizing and empowering-liberatory research and methodology, including for researchers themselves, has to include challenging the established divisions of labor in academia and beyond and especially, its hierarchy. To ignore or bypass this challenge means to subscribe to an old-fashioned, dogmatic, patronizing, and elitist—as well as also sexist and racist—understanding of research and science as comprised of already established, unquestionable canons set in stone and embodied in the currently dominant status quo in academia. The alternative is to see that science and research are never about what is already established but instead, are about what needs to change, what has to be done next, where we want and need to go in projecting into the future, and what can be accomplished from a critical and activist perspective of taking on responsibility and risks for moving forward.

In democratizing methodological work and debates, the central principle has to do with the right and responsibility of each researcher to find out answers and to develop methodologies on one's own terms, that is, to know for oneself within one's own authentic, authorial, and activist quests. Certainly, this cannot be achieved by lonely, atomic, bounded individuals but instead, by researchers as members of communities situated at particular space/time and concrete locations in history, culture, context and politics—while also questioning, challenging and transgressing these. At a deeper level, this approach is about the need to understand, reveal, and diagnose the core conflicts and dilemmas within the current situation, take them up in our own unique ways (in their unity of ethics, ontology and epistemology; see Stetsenko, 2018b, 2020), and move forward to resolving them, the best we can. This is in resonance with Frantz Fanon's (1963) striking words that "[e]ach generation must out of relative obscurity discover its mission, fulfill it, or betray it" (p. 205).

This agentive and activist approach to knowledge production as a deeply personal project can be legitimized especially in light of the ongoing and persistent sharp disagreements, debates, and controversies on even the most basic principles and theoretical positions at the very core of methodology and theory in sciences, even within relatively distinct fields such as qualitative approaches.

Indeed, although many in the qualitative community are "relatively united in the social constructionist belief that knowledge is not disinterested, apolitical, naively found (discovered, uncovered, etc.), ... they sharply disagree on what to make of that belief" (Schwandt, 2006, pp. 803–804). Another illustration of the inherent diversity of any system of ideas is that the Marxist tradition in fact exists in the format of continuing clashes and dialogues, re-discoveries, and radical dis-junctures among the discordant schemes of the many "Marxisms" that have emerged through decades.

5 Concluding Reflections

The account of sciences and research, and of their methodologies—as fluid and open-ended processes consisting of continuously mis/taking, up-taking, and re-taking reality—celebrates human agency enacted by and embodied in the process of co-authoring community practices and, thus, our shared world itself. In this approach, nothing is ever fixed or taken for granted and instead, all knowledge is constantly in-the-making, and in-the-mis/taking (!), by us ourselves as members of communities and participants in their unending dynamics extending through time. This agency, in my view, is the linchpin of being-knowing-doing and the core dimension of research and methodology. This is about insisting on the centrality of our quests to simultaneously realize the world and ourselves, in co-authoring reality through taking it up while challenging and transgressing it. These quests—and therefore, all knowledge—are understood to be achievable through us mattering, that is, through us making a difference via our own unique and irreplaceable contributions to communal practices including science and its investigative practices and projects. Accordingly, the core implication from this approach is that there is no knowledge production and no research methodology that can be separated from each individual researcher's transformative, activist engagement with, and a unique stance toward, the world and its current struggles.

To conduct research is to be engaged in current conflicts and contradictions, as social actors and agents of history—members of particular communities of practice (in their unfolding historicity), who realize them by mattering in their dynamics. This is in contrast with thinking about individuals as solo entities possessing somehow idiosyncratic characteristics, opinions, and trajectories. The argument, in other words, is for a non-solipsistic approach that nonetheless does not eliminate but, on the contrary, celebrates both our profound communality and our unique positionality, as agentive social actors who always can and do matter in the drama of history—and the drama of science and research too. This is an argument against seeing people as being passively "positioned" by others—be it external circumstances, other people, societies, cultures, contexts, and so on (on the passivity assumption in current research and theorizing, see Stetsenko, 2019b, 2020). Instead, the argument is to insist on the centrality of our own, activist taking up—primarily, through making mis/takes—the challenges and contradictions of our own time and place.

This approach is about the importance of searching for our own answers, while inventing ideas and methodologies that work for us as agentive actors of community practices, who are pursuing unique activist projects—though always in solidarity with others, as collaborative, shared endeavors—from within our own historical place and time, however mis/taken these answers inevitably turn out to be.

6 How Does the Chapter Address the Challenges of a Non-Dualist Methodology?

This chapter addresses profound questions about methodology and its roots in cultural-historical and socio-political contexts. The author's argument directly challenges the dualist vision of a split between the sciences and social practices, as science is a social practice. Stetsenko proposes a stance for CHAT methodology to push "for a more democratic and empowering-liberating research and methodology, including for participants and researchers themselves, especially those excluded and marginalized—people of color, ethnic minorities, women, scholars working in the global South—that must challenge the established division of labor within sciences and research." Stetsenko proposes to decolonize knowledge and to challenge the historical hero-figure of the white male scientist. She strongly criticizes dualist normativity, especially the claim of research objectivity and neutrality. Regarding methodology, Stetsenko suggests an analysis leading to the conclusion that even in progressive textbooks, it is highly uncommon for researchers to be encouraged to be innovative, to be creative, to take risks and to learn from their mistakes. She points out that in many Eurocentric models of science, "following the status quo can be described as an overarching adaptationist ethos" that influences the relation with the living praxis to which researchers contribute. In relation with historical context, she analyzes this adaptationist ethos of knowledge production and academic hierarchies in line with profit-driven capitalist structures of power. Stetsenko posits that from a transformative perspective as in CHAT, the process of knowledge production is about a constant struggle and striving for matters stretching far beyond the limits of what is traditionally taken as knowledge. "In it, nothing is handed down 'ready-made' and instead, everything is about overcoming, questioning, transgressing, challenging, and disrupting what is taken for granted." She emphasizes the need to challenge the established divisions of labor and power relations in academia, between methodologies, and in every social practice.

The chapter stresses the importance of a monist conception of methodology and more broadly of knowledge production. As pointed out by Vygotsky (1934), the whole inquiry process cannot be compartmentalized into separate components or steps for the purposes of analysis. All steps belong to a single dynamic and systemic whole, which can be overlooked when everything is divided into "factors." Moreover, individuals are not located outside the research process. Regarding methodology and research, the chapter discusses the dialectical link between the social and the individual. By contributing to research—which entails collaborative projects carried out in the real world of activist struggles and new practices—individuals change and make a difference through their unique individual contributions. Owing to their transformative activist stance, they also gradually change the dynamics of history and society. Each research participant and the researchers themselves are indeed, in Stetsenko's view, "active and agentive members of human communities and active agents of history-in-the-making." Therefore, the relation between society and human development is a dialectic one in its impetus and demands a methodology that can capture this ongoing and open-ended process and challenge its inherent contradictions.

Note

1 There are exceptions to this trend yet these exceptions are often limited in their critical take on science and its normativities. For example, in a book with a promising title The research imagination: An introduction to qualitative and quantitative methods (Gray et al., 2007), objectivity is addressed with an open mind, as the authors are "trying to understand [it] as less self-evident and all-encompassing than in the past." The authors state that "Research is ... a dynamic process that is more rigorous and complicated than many people realize ..." (ibid., p. 1). They helpfully note that "To learn methodology and to do research itself requires a tolerance for ambiguity and living with some uncertainty" and that making many decisions in science "is only partly a science; it is also a craft that calls for research imagination. The researcher is both a scientist and craftsperson whose toolkit includes a vibrant imagination" (ibid., p. 29). They feature and discuss, in quite some detail, feminist approaches to this topic.

Yet, throughout the text, and quite ironically, the language of standards and canons persists, with implications that overpower the authors' own claims to treating objectivity differently. For example, the authors write that "when researchers claim to be scientists, they subject themselves and their work to scrutiny and judgment according to the standards and canons of scientific investigation" (ibid., p. 4). In the same vein, they speak of "the orderly accumulation of knowledge ..." (p. 10) and insist that "The canons of science are a basic blueprint, but to do good research, we must do more than follow their direction" (p. 29). The final conclusion seems to be that "The scientific canon of objectivity does not mean that research has to be uniform and colorless"—a clear acceptance of objectivity as a canon even though moderated by an appeal to be, at the same time, creative within this canon's confines. The question remains whether one can truly be creative and non-uniform within what is presented as an orderly accumulation of knowledge which follows blueprints of objectivity, and while subjecting ourselves and our work to scrutiny and judgment according to these standards and canons? It comes as no surprise, then, that researchers explicating their value positions or commitments are seen as "indicating certain value biases" (p. 10), rather than seeing such an explication as an essential and indispensable part of research methodology itself, as suggested in the present chapter.

References

Anzaldúa, G. (1990). *Borderlands/La Frontera: The new Mestiza*. Aunt Lute.

Anzaldúa, G. (2015). *Light in the dark/Luz en lo Oscuro: Rewriting identity, spirituality, reality*. Duke University.

Arendt, H. (2018). *The modern challenge to tradition*. Wallstein.

Arievitch, I. (2017). *Beyond the brain: An agentive active activity perspective on mind, development, and learning*. Sense.

Bauman, Z. (2000). *Liquid modernity*. Polity.

Black, E. (2012). *War against the weak: Eugenics and America's campaign to create a master race*. Dialog Press.

Brinkmann, S. (2014). Doing without data. *Qualitative Inquiry, 20*(6), 720–725. doi:10.1177/1077800414530254

Bronowski, J. (1976). *The ascent of man*. Little, Brown & Company.

Charmaz, K. (2008). Constructionism and the grounded theory method. In J. A. Holstein & J. F. Gubrium (Eds.), *Handbook of constructionist research* (pp. 397–412). The Guilford Press.

Cooper, R. S. (2005). Race and IQ: Molecular genetics as deus ex machina. *American Psychologist, 60*(1), 71–76. doi:10.1037/0003-066X.60.1.71

Creswell, J. (2007). *Qualitative inquiry and research design: Choosing among five traditions*. Sage.

Critchley, S. (2014). The dangers of certainty: A lesson from Auschwitz. In P. Catapano & S. Critchley (Eds.), *The Stone reader: Modern philosophy in 133 argument* (pp. 386–391). W. W. Norton.

Dewey, J. (1960). *The quest for certainty: A study on the relation between knowledge and action.* Putnam's Sons. (Original work published 1929)

Erickson, F., & Gutiérrez, K. D. (2002). Culture, rigor, and science in educational research. *Educational Researcher, 31*(8), 21–24.

Fanon, F. (1963). *The wretched of the Earth.* Grove.

Fenstermacher, G. D., & Richardson, V. (1994). Promoting confusion in educational psychology: How is it done? *Educational Psychologist, 29*(1), 49–55. doi:10.1207/s15326985ep2901_5

Fuchs, C. (2011). *Foundations of critical media and information studies.* Routledge.

Gleiser, M. (2010). *A tear at the edge of creation: A radical new vision for life in an imperfect universe.* Free Press.

Gould, S. J. (1988). The case of the creeping fox terrier clone. *Natural History, 96*, 16–24.

Gould, S. J. (1996). *The mismeasure of man.* W. W. Norton.

Gray, P., Williamson, J., & Karp, D. (2007). *The research imagination: An introduction to qualitative and quantitative methods.* Cambridge University Press.

Griggs, R. A. (2015). The disappearance of independence in textbook coverage of Asch's social pressure experiments. *Teaching of Psychology, 42*(2), 137–142. doi:10.1177/0098628315569939

Hill Collins, P. (1991). *Black feminist thought: Knowledge, consciousness, and the politics of empowerment.* Routledge.

Jarrett, C. (2008). Foundations of sand? *Psychologist, 21*(9), 756–759.

Kincheloe, L. J., & Tobin, K. (2009). The much exaggerated death of positivism. *Cultural Study of Science Education, 4*, 513–528.

Lickliter, R., & Honeycutt, H. (2013). A developmental evolutionary framework for psychology. *Review of General Psychology, 17*(2), 184–189. doi:10.1037/a0032932

Lorde, A. (1984). *Sister outsider.* The Crossing Press.

Margonis, F. (2009). John Dewey's racialized visions of the student and classroom community. *Educational Theory, 59*(1), 17–39.

Méndez, C. L., Coddou, F., & Maturana, H. R. (1988). The bringing forth of pathology. *Irish Journal of Psychology, 9*(1), 144–172.

Moraga, C., & Anzaldúa, G. (1981). *This bridge called my back: Writings by radical women of color.* Persephone.

Morawski, J. G. (1992). There is more to our history of giving: The place of introductory textbooks in American psychology. *American Psychologist, 47*(2), 161–169. doi:10.1037/0003-066X.47.2.161

Nayak, S. (2014). *Race, gender, and the activism of black feminist theory: Working with Audre Lorde.* Routledge.

Newton, R. G. (2009). *How physics confronts reality.* World Scientific Publishing.

Ohanian, H. C. (2011). *Einstein's mistakes: The human failings of genius.* W. W. Norton.

Phillips, L. (2002). Recontextualizing Kenneth B. Clark: An Afrocentric perspective on the paradoxical legacy of a model psychologist-activist. In W. E. Pickren & D. A. Dewsbury (Eds.), *Evolving perspectives on the history of psychology* (pp. 575–606). APA.

Popper, K. (1994). *The myth of the framework: In defense of science and rationality.* Routledge.

Prigogine, I. (1997). *The end of certainty: Time, chaos, and the new laws of nature* (in collaboration with I. Stengers). The Free Press.

Reich, D. (2018). *Who we are and where we come from: Ancient DNA and the new science of the human past.* Pantheon.

Sandoval, C. (2000). *Methodology of the oppressed.* University of Minnesota Press.

Schwandt, T. A. (2000). Three epistemological stances for qualitative inquiry: Interpretivism, hermeneutics, and social constructionism. In N. K. Denzin & Y. S. Lincoln (Eds.), *Handbook of qualitative research* (pp. 189–213). Sage.

Stetsenko, A. (2005). Activity as object-related: Resolving the dichotomy of individual and collective planes of activity. *Mind, Culture, and Activity, 12*(1), 70–88. doi:10.1207/s15327884mca1201_6

Stetsenko, A. (2008). From relational ontology to transformative activist stance on development and learning: Expanding Vygotsky's (CHAT) project. *Cultural Studies of Science Education, 3*(2), 471–491. doi:10.1007/s11422-008-9111-3

Stetsenko, A. (2010). Standing on the shoulders of giants: A balancing act of dialectically theorizing conceptual understanding on the grounds of Vygotsky's project. In W.-M. Roth (Ed.), *Re/structuring science education: ReUniting psychological and sociological perspectives* (pp. 69–88). Springer.

Stetsenko, A. (2012). Personhood: An activist project of historical becoming through collaborative pursuits of social transformation. *New Ideas in Psychology, 30*(1), 144–153. doi:10.1016/j.newideapsych.2009.11.008

Stetsenko, A. (2013a). The challenge of individuality in cultural-historical activity theory: "Collectividual" dialectics from a transformative activist stance. *Outlines: Critical Practice Studies, 14*(2), 7–28.

Stetsenko, A. (2013b). Theorizing personhood for the world in transition and change: Reflections from a transformative activist stance. In J. Martin & M. H. Bickhard (Eds.), *The psychology of personhood: Philosophical, historical, social-developmental, and narrative perspectives* (pp. 181–203). Cambridge University Press.

Stetsenko, A. (2014). Transformative activist stance for education: Inventing the future in moving beyond the status quo. In T. Corcoran (Ed.), *Psychology in education: Critical theory-practice* (pp. 181–198). Sense.

Stetsenko, A. (2015). Theory for and as social practice of realizing the future: Implications from a transformative activist stance. In J. Martin, J. Sugarman, & K. Slaney (Eds.),

The Wiley handbook of theoretical and philosophical psychology: Methods, approaches, and new directions for social sciences (pp. 102–116). Wiley.

Stetsenko, A. (2016a). *The transformative mind: Expanding Vygotsky's approach to development and education*. Cambridge University Press.

Stetsenko, A. (2016b). Vygotsky's theory of method and philosophy of practice: implications for trans/formative methodology. *Educação, 39*(4), 32. doi:10.15448/1981-2582.2016.s.24385

Stetsenko, A. (2017). Science education and transformative activist stance: Activism as a quest for becoming via authentic-authorial contribution to communal practices. In L. Bryan & K. Tobin (Eds.), *13 questions: Reframing education's conversation: Science* (pp. 33–47). Peter Lang.

Stetsenko, A. (2018a). Agentive creativity in all of us: An egalitarian perspective from a transformative activist stance. In M. C. Connery, V. John-Steiner, & A. Marjanovic-Shane (Eds.), *Vygotsky and creativity: A cultural-historical approach to play, meaning making, and the arts* (pp. 41–60). Peter Lang.

Stetsenko, A. (2018b). Research and activist projects of resistance: The ethical-political foundations for a transformative ethico-onto-epistemology. *Learning, Culture and Social Interaction.* https://doi.org/10.1016/j.lcsi.2018.04.002

Stetsenko, A. (2019a). Creativity as dissent and resistance: Transformative approach premised on social justice agenda. In I. Lebuda & V. Glaveanu (Eds.), *The Palgrave handbook of social creativity* (pp. 431–446). Springer.

Stetsenko, A. (2019b). Radical-transformative agency: Continuities and contrasts with relational agency and implications for education. *Frontiers in Education.* doi:10.3389/feduc.2019.00148

Stetsenko, A. (2020). Transformative-activist approach and social justice approaches to the history of psychology. In W. Pickren (Ed.), *The Oxford research encyclopedia of psychology*. Oxford University Press. https://doi.org/10.1093/acrefore/9780190236557.013.466

Stetsenko, A., & Arievitch, I. (2004a). The self in cultural-historical activity theory. *Theory & Psychology, 14*(4), 475–503.

Stetsenko, A., & Arievitch, I. (2004b). Vygotskian collaborative project of social transformation: History, politics, and practice in knowledge construction. *The International Journal of Critical Psychology, 12*(4), 58–80.

Steuer, F. B., & Ham, K. W. (2008). Psychology textbooks: Examining their accuracy. *Teaching of Psychology, 35*(3), 160.

Sutherland, T. (2013). Liquid networks and the metaphysics of flux: Ontologies of flow in an age of speed and mobility. *Theory, Culture & Society, 30*(5), 3–23.

Thelen, E. (2005). Dynamic systems theory and the complexity of change. *Psychoanalytic Dialogues, 15*(2), 255–283. doi:10.1080/10481881509348831

Tomlinson, J. (2007). *The culture of speed: The coming of immediacy*. Sage.

Tuck, E., & Yang, K. W. (2014). R-words: Refusing research. In D. Paris & M. T. Winn (Eds.) *Humanizing research: Decolonizing qualitative inquiry with youth and communities* (pp. 223–247). Sage.

Turkheimer, E. (2011). Genetics and human agency: Comment on Dar-Nimrod and Heine. *Psychological Bulletin, 137*(5), 825–828. doi:10.1037/a0024306

Vianna, E., & Stetsenko, A. (2014). Research with a transformative activist agenda: Creating the future through education for social change. In J. Vadeboncoeur (Ed.), *Learning in and across contexts: Reimagining education. National Society for the studies of education yearbook* (pp. 575–602). Columbia University.

Vianna, E., & Stetsenko, A. (2017). Expanding student agency in the introductory psychology course: Transformative activist stance and critical-theoretical pedagogy. In R. Obeid, A. M. Schwartz, C. Shane-Simpson, & P. J. Brooks (Eds.), *How we teach now: The GSTA guide to student-centered teaching* (pp. 252–268). Society for the Teaching of Psychology.

Weiten, W., & Wight, R. D. (1992). Portraits of a discipline: An examination of introductory psychology textbooks in America. In A. E. Puente, J. R. Matthews, & C. L. Brewer (Eds.), *Teaching psychology in America: A history* (pp. 453–504). American Psychological Association.

West, C. (1999). The genealogy of modern racism. In D. Goldberg & P. Essed (Eds.), *Race critical theories: Text and context* (pp. 90–112). Blackwell.

Wright, K. (2004). Einstein was often wrong, but even his errors led to deep truths. *Discover.*

CHAPTER 3

Agency and Activity of Students from Non-Dominant Groups

Methodological and Ethical Issues

Isabelle Rioux and Patricia Dionne

Abstract

Within Cultural-Historical Activity Theory (CHAT), a growing number of studies are interested in the activity of populations that other frameworks usually considered as passive actors. In the field of education (formal and informal), this is notably the case of the works of Gutiérrez (2008) and Gutiérrez and Jurow (2017) about members of non-dominant communities. In French traditions of ergonomy, linked to CHAT's epistemological premises, some studies also take the activity of the student as research object. Those works have in common an emphasis on the active role of the subjects in their own apprenticeship and development by focusing on their activity. From this perspective, there is no more question of beneficiaries of services or of students who receive some teachings, but there are actors who, through the mediation of cultural tools, instruments and the interaction with significant others, gain progressive mastery of their learning and development. In addition, by virtue of their transformative aim, those works also contribute to stimulate the power to act of these populations. On a methodological level, this change of point of view requires some adaptations to study activity, or traces of activity, of population members of non-dominant groups. This chapter will discuss some methodological and ethical issues, based on experiences from the field and a review of literature from studies situated in CHAT. In particular, the underlying relation between the transformative and nomothetic aims of those researches will be discussed as other important ethical issues which are addressed by those studies.

Keywords

activity – non-dominant groups – transformative practices – methodological adaptation – ethical issues

Within Cultural-Historical Activity Theory (CHAT), a growing number of studies are interested in the activity of populations, such as students in the field of education, which other frameworks have usually considered as passive actors who merely receive knowledge or information—thus corresponding to a "banking model of education" (Freire, 1974). More specifically, this contribution focuses on the activity and agency of students who belong to dominated groups or are subject to *school inequities*.

The aim of the chapter is to contribute to a methodological and theoretical discussion on how different CHAT research methodologies may or may not successfully take into account the agency of students in a group that is subject to such domination. In other words, the chapter sets forth avenues for pondering the question, *How can research located in the CHAT theoretical tradition highlight the importance of agency from the standpoint of students' activity, while also taking into account the role of power relations? What role can CHAT researchers in the field play in order to create better social conditions while enhancing students' agency?* To address this question, we base ourselves on a literature review whose methodology will be briefly described further on. We begin by defining certain key concepts that guide our reading of the reviewed texts, before presenting the texts in question, which are grouped according to different types of research designs. All the texts present some empirical data stemming from research in the CHAT field. The chapter will end with a discussion of how the reviewed studies take into account students' agency and relationships of domination in the classroom.

1   Agency

In the CHAT tradition, the concept of agency is hardly new. As Haapasaari et al. (2016) point out, CHAT research examines agency in terms of action rather than personal traits or abilities, as is the case in other theoretical conceptions of agency. Stetsenko (2005) defines individual agency as "the ability to produce, create, and make a difference in social practices" (p. 78). Consistent with the works of Vygotsky, this individual agency, and all human development, is made possible and stimulated by the mediation of cultural language instruments. However, this individual agency is far from being "individualistic," in the sense that it is *not* autonomous or self-actualizing. Even inner speech and consciousness are embedded within a social relationship with the self. Moreover, merely acting out of a commitment to certain goals and ideals is viewed as a manifestation of individual agency and of how a person contributes to social life (Stetsenko & Arievitch, 2004) and its transformation; this is sometimes referred to as transformative agency (Engeström & Sannino, 2013).

Engeström and Sannino (2013), stressing the volitional dimension of agency, propose a definition along similar lines and state that "agency manifests itself when people formulate intentions and carry out voluntary actions that go beyond the accepted habits and given conditions of activity within their organization so as to then transform them" (p. 5). Basing themselves on their concept of expansive learning, these last authors discuss the development of a "new type of agency" resulting from expansive learning, that is, a learning situation that prompts a group of people to transform their activity systems. In this conception, the object of activity is collective. As such, the object of the transformation and agency is a collective object. On a collective level, agency is turned toward the achievement of a collective goal and is aimed at carrying out a collective project (Dionne & Bourdon, 2018) or solving a problem that concerns a group (Lemos, 2017). Hence, agency is neither individual nor collective, but touches upon both the individual and collective/social levels (Dionne & Bourdon, 2018). In other words, what we would like to underscore is the dialectical dimension of agency—between, on one hand, the actor's subjectivity and embeddedness in collective agency, and on the other, the agent's possibility of transforming society and the collective and in turn being transformed by them (Stetsenko, 2016). This dialectic is central to Vygotsky's (2014) conception of development: by acting on the world, humans learn and develop, and in turn this development can contribute to a new transformation of the world. Importantly, even if they conceive agency from a dialectical point of view, some research studies may emphasize one level or the other. Edwards (2005) also sheds light on relational agency. She points out that, by bringing together different individual perspectives, relational agency in joint and collective object-oriented actions can also stimulate individual development.

2   Power Relations and Inequality in the Classroom

Classrooms are fraught with multiple types of power relations. Power issues are especially obvious in the case of certain populations, for example students from socioeconomically underprivileged backgrounds (Panofsky, 2009) or cultural minorities (Gutiérrez, 2008). Indeed, without necessarily supporting a perspective of social determinism, school is often a micro-society that tends to give rise to a reproduction (Bourdieu & Passeron, 1970) of the social inequalities found in other spheres of life. This is especially true of inequalities pervading the sphere of work, where certain societal classes or cultural groups tend more often to hold a position of power (Beaty, 2013).

Regardless of students' different social or cultural status, school remains a place characterized by many forms of authority. Based on Foray (2009), at least two forms can be distinguished here. The first is teachers' personal or pedagogical authority, a very pragmatic form of authority that consists in teachers' ability to be obeyed by students in order to ensure that their groups function smoothly. The second, more symbolic, is status-related, and although wielded by teachers, has a social origin: teachers are viewed as representatives of their academic institutions, and accordingly have certain rights deriving from their position of authority. In other words, the teacher's status provides a legitimate position of authority with respect to students. These relations of dominance can also exist among students, and depending on the context, more specifically between the students in a "dominant" group and the students in a "non-dominant" group (Beaty, 2013).

From a Vygotskian perspective, actors are not destined to stay fixed in any one given role or social position. On the contrary, under the right conditions, actors (here, students) have the power to develop their agency; thus, when school norms constitute constraints, a student can use them as instruments for his or her own development; but also, in return, as instruments for transforming the academic institution. This conception thus regards the subject as an agent who is able to transform the world, in this case the world of the school, and in doing so, to transform as learner.

3   Literature Review Method

The aim of the present review is to identify certain methodological approaches stemming from the CHAT framework, including French traditions of activity analysis, that discuss students' activity with special focus on: (1) how students' agency is conceptualized; and (2) the research design and methods used/adapted to examine this activity. The review presented here, without being systematic in the sense suggested by Jesson et al. (2011), serves as an opportunity to discuss different methodological approaches to student activity. Hence, even if they are sometimes discussed, it is not the findings of these studies that is of interest here so much as the type of data that the adopted research method and framework are able to analyze, and how they are able to take into account student agency as well as relations of domination in the classroom.

In terms of relevancy criteria, the selected articles had to discuss student activity and address methodological aspects based on empirical results. Particular (but not exclusive) consideration was given to articles that addressed the activity of students belonging to minority (non-dominant) or underprivileged groups. Finally, the texts had to deal with student populations at the secondary level, in a formal education context. The literature review was conducted between April and June 2018 using the following keywords: activity, student, agency, cultural-historical activity theory or clinic of activity. The databases consulted were *Academic Search Complete*, ERIC, *PsycArticles* and *SocioIndex* for English-language texts, and CAIRN and *Érudit* for French-language texts. We sometimes also selected texts that met the criteria referenced in other reviewed texts. The texts selected were in English or in French. Without laying claim to exhaustiveness, this yielded a sample of 14 texts, mostly in connection with adolescent student populations.

4   Results

The texts were grouped according to their type of research design, which entails different methodological approaches to be able to take into account student activity or agency. Theoretically speaking, the aim was to look at how the adopted frameworks conceptualized student agency. Methodologically speaking, the aim was to look at how the adopted methods, based on their chosen units of analysis, help take into account, or analyze, the way the students' agency manifests in their activity at school. In this section we will examine norms and power relations as they relate to student agency. A summary table comparing each of the reviewed texts is provided in the Appendix. The studies are classified into 5 different types of frameworks: Social Design Experiments, Transformative Activist Stance Intervention, Change Laboratory, Clinic of Activity, and studies aimed at understanding (rather than transforming) students' activity. Considering that the review is not exhaustive, some other frameworks situated in CHAT which have studied students' agency of power relations in class should not necessarily be include here. Change Laboratory and Clinic of Activity are the methodological approaches which, in light of our review, have the most texts and empirical studies that analyze students' activity and agency. Studies situated in the Social Design Experiments and Transformative Activity Stance Interventions are less prevalent in our review; nevertheless, we begin this section with those two approaches since they are the ones that seem to put the greatest emphasis on social inequality issues.

For each framework, we will briefly describe the main methodological principles and techniques, along with some findings that we consider significant in terms of what kinds of results those frameworks and methods shed light on concerning in particular a) student agency; and b) social inequalities in the classroom context. As mentioned earlier, the populations of the selected studies are, in majority, students from non-dominant groups. Wherever possible, we will mention the type of researcher-intervention that the framework involves, although this point will be addressed in greater detail in Section 5.

4.1 Social Design Experiments

Social Design Experimentation (SDE) is a type of research methodology aimed at transforming the world and improving practises in order to foster equity and social justice (Gutiérrez & Jurow, 2016). According to its crafters, SDE seeks to design a study that is "organized around a commitment to transforming the educational and social circumstances of members of non-dominant communities as a mean of promoting social equity and learning" (Gutiérrez & Jurow, 2016, p. 565). Emphasis is placed on the researcher's designing a program or space that will create social conditions favourable to the agency and development of individuals belonging to non-dominant groups. In turn, this tends toward the creation of new learning tools or spaces that do not entirely come under the culture of the dominant group (e.g., those associated with the school institution) or of the dominated group. For this reason, Gutiérrez (2008) uses the metaphor of a "third space," a space of learning and development comparable to a zone of proximal development. This approach is largely based on developing a historicized self linked to a person's ability to use new conceptual instruments in order to interpret their experience and to understand "how one came to be a member of a historically marginalized community" (Gutiérrez & Jurow, 2016, p. 567). In terms of methodology, this approach includes *ethnographic observation* and *historical research* into the community to which the "dominated" individuals belong. This procedure also helps propose a design that will be in harmony with the culture of the community and its actors.

In an intervention research context, Gutiérrez (2008) presents a summer residential program that she set up for students from migrant farm worker backgrounds. This school program was intended to prepare the students for college, but also to develop their historicized selves. This involves that the students would be able to appropriate new tools, in this case discursive tools, for their development. The cultural mediation of writing, in a genre halfway between the *testimonio*—an autobiographical genre familiar to such students with Latin roots—and a school-type first-person essay—served as a mediating tool and a catalyst for developing the students' historicized selves. The findings show that using an instrument at the border between two cultural heritages enabled the students to develop a greater awareness of phenomena such as racism, discrimination and poverty, which exacerbate the consequences of inequality in schools. The creation of third spaces and the appropriation of new instruments by students belonging to non-dominant groups can help them act with agency in order to reduce these inequalities.

4.2 *Transformative Activist Stance Intervention*

Social Design Experiments seem to have a great deal in common with studies rooted in the Transformative Activist Stance (TAS) developed by Stetsenko (2016). Intervention research projects based on a TAS, geared, just as in SDE, toward social justice and equity, aim to develop the individual and collective transformative agency of actors, who in turn contribute to transforming the structures that generate inequity. TAS research necessarily has a transformative and critical aim, which has consequences for the methods adopted. In our view—and in this respect TAS differs in part from Social Design Experiments—TAS is more of an epistemological/methodological posture than a research method. It entails the establishment of a transformative learning group long with the conditions favourable to a critical posture and to collective actions seeking to create a future that will be characterized by greater justice and social equity.

A study by Vianna and Stetsenko (2011) illustrates the potential of TAS as an instrument for developing the agency of students in very underprivileged situations. The study examines an intervention in the context of a three-year program for young people with a Child Welfare background from very underprivileged communities. The students in question initially had a very negative relationship to formal learning. The program marked a break from traditional school instruction and one of the particularities was to pursue transformative collaboration, in which students worked on projects—with a transformational aim—led collectively and with the help of tutors, hence outside of the formal classroom context.

Relating the exceptional case of "Jay," the authors document the transformation of a student who was resisting both the institution and learning, but who, over the course of the program and the teaching/learning activity, transformed his identity while committing to plans to change society. In terms of identity, from his initial positioning as a victim, Jay increasingly positioned himself as an agent with the power to act positively on his immediate environment and on other young people in the program. He also developed a disposition to act, in the long term, as an agent capable of transforming society and more particularly the Child Welfare institution; at least, these were his plans for his career. Whereas Jay initially sought only to earn his General Education Diploma (GED), he proved to be the first student of the program to pursue a postsecondary education.

4.3 *The Change Laboratory*

The Change Laboratory is a research method which begins with an ethnographic observation phase and then implements, in collaboration with a group—traditionally, a group of workers–a formative intervention. This takes the shape of sessions in which a series of tools are used to analyze the *contradictions*[1] in their activities and to come up with collective solutions (Sannino et al., 2016).

> Change Laboratory intervention entails successive cycles of identifying and formulating problems, questioning previous problem formulations and conceptions in the search for the core source of problems in the current structure and principle of carrying out the activity. (Virkkunen & Newnham, 2013, p. 9)

The authors who adopt the Change Laboratory approach present agency as being central to their conceptual framework. Their conception of agency is very closely linked to that of *expansive learning*: "learning expansively requires breaking away from the given frame of action and taking the initiative to transform it" (Sannino et al., 2016, p. 603). This transformation takes place via the mobilization and creation of new conceptual instruments. The agent's initiative to transform action is a core condition of transformative agency. Transformative agency involves not only initiative but also a commitment on the part of workers. Expansive learning both requires and entails agency, and is conducive to the emergence of new forms of activity that entail the development of new collaborative schemes in the community, new tools and instruments, and a division of labour (Engeström, 1987/2015).

One of the three cases presented and discussed in Sannino et al. (2016) is a Change Laboratory conducted in 1998 by Engeström et al. at the middle school of an underprivileged neighbourhood in Finland. This study analyzed the impacts of an intervention ultimately aimed at transforming the "object of the teachers' work activity—the students and their learning" (p. 610), the latter being initially deemed by their teachers to be passive and unengaged. In this Change Laboratory, the first stimulus provided was the viewing of videos of the teachers' actions in order to help them become aware of contradictions in their own activities in relation to their students. This was followed by a series of sessions in which the teachers were invited, using conceptual instruments proposed by the researchers, to carry out actions in connection with the desired vision of the school and aimed at increasing student engagement.

The findings illustrate that the intervention and the process as a whole helped prompt changes in the ways the school's teachers evaluated the students, and led them to put students at the heart of their professional activity. At the end of the intervention, the teachers spoke much more positively of the students. The teachers' discursive manifestations about their students portrayed the latter as being much more actively engaged at school, which we interpret as signalling greater agency. The findings also indirectly illustrate that working on developing teachers' transformative agency can, in turn, also help develop the agency of students; nevertheless, the study does not say *how*, given that student activity was not the focus of the observations. The students were present only in the ethnographic data and were not directly involved in the Change Lab sessions. Nor is it known how the intervention may have contributed to diminishing inequalities at the school.

On a related note, although similar in several respects to the Change Laboratory, the study of Lemos (2017) differs in that it aims to study what Sannino et al. (2016) present as an *intravention*, i.e., an intervention geared toward change and originating from the initiative of a group of actors wishing to respond to the contradictions they encounter in the field. The difference between an intravention and a more traditional Change Laboratory intervention is that, in the intravention, the researcher plays a lesser role in designing the tools developed to overcome contradictions. The intravention researcher mainly plays the role of observing and analyzing the expansive learning process as it plays out.

The Lemos (2017) study examines the case of a Brazilian *favela* (shantytown) faced with flooding and unsanitary conditions. To tackle the situation, the school team decided to make a concerted effort and develop tools to create better conditions for student learning, and for the development of all school actors and the entire favela community living by the river in question. Analytically speaking, like most of the research under the Change Laboratory approach, what is involved is *collaborative agency*, defined as a "process in which participants become agents of an activity by collaboratively constructing and envisioning new possibilities for achieving a joint object in order to transform not only the focus of research or a work setting but also people's lives" (Lemos, 2017, p. 557). The findings illustrate how, following an intravention that rallied the students around the flood issue, classroom activities—for example, producing argumentative texts and envisioning possibilities to resolve the flood issue and different neighbourhood activities—helped develop collective agency. Regarding the agency of the students, however, given the focus on the activity and collective agency, and the choice of methods which primarily documented the views of the teachers and practitioners involved, it is difficult to ascertain, at least based on the empirical traces, how and to what extent student agency per se was developed through this intervention.

4.4   *The Clinic of Activity*

The Clinic of Activity is a research and intervention approach that seeks to transform activity in order to be able to understand it (Clot, 2017). A number of studies adopting this methodological perspective have examined the teaching occupation (Yvon & Saussez, 2010), and only recently has the Clinic of Activity been brought to bear on the activity of students. Previously, some French-language research from other perspectives of activity analysis (Guérin et al., 2004) had brought to light the value of also examining student activity, about which little was known.

An Activity Clinic process begins when actors from a given occupational setting request a transformation of practices. This is generally followed by an observation stage conducted by the researcher in the field. Next, *instruction to the double* and/or *self-confrontation* may be used. Instruction to the double is a method originating from the field of French ergonomics (Clot, 2017). In this method, the researcher, assuming the role of a double, asks the worker—who then plays the role of instructor—to give him detailed instructions on what to do if, the next morning, the researcher had to replace the worker without anyone noticing the substitution. In particular, this substitution serves as a planning modality (Veyrac, 2017) which helps provide access to the instructor's realized activity as well as his possible or potential activity, i.e. to the potential other actions that he could have carried out (reality of activity). The instructor, in this approach, is also asked to use the first person singular (using the French *tu*). This enunciative posture promotes some distancing from the instructor's usual activity and operating modes (Dionne et al., 2019). Finally, these last authors also point out that the researcher, as a double, prevents the instructor from narrating a "pre-formatted" version of his activity, instead requiring him to reflect on it from a different point of view. The other methods under the Clinic of Activity approach are simple and cross self-confrontation. Both of these methods necessarily involve audiovisual recordings of agents exercising their occupations, in real-life work situations. They also involve the creation of a group of voluntary actors. The participants must then be ready, first, to confront and discuss the video sequences of their real-life activity in the presence of a researcher (simple self-confrontation), then repeat the exercise but with video recordings of a peer, in the presence of this peer, who then comments on his colleague's sequences (cross self-confrontation).

Two writings (Guérin et al., 2004; Moussay & Flavier, 2014) focused on methodological issues of using the self-confrontation method to examine student activity. From a Clinic of Activity standpoint, Moussay and Flavier (2014) discuss the use of a simple self-confrontation interview to analyze the activity of students enrolled in a French *collège*[2] (secondary school) in an underprivileged neighbourhood of the suburbs of Lyon, France. The authors open a debate on the contribution of this type of analysis to fighting school dropout. The intervention research was requested by a science teacher who felt the need to "have other eyes in the classroom than the accusatory gaze of the students" (Moussay & Flavier, 2014, p. 103). Clearly, this teacher is situated in a context of tension within classroom activity. From a methodological but also ethical standpoint, a decision was made not to have the teacher view the recordings of the self-confrontation sessions with the student, or vice versa, which the authors cite as a limitation of their study. However, the feedback regarding the other party—presented by the researcher acting as the intermediary—along with greater awareness of one's own activity in the classroom enabled both the teacher and the student to get a better grasp of the other party's activity and to transform their own.

Awareness was also raised, in situ, of how the other person's activity was undergoing transformation. For example, toward the end of the process, a student remarked that the teacher was taking notes when he gave correct answers in class, even if he deviated from the norm and did not raise his hand first. This new action was viewed positively, as a form of recognition from the teacher. This awareness of how the teacher's activity had changed was conducive, in turn, to the student's engagement, motivation and classroom participation:

> I know the answer, I told her, here's the proof. I say yeah, loud and strong, and now she writes it down, before she wasn't doing that .... She notes down all the answers in her little notebook, and we talk. I understand better, this is what I want. (Moussay & Flavier, 2014, p. 113)

Moussay and Flavier (2014), following on Guérin and colleagues (2004), point out that student learning about the methodology and the culture of research in general is required for this method to be used effectively with secondary students. Indeed, a reflective posture on one's own activity is not currently a requirement in the school context in question.

Among the other Activity Clinic-based studies that use self-confrontation to analyze student activity is the one by Ouvrier-Bonnaz and Vérillon (2002). This study took place in the fourth and third-year classes of a French *collège* located in an underprivileged neighbourhood. The researchers used simple self-confrontation and crossed self-confrontation with the students. The results are insightful in terms of the role of school norms and how they can constrain the actions of certain students. Regarding the norm of having students raise their hands before they can speak, the study cites the case of a student who would raise his hand only hesitantly and not very high, and whose hand was often ignored or even, in a sense, silenced.

The study shows that, even if the school's norms sometimes proved to be a constraining factor, the students were nevertheless able to stay active thanks to the use of catachresis. For example, some might use their pens in a nonstandard way, moving them about in a writing motion but without actually writing, in order to stay alert in class and exercise their agency. The results of a study by Magendie and Bouthier (2012), who used simple self-confrontation to analyze the activity of French secondary students struggling in a given subject matter (physical and sports education), also bring attention to the dimension of what hampers students' activity by showing how emotions such as fear of rejection or discontent can burden their activity. Some students in situations of failure prefer, for example, "to be off in their own corner" (p. 34, authors' translation) rather than engage in exercises, in order to avoid potential humiliation. This last study uncovers a dialectic between emotions and agency, primarily in terms of the role they play in hampering activity.

Ruelland-Roger and Clot (2013) present a theoretical adaptation of the instruction to the double method in order to examine student activity. Their text does not specify whether the students concerned were struggling, or in a situation of domination. Nevertheless, the text was included in our review for its methodological innovation, which has the potential to transform students' activity. After recurrent interviews with teachers regarding students' actual activity, the researchers proposed and implemented the technique *instruction to the double*. Considering that analyzing their activity based on instruction to the double could seem unusual to secondary students, the authors decided to have six students in the same math class work together to perform the same task. The authors were inspired by an experiment conducted by Vygotsky (1935/1994) in which a child was asked by an experimenter to draw. Observing the student's lack of motivation to engage in this activity when addressed by the experimenter, Vygotsky then asked the child to "show another child how to do it" (Vygotski, 1935/1994, cited in Ruelland-Roger & Clot, 2013, p. 22). This change in address apparently allowed the child to re-develop his activity. Ruelland-Roger and Clot (2013) took up the same method of having peers addressed by other peers, rather than by the researcher. This change of address is the chief characteristic that the authors propose in order to adapt instruction to the double so as to help study the students' activity. In this case, the activity analysis was intended to help develop teaching-related activity. The teachers' access to video recordings of instructions to the double by their students sparked their reflection on the issue of how to develop students' activity. For example, one teacher realized that "my explanation might not be the only one, and an explanation by a classmate might be more meaningful, using his own words" (Ruelland-Roger & Clot, 2013, p. 24). Moreover, the teachers in this study realized, after viewing the students' instruction to the double, that academic engagement is in fact a broader issue than teachers perceive it to be.

4.5 Studies Aimed at Understanding Students' Activity

The texts by Andrée (2012), Beaty (2013), and Esmonde et al. (2011) adopt a primarily ethnographic research approach that is geared toward understanding students' activity in its cultural context. The aim of these research studies is not primarily transformation; rather, the interest lies in seizing opportunities for learning and development afforded by situations of error (Andrée, 2012) and episodes of difficulty (Esmonde et al., 2011) and contradiction (Beaty, 2013). All of the reviewed studies used the observation methods of informal or semi-structured interviews or audio/audiovisual recordings.

Beaty (2013) investigates video production activities by teenage students in underprivileged situations in the context of five video programs in different American high schools. The students' video recordings have a dual status: they are both what the authors call the context of the study and the data collection method. This choice of object and method was justified by the author's wish to take student agency into account, considering that video production is a school activity that is likely to foster such agency, as validated by the study's findings. Beaty (2013) defines agency as "being present in actions that create or alter events and/or structures, not by re-acting but by initiating action" (p. 6). These actions undertaken to transform events and structures unfold in relation with other students and are shaped by the possibility of affecting the school structure. The scale of agency chosen by Beaty (2013) is that of relational agency (Edwards, 2005), and throughout her study, special importance is placed on the deployment of agency through relationships with peers, i.e., the other students in the programs studied. For Beaty (2013), a structure—which from our perspective includes a division of labour and norms flexible enough to foster equity for all—can act as a catalyst to support students' agency. In another audiovisual production program considered to be particularly rigid, Beaty (2013) observes a sort of reproduction of inequalities that can also be commonly observed in society: the white students from affluent backgrounds ended up with the key production rules, whereas those from minority communities obtained much less prestigious positions. This division of labour was not observed in the programs with more flexible and collaborative structures. Hence, the results demonstrates how the structuring of school programs partly contributes to creating inequalities as well as the possibility of agency for students who are most likely to find themselves in a situation of domination.

For his part, Andrée (2012) examines the activity of a 7th grade Swedish student in a science class and focuses on her engagement in the course. The student stated she was uninterested in science and poorly equipped for this academic subject. In Andrée's view, studying students' in-class engagement first and foremost requires analyzing their activity. The relationship of inequality brought to light in this study concerns gender inequality in the context of science classes. This inequality is reinforced by the school and cultural context, including its implicit norms. The student remarked that science was mainly a male subject, and rejected the possibility of ever pursuing studies in a scientific field. However, analysis of her activity revealed opportunities where, under certain conditions—for example when the student and her group of girls chose the wrong solution in a chemistry experiment—she demonstrated genuine engagement in her learning. In terms of individual agency, these results show a discrepancy in activity, between the engagement verbalized by the student and the engagement revealed by analysis of her activity.

Esmonde et al. (2011) use an ethnographic methodology to study the collective agency of a working group of 11th and 12th grade students in math class. Drawing inspiration from Engeström's *boundary-crossing* model, i.e. a model that notably studies the contradictions emerging during actions or interactions which imply two different activity systems oriented toward different objects, these authors pinpoint two activity systems at work within the classroom situations they analyzed: The system of "doing school" and the system of "learning math." Their results illustrate that the activity system of "doing school" is often associated with the motive of pleasing and doing what is expected by the teacher. This can hinder developmental and learning potential within the activity system, in this case in relation to mathematics, since the focus has shifted away from solving mathematical problems. To a certain degree, the "doing school" activity system often remains invisible within students' activity and, in our view, can hamper students' agency if it remains unconscious.

5   Discussion and Conclusion

As mentioned previously, the aim of this chapter is to contribute to a methodological and theoretical discussion on how different CHAT research methodologies may or may not successfully take into account the agency of students in a group that is subject to such domination. In light of the elements presented above, a first observation that could be put forward is that certain methods in the CHAT tradition address non-dominant individuals and groups specifically, as a means to achieve greater justice and social equity. This is the case of Social Design Experiments (Gutiérrez, 2008; Gutiérrez & Jurow, 2016) and research that comes under the Transformative Activist Stance (TAS) (Stetsenko, 2016; Vianna & Stetsenko, 2011). Both of these approaches seek to stimulate the agency of individuals or groups, on the collective as well as individual levels, in order to produce an emerging social transformation that is constructed in the present. The aim of the research method adopted, in these approaches, is therefore explicitly transformative and emancipatory. By emancipatory, we mean that the object toward which activity is primarily oriented is the transformation of social conditions, and the way to achieve this is to enable individuals to develop a greater power to act.

In other research methodologies reviewed here, such as the Change Laboratory and the Clinic of Activity, the transformative aim is explicit, but the emancipatory aim is in the background, with the exception of the Lemos (2017) study. We have also seen that research on students' activity which primarily adopts an "understanding" posture helps shed light on certain issues, including often-invisible power issues associated with this activity. It does not explicitly seek to transform these issues; nevertheless, as in the case of the Beaty (2013) study, some research may choose to study programs that make use of tools or forms of activity that are more likely to promote agency.

As regards the dominant level of agency (individual vs. collective), a discrepancy can be noted between what is observed in terms of theory and in terms of methodology. Theoretically speaking, most CHAT research conceptualizes a dialectic relationship between individual agency and collective agency (Dionne & Bourdon, 2018). However, in terms of methodology, when it comes to the scale of the transformation that is sought and the traces of transformation that are analyzed, the different approaches tend to study one or another of these levels without necessarily taking into account the dialectic between the two in their findings.[3] We have seen that whereas many works in CHAT research—at least those under the Change Laboratory approach—mainly strive toward a transformation of collective agency, research that adopts other methodological approaches, including the Clinic of Activity, primarily highlights traces of learning or development that are associated with the individual level and are put in relation with a collective activity or occupational activity. In addition, the results related by Vianna and Stetsenko (2011) clearly detail the role of transforming a student's agency in terms of the individual's contribution to the group and the collective conditions for this transformation (role of the instructor, collective project, etc.); however, how collective agency is transformed over the course of such a research project remains unknown. Likewise, the study by Gutiérrez (2008) traces back a student's actions in order to transform inequalities that affect his social group, in this case Latinos. But the results fail to shed light on how the immediate group, rallied around a project, develops collective agency with respect to these inequality issues. Edward's scope of relational agency (2005) is only explicitly used in the study by Beaty (2013). As Edwards (2005) herself deplores, how the joint action implemented in the school has promoted students' individual agency remains unknown. This third scope of agency is scarcely taken into account in studies on students' activity in a school context.

The results of our review also uncover that, in terms of collective agency, the studies that focus on and leverages the contradictions encountered by collective actors in their activity indeed illustrate the dynamogenic effect that collective work to resolve contradictions can have on students' activity. However, it seems to us that, by putting analysis of the students' voice on the same footing as that of other school stakeholders, such a conception of collective agency risks insufficiently taking into account the inequalities between different categories of actors. Undeniably, as Schrimer and Geithner (2018) point out, such research that emphasizes the contradictions of activity view these contradictions as a source of empowerment. However, it seems that certain specific conditions are necessary for this to be the case in non-dominant groups. It is interesting to see how, or at least under what conditions, a group or individual is able to draw forth from a relationship of domination the resources that will enable it to develop and transform the world, as is reported in the Vianna and Stetsenko (2011) study.

Methodologically speaking, the researchers in the Clinic of Activity tradition, as we have seen, have developed methodological adaptations to be able to analyze real-life student activity that is fraught with power relations. However, often, such analysis is mainly aimed at developing teaching activity and does not always produce transformations in student activity, even though, in our view, it has the potential to do so. This can be seen for example in the study of Ruelland-Roger and Clot (2013), in which a methodological innovation was introduced in order to use instruction to the double to analyze students' activity. Although in this last study the method was used to develop the activity of the teacher, it could just as well have been put at the service of developing that of the students. Moussay and Flavier (2014) is such an example, with findings attesting to transformations in the activity of teacher and student alike. Indeed, in this last study, it is not only the teacher who is able to analyze the student's activity, but also vice versa. Even if this access to analysis is only partial, indirect and researcher-mediated, the findings nevertheless show traces of students' transformation in terms of agency with respect to academic activity, as we have seen.

Regarding the population targeted in the studies included in our review, it seems worthwhile to mention a few nuances about what might be characterized as individuals in situations of domination or belonging to non-dominant groups. Power relations are never stable, but rather dynamic. The findings of several of the studies reviewed illustrate how students who initially positioned themselves as "victims" (Vianna & Stetsenko, 2011) or members of a minority group can assume a prominent role as agents if they are able to affect the school structure (Beaty, 2013), or have opportunities to transform their own identity (Gutiérrez, 2008; Vianna & Stetsenko, 2011). Studies grounded in the Clinic of Activity, in particular, also raise another nuance regarding the social categorization of "dominated" status: for example, a student can very well be in a situation of vulnerability in some school subjects and not in others (Magendie & Bouthier, 2012). And what might constitute a catalyst for the agency of some students (for example, speaking up without raising their hand so that their transgression of the norm will enable them to be heard) can curb the agency of others (a "good" student who respects the norm but never speaks up, as in the study of Ouvrier-Bonnaz and Vérillon (2002). Analyzing students' actual activity helps reveal that the power relations that weigh on student agency can sometimes be found in unexpected places.

Finally, there is another form of power relation that we have not yet discussed: the one between the researchers and the actors involved. Indeed, the role that a research posture gives the researcher can be an avenue for reflection. Some authors (Engeström, 2011; O'Neill, 2016), for example, critique Design-Based Research (DBR), particularly regarding the role of the researcher, which may be associated with the "myth of the heroic designer" (O'Neill, 2016). Although DBR studies often strive to transform practices, in such a design, the researcher is the one who wields the means for this transformation. One might therefore wonder about the potential for agency in such a research design that is mainly imposed from the outside. Moreover, in certain forms of formative intervention, one could say that the researcher represents a source of intervention via the transmission of conceptual instruments (e.g., a copy of the general model of activity) intended as a stimulus and trigger for the activity leading to the transformation of the problem situation (Sannino et al., 2016). The key question, in our view, is whether dialectic research studies contribute to creating the conditions for human development (Chaiklin, 2012) and if the instruments that are conveyed, conceived and appropriated in the course of research initiatives, by expanding participants' repertoire of tools or instruments, stimulate their agency and power to act, especially when they belong to non-dominant groups. It would appear that we have an ethical duty, as researchers, in this respect. Indeed, research can be a catalyst to support student activity, especially the activity of those belonging to "non-dominant" groups, and, in so doing, to help create a more just and socially equitable future.

6 How Does the Chapter Address the Challenges of a Non-Dualist Methodology?

In this chapter the non-dualist methodology is approached from a monistic conception of students' agency. This agency is conceived in its relation to social activity instead of an individual trait, as is the case in many other approaches. As the authors state, agency is neither individual nor collective but brings into play the individual and collective/social level. The chapter specifically looks at agency in the context of power relations or inequalities and discusses how different CHAT methodologies (Social Design, TAS, Change laboratory and Clinic of Activity) can sustain the power to act of students belonging to non-dominant groups at their academic institutions. This conception thus regards the subject as an agent who is unquestionably able to transform the world and to be transformed in doing so. The subject-environment relation is examined by considering their mutual influence (non-dualist perspective). The discussion points out that certain methods in the CHAT tradition (e.g., TAS and SDE) seek to transform the relation to school and the agency of non-dominant individuals and groups specifically, as a means to achieve greater justice and social equity. In other CHAT research methodologies, the transformative aim is explicit, but the emancipatory aim remains in the background. Accordingly, the need to transform the social conditions that create inequalities for students in their relation to school can be considered a challenge for a non-dualist methodology, which strives to contribute to creating the conditions for human development. The chapter also notes that in the relationship with the actors in the research field, the researcher can have a role that is not addressed in many reviewed articles. Indeed, researchers can contribute "by expanding participants' repertoire of tools or instruments [to implement the school transformations that are important to them], and stimulate their agency and power to act." The authors invite members of the CHAT community to reflect on their role as agents of transformation or on the importance of addressing power inequalities in their contact with environments that include non-dominant groups or where power relations are entrenched.

Notes

1 Engeström and Sannino's (2011) concept of contradiction is rooted in Marxist dialectics. This conception of dialectics regards opposing forces as forming a dialectical unity during action (Dionne & Bourdon, 2018). As a dialectical concept, contradiction implies a relationship

between the collective and individual levels of activity. For Engeström and Sannino (2011) this concept refers as well to the development of historically and systemically formed tensions that arise within collective activity. Contradictions are not given from the outside, and are only recognized "when practitioners articulate and construct them in words and actions" (Engeström & Sannino, 2011, p. 371). As researchers, we cannot access contradiction directly, but we can access discursive manifestations of contradictions.

2 In France, *collège* spans years 6th to 9th of students' education.
3 In a non-formal education context, Dionne has sought precisely to shed light on this issue in her thesis (2015) by taking up a framework that incorporates the dialectic between these two levels of agency.

References

Andrée, M. (2012). Altering conditions for student participation and motive development in school science: Learning from Helena's mistake. *Cultural Studies of Science Education, 7*(2), 425–438. doi:10.1007/s11422-011-9314-x

Beaty, L. M. (2013). Confronting school's contradictions with video: Youth's need for agency for ontological development. *Outlines: Critical Practice Studies, 14*(1), 4–25.

Bourdieu, P., & Passeron, J.-C. (1970). *La reproduction. Éléments d'une théorie du système d'enseignement*. Éditions de Minuit.

Chaiklin, S. (2012). Dialectics, politics and contemporary cultural-historical research, exemplified through Marx and Vygotski. In H. Daniels (Ed.), *Vygotsky and sociology* (pp. 24–43). Routledge.

Clot, Y. (2017). *Travail et pouvoir d'agir* (2nd ed.). Presses Universitaires de France.

Dionne, P., & Bourdon, S. (2018). Contradictions as the driving force of collective and subjective development group employment programmes. *Journal of Education and Work, 31*(3), 277–290. doi:10.1080/13639080.2018.1468071

Dionne, P., Viviers, S., & Saussez, F. (2019). Discuter et réfléchir son activité par l'instruction au sosie: Émergence de contradictions et débats de métier. *Nouveaux cahiers de la recherche en éducation, 21*(2), 24–42. doi:10.7202/1061838arv

Edwards, A. (2005). Relational agency: Learning to be a resourceful practitioner. *International Journal of Educational Research, 43*(3), 168–182. doi:10.1016/j.ijer.2006.06.010

Engeström, Y. (2015). *Learning by expanding: An activity theoretical approach to developmental research* (2nd ed.). Cambridge University Press. (Original work published 1987)

Engeström, Y. (2011). From design experiments to formative interventions. *Theory & Psychology, 21*(5), 598–628. doi:10.1177/0959354311419252

Engeström, Y., & Sannino, A. (2011). Discursive manifestations of contradictions in organizational change efforts: A methodological framework. *Journal of Organizational Change Management, 24*(3), 368–387. doi:10.1108/09534811111132758

Engeström, Y., & Sannino, A. (2013). La volition et l'agentivité transformatrice: Perspective théorique de l'activité. *Revue internationale du CRIRES : Innover dans la tradition de Vygotsky, 1*(1), 4–19.

Esmonde, I., Takeuchi, M., & Radakovic, N. (2011). Getting unstuck: Learning and histories of engagement in classrooms. *Mind, Culture, and Activity, 18*(3), 237–256. doi:10.1080/10749031003790128

Foray, P. (2009). Trois formes de l'autorité scolaire. *Le Télémaque, 35*(1), 73–86.

Guérin, J., Riff, J., & Testevuide, S. (2004). Étude de l'activité « située » de collégiens en cours d'EPS : une opportunité pour examiner les conditions de validité des entretiens d'autoconfrontation. *Revue française de pédagogie, 147*, 15–26.

Gutiérrez, K. D. (2008). Developing a sociocritical literacy in the third space. *Reading Research Quarterly, 43*(2), 148–164. doi:10.1598/RRQ.43.2.3

Gutiérrez, K. D., & Jurow, A. S. (2016). Social design experiments: Toward equity by design. *Journal of the Learning Sciences, 25*(4), 565–598. doi:10.1080/10508406.2016.1204548

Haapasaari, A., Engeström, Y., & Kerosuo, H. (2016). The emergence of learners' transformative agency in a change laboratory intervention. *Journal of Education and Work, 29*(2), 232–262. doi:10.1080/13639080.2014.900168

Jesson, J. K., Matheson, L., & Lacey, F. M. (2011). *Doing your literature review: Traditional and systematic techniques*. Sage.

Lemos, M. (2017). Collaborative agency in educational management: A joint object for school and community transformation. *Revista de Administração de Empresas, 57*(6), 555–566. doi:10.1590/S0034-759020170604

Magendie, É., & Bouthier, D. (2012). Des ruptures de contrat au sens de l'activité pour les élèves: une approche clinique de l'activité réelle en EPS. *Éducation & didactique, 6*(2), 27–46. doi:10.4000/educationdidactique.1457

Moussay, S., & Flavier, É. (2014). L'entretien d'autoconfrontation: La prise en compte du point de vue de l'élève pour développer l'activité en classe. *Revue canadienne de l'éducation, 37*(1), 96–119.

O'Neill, D. K. (2016). Understanding design research-practice partnerships in context and time: Why learning sciences scholars should learn from cultural-historical activity theory approaches to design-based research. *Journal of the Learning Sciences, 25*(4), 497–502. doi:10.1080/10508406.2016.1226835

Ouvrier-Bonnaz, R., & Vérillon, P. (2002). Connaissance de soi et connaissance du travail dans la perspective d'une didactique de l'orientation scolaire: Une approche par la coanalyse de l'activité des élèves. *Revue française de pédagogie, 141*, 67–75.

Panofsky, C. (2009). Apprentissage et origine sociale des élèves, pour une théorie socioculturelle «re-socialisante» de l'apprentissage. In A. Kzulin, B. Gindis, V. S. Ageyev, & S. M. Miller (Eds.), *Vygotsky et l'éducation* (pp. 181–204). Retz.

Ruelland-Roger, D., & Clot, Y. (2013). L'activité réelle de l'élève : pour développer l'activité enseignante. *Revue internationale du CRIRES: Innover dans la tradition de Vygtosky, 1*(1), 20–25.

Sannino, A., Engeström, Y., & Lemos, M. (2016). Formative interventions for expansive learning and transformative agency. *Journal of the Learning Sciences, 25*(4), 599–633. doi:10.1080/10508406.2016.1204547

Schrimer, F., & Geithner, S. (2018). Power relations in organizational change: An activity-theoretic perspective. *Journal of Accounting & Organizational Change, 14*(1), 9–32. doi:10.1108/JAOC-11-2016-0074

Stetsenko, A. (2005). Activity as object-related: Resolving the dichotomy of individual and collective planes of activity. *Mind, Culture, and Activity, 12*(1), 70–88. doi:10.1207/s15327884mca1201_6

Stetsenko, A. (2016). *The transformative mind: Expanding Vygotsky's approach to development and education*. Cambridge University Press.

Stetsenko, A., & Arievitch, I. (2004). The self in cultural-historical activity theory. *Theory & Psychology, 14*(4), 475–503. doi:10.1177/0959354304044921

Veyrac, H. (2017). *L'instruction au sosie pour la transformation du travail : la conduit du conseil de classe par des chefs d'établissement* [Conference paper]. 52ᵉ Congrès de la Société d'Ergonomie de Langue Française, Toulouse, France.

Vianna, E., & Stetsenko, A. (2011). Connecting learning and identity development through a transformative activist stance: Application in adolescent development in a child welfare program. *Human Development, 54*, 313–338. doi:10.1159/000331484

Virkkunen, J., & Newnham, D. (2013). *The change laboratory: A tool for collaborative development of work and education*. Sense Publishers.

Vygotsky, L. S. (2014). *Histoire du développement des fonctions psychiques supérieures*. La Dispute.

Yvon, F., & Saussez, F. (2010). *Analyser l'activité enseignante : des outils méthodologiques et théoriques pour l'intervention et la formation*. Presses de l'Université Laval.

Appendix

Author	Study design and methods	Population/sample	Dominant pole of agency	Research purpose	Highlights in relation to agency and power relations
Gutierrez and Jurow (2016)	Social design Experiment	Students or persons from non-dominant groups	Individual agency	Transformative	More theoretical contribution than empirical.
Gutierrez (2008)	Social design Experiment	Immigrant students (US) participating in a summer program to prepare them for college/The case of Ave	Individual agency	Transformative	"We learn from students like Ave that racism, discrimination, and poverty intensify the consequences of inequitable schooling conditions" (p. 151).
Vianna and Stetsenko (2011)	Transformative Activist Stance (TAS) intervention-research	Adolescents boys (US) with a Child Welfare background participating in a critical-theoretical school home program/The case of Jay	Individual agency	Transformative	The program intervention has allowed and radical development of the agency of a student from a precarious background. The transformation of the student's identity has allowed him to have more agency and to contribute to the transformation of the teaching/learning program.
Sannino et al. (2016)	Developmental work research Change Laboratory	Three different school populations (including that of Lemos and of Engestrom et al., in this chart)	Collective agency	Transformative	More theoretical contribution than empirical.
Engestrom et al. (2016)	Developmental work research Change Laboratory	Teachers of a middle school located in a disadvantaged area of Helsinki (Finland)	Collective agency	Transformative	The intervention has led to changes in the way school teachers view students as the object of their activity. They spoke of their students in a much more positive way, especially regarding their agency.

(*cont.*)

Author	Study design and methods	Population/sample	Dominant pole of agency	Research purpose	Highlights in relation to agency and power relations
Lemos (2017)	Formative intervention Study of an intravention	School team of a Brazilian *favela* (shantytown) faced with flooding and unsanitary conditions	Collective agency	Transformative (analysis of a transformation initiated by the local actors)	The joint activity of the actors in order to face the flood and insalubrity situation allowed the transformation of the school and its surroundings.
Guérin et al. (2004)	Course of action (Theureau, 1992) Simple self-confrontation	College students in the Paris region situated in an underprivileged neighborhood, as part of a physical education class	Individual Agency	Transformative	Text predominantly methodological. Raises the importance of gradually familiarizing students with such a methodological device which moreover, can by very heuristic, even with population from disadvantaged neighbourhoods.
Moussay and Flavier (2014)	Clinic of activity Simple self-confrontation	French college students in an underprivileged neighborhood, as part of a Science class/ The case of a student and his science teacher	Individual agency	Transformative	Access, even indirect, to the actual activity of students is a resource for the professional development of teachers. The resulting transformations in the teacher's transmission activity have in turn an effect on student engagement in the classroom.

(cont.)

Author	Study design and methods	Population/sample	Dominant pole of agency	Research purpose	Highlights in relation to agency and power relations
Ouvrier-Bonnaz and Vérillon (2002)	Clinic of activity Simple and cross self-confrontation	French college students in an underprivileged neighborhood	Individual agency	Transformative	The results shed light on the presence of school standards that regulate student activity. To manage the constraints of school activity, students develop tactics to stay more active.
Magendie and Bouthier (2012)	Clinic of activity and Professional didactic Simple self-confrontation	3 case studies of French college students in difficulty in the subject taught (Physical Education)	Individual agency	Understanding (as resource for the teacher activity as in Professional didactic)	Student's emotions such as fear of rejection or discontent can burden their activity. Some still find opportunities for development through the realization of new activities (e.g. do what they like).
Ruelland-Roger and Clot (2013)	Clinic of activity Instruction to the double	A group of six French college students from the same class and a group of six teachers in mathematics	Individual agency	Transformative	Teachers discover the difference between what they think of the apparent activity of the student and the "real activity" of the student. Students may actually be much more involved in the learning activity than appearances might suggest.

(*cont.*)

Author	Study design and methods	Population/sample	Dominant pole of agency	Research purpose	Highlights in relation to agency and power relations
Beaty (2013)	Ethnographic study	Case studies of minority students (US high school) in 5 school programs related to video production	Relational agency	Understanding	Different forms of authority/collaboration in student activity have benne observed "from complete cooperation, subtle resistance, and open defiance." The possibility for the students to affect the school structure can act as a catalyst to support their agency.
Andrée (2012)	Ethnographic study	Swedish Students of 7th grad in a science class/The case of Helena	Individual agency	Understanding	Findings of inequalities, reproduced in part by the school environment, of girls vis-à-vis sciences. Altering the conditions of students' school activity can opens new opportunities for student participation and engagement.
Esmonde et al. (2011)	Ethnographic study	American students of 11th and 12th grades in math class/the case of a student work team	Collective agency	Understanding	Moments of difficulty, confusion or disagreement are productive for collective learning. Students learn more when they are in what the authors call the "learning mathematics" system and are less active in the "doing school" activity system.

CHAPTER 4

THE CONSTANT or Person-as-Place, and Research-Life

Sustaining Collaboration between University-Based and Field-Based Co-Researchers

Beth Ferholt and Chris Schuck

Abstract

To be able to have one's research shaped in part by people whose lives and livelihoods reside in settings very different from the university, at those moments when suggestions "from the field" fundamentally challenge conventional social scientific inquiry and concurrent ways of thinking and being, is nearly impossible. Our chapter addresses this dilemma by presenting the *research-life* process. Research-life consists of a mutual dependence of life and research questions that is bidirectional, ongoing, and evolving. One continues generating questions through the research to solve questions in one's life, and one's life becomes a means of generating questions so one can study these questions through research. Research-life thus maintains its access to a phenomenon's full, dynamic complexity and, by bringing attention to the frame between research and life, simultaneously includes its researchers in the research process. For these reasons, it may be useful to many researchers designing studies in which they hope to sustain collaboration between university-based and field-based co-researchers throughout the research process. Such studies open up possibilities for new, hybrid methods, which could make visible to researchers phenomena previously considered to be inaccessible to science.

Keywords

play – playworld – consciousness – early childhood – imagination – emotion – perezhivanie

∴

> You cannot force someone to love something,
> and if there's no love, there's not a playworld.
>   MICHAEL (personal communication, February 3, 2019)

∴

One of the things that I, Beth, have learned from my reading of Vygotsky's work and my engagement with studies inspired by his work is that designing research to benefit people who are immersed in the activity that you are studying is an important way of coming to understand this activity. One perspective is not enough and the perspectives of the people with the most at stake are particularly valuable. I work with early childhood teachers and young children in my research and one of these teachers, Michael (a pseudonym), in the midst of a study in which we were both participants, suggested a new way of conceiving of—and so conducting—our research process. What Michael suggested made sense to me as someone who had worked for many years as an early childhood teacher and made sense to me when I was working alongside Michael in our study, but I could not figure out how to incorporate Michael's suggestion throughout a research process.

After many years of failed attempts and ongoing discussion with Michael I concluded that his suggestion, which he and I had come to call *THE CONSTANT* (Michael often writes this word/term in capital letters and so we will here, too) or Person-as-Place, required—if researchers were to make use of it—something commonly found in preschools but not in universities: At least two researchers needed to be working together to shape the development of a life. I decided to try to better understand Michael's suggestion by engaging in what I came to think of as a trial research study of the suggestion itself. This would be a study of an aspect of the study's own method. I then eventually, conveniently, found myself at a point in time when I had both sufficient job security—an important point as it concerns the difficulties of conducting such a project, one which is by-definition not primarily concerned with the immediate demands of the institutions that support researchers—and a life (my own) that was about reach a developmental transition that might prove difficult to navigate. So I invited Chris to join me in coming to better understand Michael's suggestion. Chris was a perfect candidate to be my co-researcher—perhaps the only candidate—because he had worked with me to shape the development of my life as my friend since we were teenagers, and was now in the early stages of a midlife transition to working as a scholar and a researcher.

In my work with Chris we came to understand Michael's suggestion in such a way that we saw this suggestion manifesting itself in our trial study as a process of conducting research inside a life (while, at the same time, living a life inside the research), and so I named this process *research-life*. Research-life could be categorized as a form of autoethnography, but its primary contribution does not lie in the fact that it shapes the development of a life or helps us to understand aspects of this life. Research-life addresses instead a practical dilemma: that an effort to have one's research shaped in part by people whose lives and livelihoods reside in settings very different from the university is, at those moments when suggestions "from the field" fundamentally challenge conventional social scientific inquiry and concurrent ways of thinking and being, nearly impossible. Using a recursive logic, research-life is based on a hunch that preschool teachers, when they are able to augment their expertise at including young children in classroom activities with techniques learned from young children who are experts at including each other in play, have something to teach researchers about including field-based researchers in the research process.

This chapter thus resembles an effort to jump into an already-swinging jump rope. Its two authors are hoping that Beth, by paying close enough attention to Michael's suggestion despite her position outside his activity of teaching, has been able to jump into another activity that is similar to Michael's in key ways, i.e. her research-life with Chris. This research-life will in turn allow Beth to experience something of what Michael described (his suggestion) *and* both analyze and write about this experience while she remains inside this activity.

The heart of this chapter consists of Michael's suggestion, or thoughts of Michael's that Beth has come to understand as a suggestion, using his own words. However, to make these words comprehensible there are several layers of context we must provide. We will first describe early childhood teachers as key collaborators for researchers who are interested in studying human development through a non-dualist methodology, including what we introduce here as the research-life process. We will then briefly present the activity in which Michael was able to learn from the children in his classroom about play, an activity called *playworld* (Lindqvist, 1995); and describe a methodological contribution based on suggestions from the children that allowed this particular playworld to continue, a method called *film-play* (Ferholt, 2018). This background information will allow us to meaningfully describe, at some length, one example of Michael's "including" a child in this playworld using a technique that he learned from the children. We then conceptualize Michael's act of including, drawing upon Bateson's (1972) theory of play in order to present Michael's *own* conceptualization of this aspect of his playworld experience in terms of a work of art—the suggestion which had been previously excluded from Beth's research processes. We will conclude the chapter with a description of our own trial research-life project, which generated all of these layers of context that made Michael's suggestion comprehensible to us, and hopefully to our reader as well. (Usually the method section is placed before the analysis and findings sections when a research study is presented, but as it was life that guided this study and our methods were our findings, the outline described above is most feasible.) All the steps described above serve the larger project of identifying, analyzing and describing a phenomenon whose existence was intuited by Beth and Michael in a playworld, many years ago.

Meanwhile, it is important to contextualize this chapter as the second paper in a series of three interrelated papers. The first titled, "A multiperspectival analysis of creative imagining: Applying Vygotsky's method of literary analysis to a playworld" (Ferholt, 2018), turned out to be only an initial analysis or, more precisely, only an identification of a unit of analysis. With hindsight (provided by this chapter), this first paper also provided a rule of thumb that we would need to apply throughout our own research process. Namely, in some cases, we can only observe the contours of our object of study, *and also only analyze and present our findings concerning this object*, when we evoke and manifest this object, such that our research *repeatedly* constitutes an example of our object of study; thus challenging the divide between method and object in conventional social sciences. The current chapter, in other words, describes both research-life and what research-life has been developed to analyze. Findings from this extended study will be presented in a third paper in the trilogy, and this presentation of our findings will also constitute an example of our object of study.

We realize that some of the description and background above may come across as a bit abstract. For purposes of clarity, before proceeding any further we shall lay out a brief summary of what we consider to be the key elements of our research-life process.

1   Summary of Key Elements of Our Research-Life Process

1. Unit of analysis: Originally this was perezhivanie (as elaborated in the first paper (Ferholt, 2018)), but gradually we found ourselves working toward what we anticipate becoming a new unit of analysis. The presentation of these latest findings in the upcoming third paper should be required to make that case; as such, the present chapter can be regarded as simultaneously a transitional work, and a proleptic one.

2. Research question: "What is a new way in which we can explore what Michael and Beth shared in the U.S. Narnia playworld; a method which we believe may have potential to describe aspects of human development not normally conducive to scientific research, but which we have only, now, been able to pursue more fully in this chapter?"
3. Method: There were methods for the original playworld studies that have been presented elsewhere (Ferholt, 2009, 2018; Ferholt & Lecusay, 2010), but film-play (Ferholt, 2018) emerged as the significant method for data collection. In this chapter, research-life emerged as the significant method of analysis. In the prospective third paper, we expect to discover what we are studying via yet another method.
4. Theoretical background and inspiration for the study: We primarily work from Vygotsky (1971, 1978, 1987, 1994), Bateson (1972), Lindqvist (1995), Paley (1986), Rouch (1978), Vasilyuk (1988), and Buber (1970).
5. Data: Data consist of our email communications; records of our verbal conversations (phone and in person); and some written notes concerning Beth's development, Beth and Chris's relationship and the analysis.
6. Findings: For this chapter the finding was the method of research-life. There was also an initial finding concerning the object of study, but this cannot be fully described before the third paper is completed. In a sense, each of the three papers are studies of methods: methods of isolating objects of study, analyzing these objects and presenting findings. The findings will not be visible until the method for presenting the findings has been developed and presented, using, as in the first paper, Vygotsky's method of literary analysis.

2   Why Preschool Teachers?

Vivian Paley is a preschool teacher and author who has shaped the field of early childhood education in the U.S. and whose work can be well described as avoiding "the arrogance of adult to small child; of teacher to student; of writer to reader" (Leach, 1986). Paley developed a method of regularly writing down her young students' stories for them, helping them to act out these stories together, and also regularly audio recording and transcribing the words of the children in her classrooms. One of Paley's many books, *Mollie is Three* (1986), is preceded by a foreword in which Michael Cole makes two points about psychology in the 1980s that are equally true today, several decades later. First, "'(s)cience can not utter a single word about the individual molecule, thing, or creature in so far as it is an individual but only in so far as it is like other individuals' (Walker Percy, The Message in the Bottle)" (1986, p. VII). Cole notes: "Applied to psychology, the discipline which studies *individual* behavior and consciousness, this limitation on the scientific method is particularly disheartening" (1986, pp. VII–VIII). And second, while development occurs over time and should therefore be studied over time, for a variety of reasons this rarely takes place in psychological studies.

Cole responds to these two critiques of the field as a whole by stating that a person "responsible for guiding the development of individual children as a professional commitment (for example, if one happens to be a nursery school teacher) … is in a unique position to resolve some of the very issues left unresolved by others who study children and their development" (1986, p. IX). What the preschool teacher can do to resolve some of these issues left unresolved by others is to "combine the observational/interventionist strategy favored by the ethnologist with the participant methods of the anthropologist" (1986, pp. IX–X) and to do so over a long period of time and many contexts. It is in this way, Cole claims, that Paley "presents us with a picture of the formation of human consciousness that provides a flesh-and blood representation of William James's intuition about human consciousness at all stages and the process by which we all wrest pattern from the flux of experience" (1986, p. XIII).

Recent preschool pedagogical research in Sweden that has described and illustrated a framework for future research studies called *early childhood education research from within* (Nilsson et al., 2018) and which, like Paley and Cole's work, is heavily influenced by Vygotsky's work, is closely related to Cole's claims above. "Early childhood education research from within" is an encounter between the academy and the preschool developed on the assumption that if teachers who believe that children are capable and competent, and who therefore listen closely and respectfully to children, participate in such research, then children are indirectly a part of a research team and their voices can potentially influence early childhood education and scholarship in the field via the academy—i.e., life (the realm of practice) influencing and shaping scientific study of life. Simultaneously, if researchers in preschools strive to have this research guided by the interests and knowledge of the teachers, then these researchers can act as catalysts, helping preschool activities to change in response to contradictions within these activities—i.e., science (the realm of study) influencing and transforming life in the process of studying it. "Early childhood education research from within" was developed within a research project in which Monica Nilsson and Beth were university-based researchers, and it does allow research to be shaped in part by people whose lives and livelihoods reside in settings very different from the university, in this case preschool teachers. The book that the project generated (Nilsson et al., 2018) is co-authored by Monica, Beth and the three preschool teachers in whose classroom the study took place. But "early childhood education research from within" does not focus on those moments when suggestions "from the field" fundamentally challenge conventional social scientific inquiry and concurrent ways of thinking and being.

Observational/interventionist strategies combined with participant methods, practiced over time, are important potential contributions from preschool teachers to the field of psychology. Bringing children's voices to research in the field of early childhood education and care is also an important potential contribution from preschool teachers to the academy. This chapter builds on these observations of Cole (Paley, 1986) and of Nilsson et al. (2018) by turning to Paley, herself, to see what preschool teachers might have to teach researchers about research. Paley states: "If ... (a) preschool activity cannot include all the children in the classroom in some way, then the activity has to be reexamined or the way one is doing the activity has to be reexamined" (Armstrong & Dawson, 2004). She says of her own teaching practice that if she did not include all of the children in the classroom, she "might as well have stayed home" (Armstrong & Dawson, 2004).

That such inclusion would be the expertise of people whose profession consists in great part of raising the youngest children to be human, makes sense to those of us who understand raising young children to mean including these children in human social activities at the very time when they are just being introduced to human social activities (the very start of their lives). Vygotsky writes: "Few understand why it is imperative not only to have the effect of art take shape and excite the reader or spectator but also to explain art, *and to explain it in such a way that the explanation does not kill the emotion*" (1971, p. 254). Preschool teachers must, in a sense, explain being human, being social, to newcomers to the activity of living, and they must do so in such a way that they enact this social/human way of being with the students, or the children will not understand what the teachers are explaining.

For instance, as those familiar with preschool classrooms may appreciate, the novice preschool teacher is often found enforcing proximity to preschool activities only to find the children imitating the enforcing as best they can. This process is too exhausting to maintain for long and so even the moderately experienced preschool teacher can be found eating with the children as they explain how to eat at mealtimes, touching the children gently and speaking softly as they explain how to work safely with noisy and heavy toys, nodding off with the children as they explain that naptime is for sleeping, etc. Master teachers (or at least those teachers who are of interest to us here) have a variety of nuanced means of including all the children in the classroom activities.

3 Playworld and Film-Play

3.1 *Playworld*

When Michael made his suggestion concerning a new way of conceiving of and so conducting our research process, he and Beth were co-participants in a playworld (Lindqvist, 1995). Playworlds (Lindqvist, 1995; Marjanovic-Shane et al., 2011; Nilsson & Ferholt, 2014) are activities that combine adult forms of creative imagination (art, science, etc.), which require extensive real life experience, with children's forms of creative imagination (play), which require the embodiment of ideas and emotions in the material world (Vygotsky's "pivot") (Vygotsky, 1978). Accordingly, in the example that we will present below we argue that Michael's including of a child in his class in a classroom activity was shaped by his students' expertise as players as well as his own expertise as a preschool teacher.

Playworlds engage adults in learning from children how to play by intentionally addressing epistemological and ethical dilemmas that are of interest to people in a variety of life stages (Ferholt & Lecusay, 2010), so that the adults as well as the children who are participating in a playworld are invested in solving this dilemma. Furthermore, these dilemmas are such that it is the combination of different perspectives, rather than skills or experience that come with age, which produces solutions (e.g. What is real?, What to do if someone you love is doing something harmful to themselves and others?, What does one do in the face of conflicting options? etc.) (Nilsson & Ferholt, 2014). If we understand play to be imagination in the material world (Vygotsky, 1978), then it makes sense that adult participants would want to remain in playworlds in order to access a powerful form of imagination that is not always available to them and that is rarely available to them along with coaching from an expert player (Ferholt, 2009).

Playworlds also cultivate and highlight teachers "stepp(ing) out of their 'teacher roles' and leav(ing) behind the institutional language which is part of the teacher role in preschools and schools. By virtue of the fictitious role, the teachers have dared to try new attitudes and ways of acting" (Lindqvist, 1995, pp. 210–211). In Michael's words: "(H)ere is an analogy ... I have on my football helmet ... and everyone else is playing basketball. The kids are playing basketball ... and if we want to play, we need to get rid of the helmet" (personal communication, January 25, 2009, cited in Ferholt, 2009, p. 17).

This pressure on the teacher to "remove one's helmet" in a playworld is effective because the teacher is personally invested in the playworld continuing. In Michael's words, again:

> I [when not in a playworld] imagine the things I cannot be. I do not BE the things I cannot be. In the PW [playworld] I can BE a witch. A kid has to act because he cannot imagine. I have to act like the things that I know that I cannot actually be ...
>
> A PW [is] kids and adults HAVING to act. Adults [are] acting things they cannot be. Kids [are] act[ing] things they cannot internally imagine. (personal communication, January 25, 2009, original emphasis, cited in Ferholt, 2009, p. 16)

Playworlds thus gave Michael access to a venue for augmenting his own expertise at including young children in classroom activities, with techniques learned from these children, while providing Michael and the participating researchers (who were also in role in the playworld described below) with a fine example of teachers "bridging [of] segregated and differently valued knowledges, and drawing together legitimated as well as subjugated modes of inquiry" (Conquergood, 2002, pp. 151–152).

3.2 Film-Play

In the playworld where Michael and Beth were collaborating, this drawing together of modes of inquiry was extended to include researchers developing a new method of analysis based on suggestions from the child participants. Jean Rouch wrote of the detailed parallel between his ethnographic filming and the possession dance, magic and sorcery he filmed, that "[i]t is the "film-trance" (ciné-trance) of one filming the "real trance" of the other" (1978, p. 64). Beth was studying perezhivanie (Blunden, 2016; Ferholt & Nilsson, 2016a, 2016b; Vasilyuk, 1988) in this particular playworld, and just as Rouch's ciné-trance is part ethnographic filmmaking and part trance (the subject of his film-making), she and her fellow researchers combined film and perezhivanie, producing what Beth later termed film-play.

Concretely, film-play is a form of adult-adult interaction incorporating the playful creation and appreciation of ethnographic films that are both social-scientific documents, and also works of filmic art. In the context of the Narnia playworld, the researchers used various ensembles of methods of representation, including film-play, which itself evoked and manifested the perezhivanie it was supposed to represent. This made perezhivanie available for analysis by avoiding breaking perezhivanie into its component, and thus static, parts (and so losing its momentum) (Ferholt, 2018).

The reason Beth named this method film-play and not film-perezhivanie is that the way that film-play and ciné-trance work—by constituting examples of phenomena that they are intending to represent, making both particularly useful in the study of phenomenon that are at least partially characterized by their momentum—is play-like. For Bateson (1972), play is a paradox because it both is and is not what it appears to be. The (play-like) quality of film one is striving for in film-play is the illusion of time flowing that we, the audience, fall into, even as we are aware of—in fact because we are aware of—the disjointed still photographs that film actually is. Sobchack (1992, 2004) calls this quality of film "lived momentum." Sobchack's argument is that film shows us the frame through which it is created and that the paradox of film is that our knowledge of this frame—our knowledge that the movement we experience is just an illusion—is what makes this illusion convincing.

Furthermore, because it has momentum, which is the ability to develop towards a future, film is alive. Sobchack (1992) claims that film has an active life of its own. You can live in the film, but film also lives within your life. To quote Rouch (1978) again: When the filmmaker-observer shows the film to the subjects of the film, "a strange dialogue takes place in which the film's "truth" rejoins its mythic representation" (p. 58). In our case the development and then use of film-play literally showed the researchers, and confirmed for the teacher, certain aspects of the playworld that made this playworld's continued development possible. Specifically, the adult participants in this playworld had to believe that the children believed that an evil character (the White Witch, discussed below) had arrived in the playworld when Michael went into role as this character, or they could not continue with Michael in the playworld. And the researchers were not convinced of this character's existence until they saw the products of their own film-play (Ferholt, 2018).

4   An Example of Michael's Including a Child Using a Technique That He Learned from the Children in a Playworld

Film-play differs from the research-life process in several ways, including the fact that it has specific constraints due to its reliance on film (for instance, it is constrained to relatively short time spans); and that no one has yet figured out how to continue film-play throughout the research process. However, in the context of the playworld, several key similarities between film-play and research-life emerge that offer insight into the perspectives of Michael, Beth, and the other researchers as they attempted to make sense of the event that we will describe, below. In the following example, we will describe how Michael revealed the frame through which the playworld is created; the awareness of which invests the playworld with its very power, making the playworld compelling—perhaps because an illusion has been made convincing in some respects. (The following example is taken from two discussions of related issues: perezhivanie and film-play (Ferholt, 2009), and inclusion and ambivalence (Ferholt & Rainio, 2016).)

4.1 *An Overview of the Playworld*

The playworld, called the U.S. Narnia Playworld, took place in a kindergarten and first-grade class of 20 children in a public elementary school on a U.S. military base. It was based on C. S. Lewis's *The Lion, the Witch and the Wardrobe* (1950). Over the one-year period during which the playworld took place there were 14 sessions, each of which lasted approximately two hours.

Most of these sessions included reflection upon the enactments in the form of discussion, which was followed by free play or art activities. All of these playworld sessions involved set pieces and props created by both the adults and children, including some props that were designed to appeal to the participants' senses of touch, smell, and sound. Many of these set pieces remained in place throughout the school day—most of the classroom furniture had been removed—and the set piece that served as a "portal" to the playworld was a wooden wardrobe with a false back, which could be removed easily when the children were out of the room but which appeared to be permanent.

Most of the 14 playworld sessions included all four researchers, who played the child heroes of the playworld. The teacher joined in role for the first time during the seventh of these sessions, playing the evil White Witch. The children joined in role for the first time during the eighth of these sessions, as themselves, and for the final of these sessions the children were the primary planners of the adult–child joint play.

4.2 *Pre-Recess Negotiation*

The event included a planning session that has a pre-recess negotiation and a post-recess confrontation, and also a final acting session of the playworld. The example that concerns us took place during the post-recess confrontation. We will provide a brief description of the pre-recess negotiation here, and after describing our example in the next section, then provide a brief description of the final acting session.

During the pre-recess negotiation of the planning session, the children meet to try to decide upon a plan to save Mr. Tumnus, a faun and their friend, from the White Witch. During the meeting one child, Milo, is rolling around on the floor and interrupting people. Michael asks Milo to sit apart from the group twice during the meeting, to calm down, saying that Milo can return whenever he wants. The first time Michael does this, two children go to bring Milo back to the group after a short while. The second time Michael does this, Milo starts to cry and Michael goes to talk to him, and then brings him back to the group looking much calmer. Milo explains his plan, which is that the children and child heroes of the story blow up the whole school to save Mr. Tumnus from the White Witch. Michael includes this plan in the group discussion and the class decides to have all of the children's methods of conquering the White Witch combined into one plot for a final playworld session. When the children return to the meeting after a break, Milo raises his hand and says to the class that the plan they have all decided upon "is a good plan because everyone gets to do their plan [the plan that is derived from their own picture]."

4.3   Post-Recess Confrontation: Michael's Including

When the children have returned from a recess and start rehearsing the plan, Milo is being inattentive and disruptive. *Michael speaks right to Milo in front of all the other children, saying he is sorry to single Milo out but that Milo cannot be part of the plan unless he commits to go through with it because they all need him (to save Mr. Tumnus from the White Witch without their all being caught by the White Witch).* Then Michael asks Milo what he will choose to do.

Milo's response makes it sound like he does not want to be in the playworld, but this is because he misunderstood the grammatical construction of Michael's question. When Michael responds to Milo's mistaken response, Milo bravely and clearly, with great focus and impressive articulation, states several times that he has been misunderstood (that he does, in fact, choose to be included). Milo's voice and posture are powerfully respectful and self-respecting.

4.4   Final Acting Session

The following day is the incredibly emotional penultimate acting session, in which Mr. Tumnus is rescued and the White Witch is transformed. In this final acting session, Milo's part of the plan has been reduced from blowing up the whole school to blowing up the 4 thrones after the 4 child heroes, and also the 20 children, have sat on these thrones. When it is time for Milo to carry out his part of the plan, during the final acting session of the playworld, he throws a "hand grenade" that he has brought through the wardrobe into Narnia and then engages everyone in a dramatic countdown to the explosion after making sure, in a very assertive and sincere tone of voice, that everyone is standing clear.

However, Milo then refuses to stop destroying thrones. After the explosion he spends many minutes tearing apart the cardboard thrones, first with a few other children and then on his own, with no signs of tiring. A researcher/actor reminding him that we need him to finish the plan finally convinces Milo to join his classmates in bringing the stone Mr. Tumnus to life, although he soon leaves the group again to return to his broken thrones, and then to trying to break other things in the room.

4.5 Analysis of Michael's Inclusion of Milo

Many things are happening during this event (see Ferholt, 2009; Ferholt & Rainio, 2016, for discussion of some of these), but we will focus on Michael's first including of Milo, italicized above. During the first part of this event Michael welcomes Milo's plan to blow up the school as a part of an in-school activity. A variation on this same move occurs during the confrontation when Michael tells Milo that Milo cannot be part of the plan unless he commits to go through with it because they all need him to save Mr. Tumnus from the White Witch without their all being caught by the White Witch. Here, Michael is again bringing Milo's challenge, itself, to the activity, into the world that the activity is creating.

Furthermore, during this confrontation Michael appeals to Milo not only on the behalf of the class as a whole but also on the behalf of the class in Narnia and Mr. Tumnus, whom the class is endeavoring to save. And it is the narrative of Narnia that creates the urgency in Michael's asking Milo what he will choose to do. It is authentic urgency on Michael's part because he is in role within the world of Narnia during the playworld activity: Michael is, literally to some extent, also scared of the White Witch's arrival before their plan of attack has been fully prepared and rehearsed.

To be clear, Milo's inclusion is essential to the playworld's existence because Michael agrees with Paley that if Milo, or any other child in the classroom, is not included, then the playworld activity (the activity itself) has to be reexamined or the way they are doing the playworld activity has to be reexamined. Milo's inclusion is also essential to the playworld's existence because for Michael not to be scared of the White Witch along with the children is for him to not play in the playworld—both through his not believing in a character, and doubly so because in the playworld this character is himself—and if Michael does not play, then it is children's play but not the intergenerational play that makes a playworld. On both counts, if Milo was not included when the play, the "rehearsal," began, then Michael "might as well have stayed home."

Another facet of this confrontation, in which Michael explicitly states that the class needs Milo to be committed in order to proceed, is that because Milo's commitment is essential, it is important for all participants in the playworld not to judge but instead to accept Milo's ideas and contributions as they are offered. The burden of commitment does not rest on Milo alone. Instead this burden is shared by Michael and the whole class / all of the characters in Narnia.

4.6 Beth's Role in This Playworld Event

This event took place on the middle of three pivotal days in this playworld's development. These were significant days for all or most participants, but we will highlight Beth's experience here. The reason for our doing so will become clear in the next section.

The day before this playworld event, Michael asks Beth to sit in the wardrobe for an interview. Beth had been interviewing all the adult participants and filming these interviews, while interviews of Beth were conducted and filmed by each of the other adult participants. Michael's interview style is to ask many specific questions, and after borrowing one of the children's (Martina's) question (a question that she had asked when conducting and filming her own interviews of participants), "What is your favorite part of the playworld?", he insists that Beth and he switch seats, Beth taking the camera, as he wants to answer this as one of his own questions right away.

Throughout the remainder of the playworld, Michael's eagerness to answer this question continues, and this eagerness is soon shared by almost all of the other adults, and also the children. In interviews, rehearsals and classroom discussions it is not uncommon to hear someone saying: "Can you ask me: 'What is your favorite part of the playworld?'" or "My favorite part of the playworld is ..." This also comes to be the question that shapes further development of filmplay, as part of the film-play process is to select footage of participant's favorite parts of the playworld and to make the films primarily from this footage. Beth's own favorite part of the playworld, up until the completion of this chapter, was the day of the event in question. It was her favorite part of the playworld because she felt included in the role of teacher on this day, and she sensed that this would be very important to development in her own life, across a time span of decades.[1]

In morning meeting the day after this interview (which was also the day that Michael included Milo), the following question arises while planning the final acting session: "Why sit on the four thrones if there is a prophesy that this will kill the White Witch, and she has already been made into a good person?" This seems to stump Michael and all the children, so they begin to reorder their storyboard. Beth tries not to interrupt; she has never offered an unsolicited contribution to a class discussion before, but she cannot restrain herself: She suggests a close reading of the poem in the novel that contains the prophecy. Then she waits nervously until her contribution has been made use of in such a way that it is helpful, not disruptive. Nancy recites the poem, from memory, and Michael and some of the children realize that the evil *times* will be over and done when the thrones are filled but that the Witch will not die. Beth thinks to herself that it has been a breakthrough of some sort, for her, to step into this class discussion successfully, and she observes that she feels deeply and joyfully relieved.

Michael then stops the discussion. He tells the children that they look tired and tells them to do whatever they want to do, that they can even just lie down for a while if they want to. Beth experiences a second surprise of the day. As she watches the children take their "rest" among the props, preparing to finish their play by lying and playing in and on the setting of Narnia that they and Michael have created over the course of the school year, she sees the world of the classroom and the world of Narnia lying right next to each other, breathing together, both porous. She sees the room anew and feels a sense of great awe for the children: It seems to her that when she first came to this classroom she couldn't believe that she would find anything new here, but that she is, right this moment, being shown a newness. When Beth describes these feelings to Michael he says that he forgets that Beth and the other researchers don't see what he sees all the time, the children's free play in the classroom with its wardrobe, trees, lamppost, cave, beaver dam, castle and cage, but she is not convinced that he sees daily what she is seeing now.

When the children return to the meeting Milo says that this plan is a good plan because everyone gets to do their plan (the plan that is derived from their own picture). The children are now sitting facing the board, and Michael works with them to make a list of all the things to do and who will do them. He wants the numbers to work out evenly: 7 tasks and 20 children, and just two children do the first task, so three children to each task. But Pearl repeats Milo's suggestion that they each do the task that derived from their own picture. Michael sees the wisdom of Milo and Pearl's point immediately, and the children literally cheer after Pearl has spoken. It occurs to Beth that the children have hit upon a central lesson of this playworld: that we each must live in this joint world in our own way, simultaneously.

Beth stays for lunch and during lunch Rachel, one of the oldest and most mature first graders, asks her why she is still in the classroom, as adults from the university rarely stay for lunch. Beth responds that she is still in the classroom because she is having too much fun to leave, and then she realizes that this is true. As well as the events described directly above, this morning has included another wonderfully fun time for Beth: the recess in which Luke and Albert and she were in the castle, recording and viewing the boys' dreamtelling in an endless spiral.

After lunch, when the class returns to their classroom from recess, Michael decides that they are too noisy and makes them come in and out again and again, over and over. He finally raises his voice and almost yells at his students as they stand outside the door, waiting to enter, yet again. Beth is so troubled by this that she oversteps another boundary that she has set for herself as a visiting researcher in Michael's classroom: She gives Michael unsolicited advice while he is in the midst of teaching. She touches Michael's arm and says to him, "Chill."

As soon as she has spoken this one word Beth immediately thinks, "I've surely done it (made Michael wish I was not in his classroom) now." But she also worries that she and Michael are somehow messing the whole thing up, that the rehearsal for the next day's finale will never take place and that they are losing everything they have built with the children if they become authoritarian, now. Just a short while later this last concern seems founded. The rehearsal of the plan has finally begun and Milo is being inattentive and disruptive, and Michael confronts Milo in such a way that Beth suddenly thinks that Michael is being selfish and that he is demeaning Milo. However, it turns out that Beth is wrong on all counts: Michael will express his appreciation of Beth's intervention when the researchers talk on the phone in the evening, they will finish the rehearsal this day, and Michael appears to strengthen his relationship of mutual respect with his students through his difficult interaction with Milo.

When the researchers call Michael in the evening to consult about final details of the next day's performance, Beth apologizes for saying "Chill" to Michael earlier in the day. Michael says that Beth helped him calm down, that he really appreciated this, and that he really appreciated the benefit of having another adult in the room. Michael also tells us that when the children had finished writing down their plan, so they could read it to the four siblings the next day, they asked Michael to keep the plan safe from the White Witch by sleeping with it under his pillow. He says that he knew he would do this if he said he would do it, and that he could not sleep well with a piece of large paper folded under his pillow, so he asked the children if he could keep the plan under his bed. They said no, this was not a good idea, so he suggested sleeping with the plan next to his bed and under a set of noisy keys and they did agree to this plan. The children are definitely concerned that the White Witch will leave Narnia to steal their plans from Michael's house, and Michael seems quite concerned as well!

When Beth told Michael to "chill," she experienced this as a significant change in her identity with respect to the class. Before her evening phone call with Michael, she felt the most intense anxiety of her entire year in this playworld. During the day of this event Beth felt, in her words: "trapped in the classroom, as if I would never be able to return to the university, a feeling so intense that I felt physically incapacitated" (Ferholt, 2009, p. 238).

5 Our Conceptualization of Michael's Act of Including

Michael told Milo that he cannot be part of the plan unless he commits to go through with it because they all need him (to save Mr. Tumnus from the White Witch without their all being caught by the White Witch). First, Michael's explicitly stating that Milo needs to choose to be in the playworld, in order to be in the playworld, expresses an essential aspect of play: you cannot force someone to play because play is not play if its not voluntarily chosen. Therefore, if you want a new player to join your play, you need to make them want to play. So, second, Michael tries to make Milo want to be in the playworld by making him feel invested in the playworld's continuing.

This gesture of Michael's is a gamble. His offer could certainly be refused. But Milo has been surrounded by many people who are in the playworld and the playworld trappings for a good part of every weekday over the course of many months, so there is a good chance that the logic of the playworld will appeal to him.

Our third point, and the point that is of most interest to us here, is that Michael also harnesses the "lived momentum" of the playworld in his appeal to Milo to choose to enter the playworld. In his statement, Michael simultaneously acknowledges the playworld's frame (you can choose to exist outside of the playworld) and ignores this frame (telling Milo that if he does not enter the playworld to save Mr. Tumnus from the White Witch they all risk being caught by the White Witch). This acknowledgement of the playworld's frame, as Sobchack explained concerning film, solidifies the illusion of the playworld's being real and Milo, formerly a mere audience, falls into the playworld; even as he is aware of—in fact because he is aware of—the playworld *and* the school in which the playworld exists. This is why Milo's anticipation of blowing up the school must be maintained (his plan included along with the others), and this may be why the "blowing up the whole school"—not just the thrones—appears to have remained Milo's plan throughout the final acting session. It is certainly why Michael must widen his vision of the playworld to encompass hand grenades (not a distant threat in a school on a military base) if Milo is to be included, making the continuation of the playworld possible through his inclusion.

Michael shows the frame through which a playworld is created, and that the paradox—that Milo's knowledge of this frame, his knowledge that the danger caused by the presence of the White Witch is just an illusion—is what makes this illusion convincing. For Bateson (1972) play is a paradox because it both is and is not what it appears to be. For instance, the play bite is a bite but in play it is not. "The playful nip denotes the bite, but it does not denote what would be denoted by the bite" (Bateson, 1972, p. 185).

Furthermore, for Bateson play is also a paradox because it is metacommunicative: Play is not just play, but is also a message about itself. The message "This is play." sets a frame for the play, creating a paradox by drawing a line between categories of different logical types. As Bateson explains, the picture frame (the equivalent of "This is play.") is an instruction to the viewer to not extend the premises that obtain between the figures within the picture to the wallpaper behind the picture, and this is a paradox because the frame does delineate things that are not of the same logical type (Bateson, 1972, p. 185).

Bateson claims that what we consider sanity requires these paradoxes of abstraction. He argues that without these paradoxes there could be no communication, change or humor. And as Lindqvist explains, play is creative in the sense that it allows children to think the new, but also creative in that it reflects the self-reflexive and proleptic process that Vygotsky identifies with art and with consciousness:

> Vygotsky's view of the dynamic structure of consciousness corresponds with the aesthetic form of art. In play, a meeting between the individual's internal and external environment takes place in a creative interpretation process, the imaginary process, in which children express their imagination in action. Play reflects the aesthetic form of consciousness. (1995, p. 40)

In Vygotsky's own words: "The potential for free action that we find associated with the emergence of human consciousness is closely connected with imagination, with the unique psychological set of consciousness *vis a vis* reality that is manifested in imagination" (1987, p. 349).

Michael is both Milo's teacher and the White Witch and so he literally embodies the frame, the awareness of which allowed Milo to fall into the playworld. In Michael's conceptualization of what we understand to be this same aspect of this playworld, which we present below, Michael stresses a person functioning as a frame in this way. It is this person as a frame that Michael calls THE CONSTANT, although Beth often uses the term "person-as-place" in her conversations with Michael, presumably because one falls inside the place that their CONSTANT frames.

THE CONSTANT is not a scholarly concept in a traditional sense. It is perhaps a concept-in-the-making or tool for the construction of playworlds, as it has been especially helpful in the making of several playworlds since Michael coined it. Person-as-place could similarly be a metaphor or tool for the development of research-life. Beth generated it from a temporary habit she had of speaking Michael's name when she was managing a serious health threat to a loved one in real life, somehow summoning the magic of the Narnia playworld when it was needed, and she thinks of it as a term evoking this descriptive phrase of Martin Buber's: "As long as the firmament of the You is spread over me, the tempests of causality cower at my heels, and the whirl of doom

THE CONSTANT OR PERSON-AS-PLACE, AND RESEARCH-LIFE   89

congeals" (1970, p. 59). It was important to us to keep both terms alongside "research-life" in this chapter because our argument concerns, in part, imperfect efforts to translate these terms across stages of the research process.

6   Michael's Conceptualization of THE CONSTANT

6.1   *The Wall on Which the Picture Is Hung: Nested Narratives*
In the following excerpt from the video field note of Michael's—while he is again thinking about favorite moments—he describes the playworld as situated within two larger, concentric fields, what he calls "narratives." The note is transcribed from a video recording of Michael speaking to the camera; some gestures are described in parenthesis and italicized, and line breaks show long pauses. "The day that Beth walked in" refers to the day that Beth, the researcher chosen to first meet Michael when the research team was looking for a teacher to participate in a new playworld research project, walked into Michael's classroom to visit and then invited him to join the project.

> But I think for me personally, my favorite moment, you know, just me personally—not being altruistic—was, the day that Beth walked in.
>   Yeah. If it ca— if it can't be the one—because ultimately A (student). being nice to L (student). is my ultimate goal. So that kind of signifies my favorite moment, also.
>   It's tough. Those three.
>   But I'd have to say, as a teacher ... (*He points in front of himself, down at the floor, then raises his hand to the height of his neck and draws a circle with his hand*). Uh, for what I do in the classroom, A. being nice to L. was the ultimate time.
>   As a teacher involved in *this* (he means the Narnia Playworld as he points to the cardboard sets of the playworld that are around him in his classroom), it was (*His hand is now drawing a slightly larger circle in front of his neck*), it was the box on the head (referring to when he as the White Witched was trapped in the Narnia Playworld). (*He points to his head*)
>   And as me personally, as a teacher as well but as me personally (*The circle he is drawing with his hand becomes larger still*), is was when Beth walked in the door.
>   Does that clarify things?
>   I know it sounds like I'm choosing three but it's actually one for each of my ... three narratives: teacher, teacher involved in how I ... (*He was pointing with a finger for each of these three 'narratives,' but then he starts*

the list again while making a small circle with his left hand by his left ear each time he names one of the three 'narratives')

Person—being a human in the world. Teacher in the classroom. And then teacher involved in this Narnia.

So those are my three moments for each of those ... narratives.

So that's three for you, Beth." (video field note, May 6, 2005)

6.2   The Frame Delineating Things That Are Not of the Same Logical Type: A CONSTANT

Michael explains (in an email sent March 15, 2009) that a "constant is someone who helps you reflect back on what you yourself did ... (a) constant helps you remember your own experience (and this person may/may not have experienced anything you did)." Michael adds: "A constant is sort of like a beacon ... guiding you back on course. But, also giving you hope." In the episode of the show "Lost" (Cuse & Lindelof, 2008) to which Michael is referring, someone who will need help in the future literally tells their CONSTANT to answer the phone at a certain time at a certain date in the future, as they have a premonition that they will need this person at this point in time, and the fact that their CONSTANT does answer the call is what keeps the main character from melting in a sort of supernatural borderland.

Michael also explains that Beth is his CONSTANT in an area encompassing the playworld that he and Beth created. Four years after recording the field note, a portion of which is transcribed above, Michael explained that, through the Narnia Playworld, Beth became his "constant for when I am teaching": "When all is chaotic (in my classroom) and I need something to 'right my ship' I think of (Beth). I do not have to consciously think about you: you just appear in my brain." Beth was also herself in the playworld in role, and apparently, from the email above, in Michael's narrative of "person—being a human in the world."[2]

What Michael's description of A CONSTANT and delineating of nested narratives offered Beth was, ultimately, a suggestion of a new way of conceiving of the research process; yet it was not until she had designed the trial research-life study with Chris that she would come to understand this. Initially, she only knew that she wanted to better understand Michael's insight, such that it could, perhaps, contribute to the design of a research study—and that at least two researchers needed to be working together to shape the development of a life. Beth did not extrapolate this last tip for proceeding from Michael's suggestion on her own, although she did proceed quite intuitively into the new study with Chris, even believing at the start that she was simply inviting Chris to think and write with her about a means of studying perezhivanie. Michael fully appreciated that Beth was primarily concerned with working to include early childhood teachers throughout the research process by helping herself to avoid dismissing those claims of teachers that made sense in the classroom but not in the university. And Michael raised and discussed the topic of CONSTANTS with Beth over many emails and talks, which took place over the course of many years, such that Beth considers Michael to be a co-designer of the trial research-life study, or at least of precursors to this trial study. (Beth (Ferholt, 2009) describes a precursor to this study that Michael and she executed within the Narnia playworld study, a visual mapping of perezhivanie across the year-long timespan of the Narnia playworld, although this effort has yet to produce any findings.)

7 Beth and Chris's Trial Research-Life Study

As stated earlier, Chris was a perfect candidate for Beth's co-researcher in a trial research-life study because he had some scholarly interests related to the project and most importantly, a history of working with Beth and influencing the development of her life since their teenage years. What we came to understand through the course of our study is that Chris was also Beth's CONSTANT between her life and the study we were creating, and moreover that he had played this role for over three decades, as both her life and her research had evolved. This life "narrative" was not Beth's whole life, but a portion of her life on which the study was "hung" not unlike a picture on a wall (i.e., which encompassed the study), so we will begin with a brief description of this "wall" and what it encompassed.

Beth will write the next section in the first person, as she wrote the introduction in the first person, because there were two points in our research process during which Beth could not collaborate with Chris. When the research that led to this study began, during Beth's early childhood (one of the key contributions to our development of our study came from a book, *A Book of Seagulls and Other Water Birds* (Ferholt, 1977), which Beth "published" in her preschool one week before her sixth birthday), Beth had not yet met Chris. Three days before we submitted a nearly final draft of this chapter Beth found that she needed to rewrite the introduction to the paper on her own, thus ending the study (by ending the collaboration, although we both did make final edits to the chapter), because the life component of the research-life process seemed to be precluding all other ways of ending the study (barring someone's dying).

7.1 *Beth's Nested Narratives and* THE CONSTANT *between Them*
When I was a young child, one of my primary caregivers appeared to suffer from bouts of despair. I often wondered how people get from one end of their

life to the other with a sense of coherence and the motivation to keep living. Over the course of my own life, I found this question and various means of responding to it in young children's play; the work of preschool teachers; Virginia Woolf's novels; and in Vygosky's writing, particularly his writing on imagination, creativity and consciousness, and on perezhivanie (1994), when combined with the work of Vasilyuk (1988) on perezhivanie.

Fyodor Vasilyuk (1988) adapts Vygotsky's use of the term perezhivanie to describe a form of inter-subjectivity in which we insert ourselves into the stories of others in order to gain the foresight that allows us to proceed. He describes perezhivanie as an internal and subjective labor of "entering into" which is not done by the mind alone, but rather involves the whole of life or a state of consciousness. And although, for Vasilyuk, perezhivanie is the direct sensation or experience of mental states and processes, another person is needed for this experience: It is this inclusion of another person that allows the first to overcome and conquer despair through perezhivanie.

Vasilyuk describes the proleptic nature of perezhivanie through a discussion of the development of Raskolnikov, the main character in Dostoevsky's *Crime and Punishment*, but the non-technical definition of the word "perezhivanie" can also include this temporal pattern, as Robbins most eloquently explains:

> "(P)erezhivat" means, if you look at it closely, that you have passed as if above something that had made you feel pain ... There, inside of a recollection that we call an "again living"—lives your pain. It is the pain that doesn't let you forget what has happened. And you keep on coming back to it in your memory, keep living through it over and over again, until you discover that you have passed through it, and have survived. (2007a, n.p.)

Robbins adds that "(p)erezhivanie ... is an anchor in the fluidity of life, it represents a type of synthesis (not a concrete unity of analysis), but an anchor within the fleeting times we have on this earth, dedicated to internal transformation and involvement in our world" (2007b, n.p.). I think this anchor designates the part of perezhivnie that is the other person, THE CONSTANT, who (per our earlier discussion) is the frame, delineating the things that are not of the same logical type. When you use this person to simultaneously inhabit both the picture and the wall, and so remain aware of the paradox, then you have a sensation of falling into a new time, new "lived momentum."

When I turned 15 years old my primary caregiver's state made it nearly impossible for me to navigate a new developmental transition. I met Chris discussing our assigned book for our high school English class, *1984* (Orwell, 1949). As our friendship developed through our reading and writing and discussing ideas together, Chris showed me certain ways of being and listened to me in ways that allowed me to first realize that my caregiver's love lived on in me, and then move on with my life while letting my caregiver move on towards their death. For a series of complicated reasons, I anticipated having difficulty navigating a new developmental transition (again) when I was approaching my 46th birthday. I was facing becoming my former caregivers' caregiver, as they aged, and with their descending into a more joyless place than I had yet been able to imagine. I "called" Chris again, and our trial research-life study was the result. This eventually developed into the current chapter and also my living through, over and over again, until I realized that I had passed through my pain, passed as if above those things that had made me feel pain in my childhood and adolescence, and survived.[3]

7.2 *How Our Trial Research-Life Study Worked*

Conducting our trial study inside my life did indeed allow me to sustain my collaboration with Chris throughout the research process. Our email communications, written over the span of several years, consisted of discussions of our life challenges and humdrum details, intertwined seamlessly with work on this chapter's arguments, structure and nuances. And how this happened did, as anticipated, mirror the example of Michael including Milo in several ways. For instance, when Chris suggested something that I thought, as a researcher, was incorrect, his role in my life led me to continue listening, even when he challenged my most deeply held beliefs about the research process, because more than I wanted a publishable paper I wanted to continue my collaboration with Chris for the sake of my development in my life. My life was more important to me than the paper and it was for this reason I repeatedly chose to continue the research collaboration by hook or by crook; just as for Milo, his teacher and classmates' safety from the White Witch was more important than the playworld, so that he chose to be included in the playworld despite the fact that he had been resisting this collaboration up to this point.

Chris, like Michael, was literally the embodiment of the frame between the research and my life because, just as Michael was both the teacher in the classroom and the White Witch, Chris was my friend in my life and my co-researcher. And consistently, across hundreds of concrete examples spanning a range of time scales and degrees of emotional intensity, from many emails about life and the trial study (such that they are available for further analysis)—emails in which a 'strange dialogue takes place in which my life's "truth" rejoins its mythic representation' (Rouch, 1978, p. 58) in our trial study—I am made aware of the disjointed still "photographs" of life that research actually is, the arbitrary and momentum-stopping practices that constitute the activity, and because I am aware of this, I fall into the illusion that constitutes our joint research, and can, again, expand my understandings to include Chris's input.

8 A Problem—Or a Question—Or Maybe Just The Question

All of this may look like a storybook ending. But the reality (and this is research-life, where reality is never far away but where endings can be elusive) is less simple. We must now broach an important topic, which we have left aside until this point as it requires some context and mentioning it earlier would be premature.

It cannot be ignored that despite the collaborative nature of the chapter that had both co-authors extensively involved in the discussing, researching and writing process, and our ongoing exploration of this collaboration, Beth's role and voice is much more visible than Chris's throughout. Indeed, several readers of an earlier draft commented on this lack of a joint authored voice. As one put it: "I understand that Chris functions for Beth in the role of The Constant … I believe the claim is being made that this paper could only have come into being through his functioning as such a Constant. But I don't find very much in the paper that I can use to explicate just how this may have been so," adding that they didn't "feel or hear Chris's own voice or a distinct joint voice of the co-authors." This reflects what Chris himself has described as an "asymmetry or discrepancy" between what the project signified for Beth and what it signified for Chris, who viewed himself as primarily assisting Beth in conducting her own research-life study, and was sometimes ambivalent about his role as her CONSTANT. In this sense, he often experienced himself as more "outside" the study, even while remaining "in" as a committed collaborator, co-author and friend. Moreover, the co-authors disagree about the very implications of these diverging experiences of and relationships with the larger project. In an email exchange from July 17, 2018, Chris struggled with this issue:

> Strangely, the [supportive] role you describe for yourself is exactly how I have experienced MY role with respect to you. It feels as though I join you while you are doing this lifelong project that has special significance for you and which I don't necessarily understand. I listen and support and try to understand the best I can, and have a dialogue with you about it, and somehow give you something in the process that makes a lot of sense to you even if I don't know why it was so important. In other words, it feels as though you keep wanting to attribute to me things that I want to attribute to you (that I see you doing and not me).

It seems urgent to consider whether this ambivalence and confusion on Chris's part about the nature of his connection to the project (to the point that he often felt tempted to call it "your paper, not mine") constitutes a crisis; perhaps even a fatal flaw in the chapter. If the viability of research-life is prefaced on one researcher's significant relationship with a CONSTANT who enables her to continue, yet for the CONSTANT this project could be simply ... another project—a gesture of friendship and assistance, or an interesting intellectual activity—what does this tell us about research-life? And what does that say in turn about our particular foray into research-life? With this in mind we have embedded here, in nested fashion, Chris's own suggestion "to discuss that [the absence of my personal voice] directly, in the later section detailing our collaboration ... that there were reasons this was not feasible .... Perhaps it is even an interesting and essential feature of this particular project, that one of the collaborators is [seemingly] invisible (or maybe not, and it's just a weakness). We could always throw that out as an open question."

Chris will now continue in the first person for all of the remaining section, because he is speaking about an aspect of the study in which he must distinguish himself from Beth.[4]

Such glaring absence of a "joint authorial voice," as noted, would appear to indicate a major limitation and crisis. However, this assumption is based on a pair of fallacies:

1. To the extent that I contributed enough of my own writing (or rewrote key passages), influenced the framing of ideas and what was put out and left in, worked on edits, discussed, put in the requisite time, and Beth can attest to all this: I qualify as a second author. However, having a professional role as second author is not an automatic commitment to being your CONSTANT and fully "in" an intimate research-life dyad; it simply means I was second author of the document. We should conceptually distinguish these two things.

2. There is a presumption that the foregrounding of Beth's point of view and not mine means that we failed at being co-authors, with the implication that a "joint authorial voice" must entail both authors sharing their experience of the research-life or the meaning it held for them—or even agreeing in the first place that research-life is inevitably reciprocal in the sense Beth suspects—and that we must agree for this research-life to "count." Yet, it is conceivable (if hardly certain) that this discrepancy—what I have called at various times an "asymmetry" or "disconnect" or "tension" between how Beth related to the research-life study and how I related to it—could actually be a strength and interesting feature of the paper. It raises the relevant question: must research-life always involve two people and if so, must they each be invested in analogous ways or to the same degree? Does the CONSTANT have to know they are a CONSTANT, or even care? Must someone's CONSTANT in a research-life project be using the

research to negotiate problems in their life and vice versa, as is the case for the other person (whom I am tempted to label the CONSTANTATOR)? What are the various configurations this dynamic can take, some of which may appear asymmetric or unreciprocated out of context? As I once asked Beth in a moment of confusion: "I mean, there can't be one research-life spread out among two lives, can there? Or two different research-lives somehow fitting together as the same research-life project? Feel free to explain ... It's honestly a piece of this that I've never understood."

Even if research-life *is* inherently two-way, I don't see why it follows that our authorial voice must manifest in the specific way that some readers found lacking. What if my main contributions do not show up as some idealized joint author voice, but as joint *thinker* and *discusser* voice (all reflected in the emails as data)? Or if I am a truly a joint author, why must this include speaking in the first person; how do they know my voice isn't a background overtone mixed in with Beth's louder one? What if much of the time I don't even care about the research or Beth's presence for navigating my own life (whether from a different positioning to the material, or a limbic system that is hooked up differently, or simply despair)—but then occasionally, like Pierre in the Maurice Sendak story, I remember that I do, in fact, "care"—even if this might look very different from how Beth cares?

In short: what would it mean for something to reflect "joint authorship," and how might that be expected to show up in "voice" as well as other ways? And why does joint authorship matter?

So what I am suggesting is: research-life may be much more heterogenous as a method or process than we have made it sound or the reader is inclined to assume—and the way this type of collaboration is actually reflected may not line up with the assumptions that have been made about it (or at least, take a much more diverse range of forms than assumed). Certainly, we need to interrogate this gap that Beth and I evidenced in our respective experience of, and engagement with, research-life—but the implications are not at all obvious. To the extent that research-life is a reflection and expression of living, what appears lopsided, inconsistent or incomplete may simply affirm that much more its status as research-life.

If all of this (or even some of this) is true, then that suggests that these "problems" are simultaneously unresolved questions, which may turn out to be quite valuable. In fact, we have wondered more than once whether having generated them, and now beginning the process of trying to answer them, might constitute the very heart of our chapter (not the death of the chapter). We hand this back to you, the reader, in case you want to help us decide.

9 Conclusion

Cole quotes William James at length in his foreword to *Mollie is Three*, writing that as James said of history, we can say of Mollie that her world:

> Is full of partial stories that run parallel to one another, beginning and ending at odd times. They mutually interlace and interfere at points but we cannot unite them completely in our minds ... It is easy to see the world's history pluralistically, as a rope of which each fiber tells a separate tale; but to conceive of each cross-section of the rope as an absolute single act, and to sum the whole longitudinal series into one being living an undivided life, is harder ... The great world's ingredients, so far as they are beings, seem, like the rope's fibers, to be discontinuous, crosswise, and to cohere only in the longitudinal direction. (Paley, 1986, p. XIII)

This longitudinal direction is made visible, analyzed, conceptualized and presented by Paley, who was a scholarly researcher and writer, and simultaneously a preschool teacher when she wrote this book. But to perform this same feat most of us would need to—as our starting point—sustain collaboration between university-based and field-based researchers throughout the research process. This is a feat that is only very rarely accomplished and Chris and Beth's trial study may prove to be no more than a "limit case," delineating an area for future exploration in response to this challenge.

The research-life process consists of a mutual dependence of life and research questions that is bidirectional, ongoing and evolving. One continues generating questions through the research to solve questions in one's life and one's life becomes a process of generating questions so one can study these questions through research. Research-life, thus, maintains its access to the longitudinal direction of life, phenomena's "lived-momentum," and, by bringing attention to the frame between research and life, simultaneously includes its researchers in the research process.

It is for these reasons that research-life may be useful to many researchers who are designing studies in which they hope to sustain collaboration between university-based and field-based co-researchers throughout the research process. These new studies could, perhaps, develop and apply new, hybrid methods that would make phenomena previously considered inaccessible to science, visible to researchers in their full dynamic complexity. Research-life could also prove to be completely impractical for a variety of reasons, but primarily because most people do not have a research-life CONSTANT, and if they have one this person is unlikely to be available to engage as a co-researcher and co-author (as Chris was available in this case), when the researcher's life is at just the right stage for such a study.

Beth is in the process of determining if our research-life trial study might be expanded to constitute a longitudinal study of the development of perezhivanie using empirical data, which would make perezhivanie across a three decade long time span available for analysis whereas film-play has only been able to make perezhivanie across a three second long time span (perezhivanie without its consequences on a life, so incomplete perezhivanie) available for analysis. If so, this trial study would mark the start of a successful example of romantic science: as Alexander Luria states, "When done properly, observation accomplishes the classical aim of explaining facts, while not losing sight of the romantic aim of preserving the manifold richness of the subject" (Luria et al., 2006, p. 178).

Beth is also looking forward to searching the playworlds of Michael and other early childhood teachers for other examples of Michael's suggestion in action, particularly examples in which teachers and researchers are included in playworlds, which might allow for the development of processes that are more practical than research-life but which also make use of Michael's concepts to help researchers to include from-the-field methodological input throughout the research process. It is with this future project in mind that we conceive this chapter and the trial research-life study that produced it as an attempt to respond to what we consider to be an urgent call to scholars and researchers: the call to "bridg[ing] [of] segregated and differently valued knowledges, [and] drawing together legitimated as well as subjugated modes of inquiry" (Conquergood, 2002, pp. 151–152).

Thus, our chapter is incomplete, but it is incomplete by necessity. The final paper in the trilogy should allow us to see that some of our conclusions in this chapter were incorrect—for instance, perhaps, the relationship between research-life and science (see below)—just as this chapter showed us that in the first paper we were not identifying our object of analysis correctly. Furthermore, in this chapter Beth is "her present and future self simultaneously": she anticipates being the sole author of the third paper and in this sense imagines herself as a future author; while in this chapter, now, she is merging her voice (albeit inelegantly and sometimes unsuccessfully) with Chris's. The two co-authors of this chapter are not fully in agreement, which also leaves the paper incomplete. But this is, of course, to be expected, as Chris was invited to be a co-author for life as well as research reasons. Yet another reason for this chapter being incomplete is that written text and especially scholarly writing are insufficient when one wants to work against linearity, as we do. The third paper in the trilogy will incorporate film and art in an effort to bring this three-part (four-part, if one counts the original playworld itself) study to a conclusion.

We may ultimately conclude that the research-life process cannot be integrated into social science, but it is also not simply life or therapy or art. The research-life process could be said to be aiming both to "explain the facts" and to *create* the rich subject whose individual life provides the facts that must be explained. Instead of endeavoring to base our research on a problem to be solved and then show how we solved or answered this problem, in this chapter we have generated and continued to regenerate a problem, so that we can solve it (together). In doing so, we have attempted to investigate how science can influence life, and vice versa, and the nature of the connections between the two. Just as play is creative, life and science generate something new in their engagement with each other, and the research-life process is as much or more a use of science in life, for life, as it is an attempt to bring life to science.

Acknowledgements

Thank you to the several people who read a draft of the paper for their important feedback; and to Anna Pauliina Rainio, Robert Lecusay, and Jay Lemke for their essential feedback.

Notes

1 We do not have space in this chapter to discuss the ways that this sense is a "memory of the future" that drives the development of research-life (as Vasilyuk writes of perezhivanie: "Bliss is conferred even at the beginning of the road to redemption, as a kind of advance payment of emotion and meaning, needed to keep one going if a successful end is to be reached" (1988, pp. 190–191)), but Beth and Chris's trial research-life project culminates in Beth's remembering that she is a teacher. This is the realization that allows Beth to re-find this very section of this chapter and so allows Beth and Chris to complete the chapter. Analysis of the proleptic nature of research-life will have to be left for another paper.
2 If the teacher narrative was situated between the teacher involved in Narnia narrative and the being-a-human-in-the-world narrative, Beth may have been a double CONSTANT for Michael, framing the teacher narrative from both sides. However, we cannot, in this paper at least, tease apart what functions Beth's role as Michael's CONSTANT between these areas may have served in this playworld; or from which border-between-narratives she framed Michael's teacher narrative; or if, perhaps, she was actually working as a frame between Michael's teacher and teacher involved in Narnia narratives in such a way that she helped Michael to enter the place of the playworld rather than, or as well as, the place of his teaching. A fruitful moment to explore if we were to consider these questions might be Beth's telling Michael to "chill" directly before he successfully saved the playworld by including Milo.
3 The chronology in the research-life process is hard to determine: "this does not mean that the later elements in the series appear in consciousness only after the earlier stages have been traversed. They respond to one another psychologically and all exist at once in consciousness,

as a Gestalt, though it is true they are expressed with varying degree of clarity as the series is gone through" (Vasilyuk, 1988, pp. 190–191).

4 Chris has chosen not to describe this transition to first person voice using the construction "I, Chris," as Beth had done earlier, but instead use third person voice, precisely because Beth's style does not feel like his style.

References

Armstrong, D., & Dawson, M. G. (2004). *Vivian Paley and the boy who could tell stories* [Film]. Xxx.

Bateson, G. (1972). *Steps to an ecology of mind: Collected essays in anthropology, psychiatry, evolution, and epistemology*. Chandler Publishing Co.

Blunden, A. (2016). Translating *perezhivania* into English. *Mind, Culture, and Activity, 23*, 3–12. doi:10.1080/10749039.2016.1186193

Buber, M. (1970). *I and thou*. Simon and Schuster.

Conquergood, D. (2002). Performance studies: Interventions and radical research. *The Drama Review, 46*(2), 145–156.

Cuse & Lindelof. (2008). *Lost* [Television show]. Xxx.

Ferholt, B. (1977). *A book of seagulls and other water birds*. Self-Published.

Ferholt, B. (2009). *Adult and child development in adult-child joint play: The development of cognition, emotion, imagination and creativity in playworlds* [Unpublished dissertation]. University of California.

Ferholt, B. (2018). A multiperspectival analysis of creative imagining: Applying Vygotsky's method of literary analysis to a playworld. In C. Connery, V. John-Steiner, & A. Marjanovic-Shane (Eds.), *Vygotsky and creativity: A cultural historical approach to play, meaning-making and the arts* (pp. 163–180). Peter Lang.

Ferholt, B., & Lecusay, R. (2010). Adult and child development in the zone of proximal development: Socratic dialogue in a playworld. *Mind, Culture, and Activity, 17*(1), 59–83. doi:10.1080/10749030903342246

Ferholt, B., & Nilsson, M. (2016a). Early childhood perezhivanija. *Mind, Culture, and Activity, 23*(4), 25–36. doi:10.1080/10749039.2016.1199701

Ferholt, B., & Nilsson, M. (2016b). Perezhivanija as a means of creating the aesthetic form of consciousness. *Mind, Culture, and Activity, 23*(4), 25–36. doi:10.1080/10749039.2016.1186195

Ferholt, B., & Rainio, A. P. (2016). Teacher support of student engagement in early childhood: Embracing ambivalence through playworlds. *Early Years: An International Journal of Research and Development, 36*(4), 413–425. doi:10.1080/09575146.2016.1141395

Leach, P. (1986, July 6). Daily life among the children. *New York Times*, p. 8.

Lewis, C. S. (1950). *The lion, the witch and the wardrobe*. Macmillan Publishing Co.

Lindqvist, G. (1995). *The aesthetics of play: A didactic study of play and culture in preschools*. Uppsala University.

Luria, A., Cole, M., & Levitin, K. (2006). *The autobiography of Alexander Luria: A dialogue with the making of mind*. Laurence Erlbaum Associates.

Marjanovic-Shane, A., Ferholt, B., Nilsson, M., Rainio, A. P., & Miyazaki, K. (2011). Playworlds: An art of development. In C. Lobman & B. O'Neill (Eds.), *Play and culture studies* (Vol. 11, pp. 3–31). University Press of America.

Nilsson, M., & Ferholt, B. (2014). Vygotsky's theories of play, imagination and creativity in current practice: Gunilla Lindqvist's "creative pedagogy of play" in U.S. kindergartens and Swedish Reggio-Emilia inspired preschools. *Perspectiva, 32*(1), 919–950. doi:10.5007/2175-795X.2014v32n3p919

Nilsson, M., Granqvist, A. K., Johansson, E., Thure, J., & Ferholt, B. (2018). *Lek, lärande och lycka: lek och utforskande i förskolan* [*Play, learning and happiness: Play and exploration in preschool*]. Gleerups.

Orwell, G. (1949). *1984*. Harville Secker.

Paley, V. G. (1986). *Mollie is three: Growing up in school*. University of Chicago Press.

Robbins, D. (2007a, December 1). *Online discussion forum: XMCA*.

Robbins, D. (2007b, December 29). *Online discussion forum: XMCA*.

Rouch, J. (1978). On the vicissitudes of the self: The possession dancer, the magician, the sorcerer, the filmmaker, and the ethnographer. *Studies in the Anthropology of Visual Communication, 5*(1), 2–8.

Sobchack, V. C. (1992). *The address of the eye: A phenomenology of film experience*. Princeton University Press.

Sobchack, V. C (2004). *Carnal thoughts*. University of California Press.

Vasilyuk, F. (1988). *The psychology of experiencing*. Progress Publishers.

Vygotsky, L. S. (1971). *The psychology of art*. MIT Press.

Vygotsky, L. S. (1978). *Mind in society: The development of higher psychological processes*. Harvard University Press.

Vygotsky, L. S. (1987). *The collected works of L. S. Vygotsky: Vol. 1. Problems of general psychology*. Springer.

Vygotsky, L. S. (1994). The problem of environment. In R. Van der Veer & J. Valsiner (Eds.), *The Vygotsky reader* (pp. 338–354). Blackwell Press.

CHAPTER 5

Dialogical Epistemology as a Resource of CHAT Methodology in the Close Interaction of Science and Society

Ritva Engeström

Abstract

CHAT emerged as a theory of the development of higher mental functions and allowed a way of focusing on the possibilities of humans to become conscious creators of both themselves and the world. In interconnecting the developmental process with an open approach to the future, CHAT approach has been used in developmental projects as a potential tool for societal transformations by directing the research towards the formation of consciousness rather than simply describing what can be found in societal activities. To bring together the practice-driven approach and the idea-driven construction of future forms a purposeful blend between different contexts and facilitates the move away from the decontextualized segregated model of science to an approach that is integrated with its social context. An increasingly acknowledged close interaction of science and society brings into the forefront the heterogeneity of meaning systems and, thus, dialogical epistemology into the core of science. While elaborating a dialectical concept of development, Vygotsky emphasized a two-fold process of human interaction with the world. This view raises the meta-level complexity of doing science through its own sign systems and conceptualizations. In activity-oriented tradition (in CHAT) the model of activity system has a central role of a unit of analysis comprising the realms of 'individual', 'social' and 'societal' from the perspective of development. The model itself has rarely been examined but rather assumed as foundational while playing its role as unit. In the chapter I turn my look to a unit of analysis as a researcher's artifact (sign and tool) to construct the link between the world of phenomena and research practice. I use the model as a case of unit for researching the unity of knowing, consciousness and acting.

Keywords

individual-collective development – dialectic – dialogic – subjectivity – sense making

∙ ∙ ∙

> [I]deology is in some respects unfortunate, for our word suggests something inflexible and propagandistic, something politically unfree. For Bakhtin and his colleagues, it meant simply an "idea system" determined socially, something that means ...
>
> CAROL EMERSON (1986, p. 23)

∴

Empirical research based upon Cultural Historical Activity Theory (CHAT) faces a number of strong methodological challenges. These arise because the CHAT approach is intended to help us to understand conceptually the unity of thinking, human development and practice which grounds on the sociocultural and material world. Further, CHAT requires us to deal with the complexities of different dimensions and layers of this integrated view in the context of each unique investigation. As an attribute of scientific practice, this complexity gives rise to a meta-level problem because science depends on and advances through its own sign systems and conceptualizations. These cannot be taken for granted, accepted without question, or conceived as unchanged in a changing society around the world which provides a variety of purposes and interests for doing research. My chapter draws upon empirical studies carried out in the "developmental work research" (DWR) as a program of "activity theory" tradition in CHAT. Thus, my experiences, thoughts and claims make reference to CHAT theoretical ideas generated in DWR research practice. There are certain discernible features of DWR which are particularly relevant to the present chapter.

First, in approaching human activity the DWR methodology treats consciousness in movement (Vygotsky, 1978) to be open to the unknown in change and capable of producing future-oriented thinking, visions, and new practice. In research practice this has meant that the main data gathering takes place in natural settings in which human cognition interacts with an environment rich in organizing resources (for an ecology of thinking, see Cole, 1996). Second, to keep context at the center in the methodology and overcome the classical epistemological distinction of science between the objective knowledge of science and the subjective knowledge of the people being studied, DWR approach has been oriented to building collaboration outside a disciplinary structure and working with a wider array of people and expertise in order to form a purposeful blend of different conceptual structures and contexts of thinking. The method of the Change Laboratory (CL) has become known as a tool of integrating science with its social context (Virkkunen & Newnham, 2012). Third, the model of activity system has a central role as a unit of analysis comprising the realms of 'individual,' 'social' and 'societal' from the perspective of development. The model conceptualizes activity as an object-oriented and collective unit that has become a distinctive mark of DWR/CL research (Engeström, 1987/2015).

In this chapter, my focus is on the activity system model which provides a methodological basis for doing empirical research on human practice. The model itself has rarely been examined in DWR/CL studies but rather assumed as foundational while playing the role of a unit of analysis. My long-standing interest in theory of dialogue in the DWR/CL framework has inspired me to probe the epistemological boundaries of activity system for studying subjective processes as activities from the perspective of the relation of 'the self' and society. I begin the chapter with theoretical discussion about activity-oriented research and dialogue. These sections are followed by the research examples which turn the look at doing science through advancing its sign system and conceptualizations. As an end goal, I search for a stance in which to position myself in relation to a changing society as a researcher in the framework of DWR/CL and as a member of CHAT community.

1   From Object-Relatedness of Mind to Object-Oriented Activity

A way to introduce activity theory, particularly, when drawing upon the model of activity system, is to display the generations of the model through which activity-oriented theory has evolved (Y. Engeström, 2001, 2009). By now, the literature addresses four generations starting with the original idea of *mediation* as the first generation. The unit of analysis equates with Vygotsky's (1978, p. 40) triangular model in which the direct connection between stimulus (S) and response (R) is transcended by "a complex, mediated act." Seeing this model as an individually focused unit of analysis, Engeström (1987/2015) elaborated, utilizing A. N. Leontiev's (1978) theoretical work, an extended model which conceptualizes activity as a collective phenomenon explicating the societal and collaborative nature of individual actions (Figure 5.1). This model denotes the start of the second generation. Over time the scope of the unit has become enlarged. In the third generation, the basic unit is expanded to include interacting or networking activity systems. The recent research has brought into discussion the fourth generation of theory, which focuses on activities having largely invisible and weakly bounded forms.

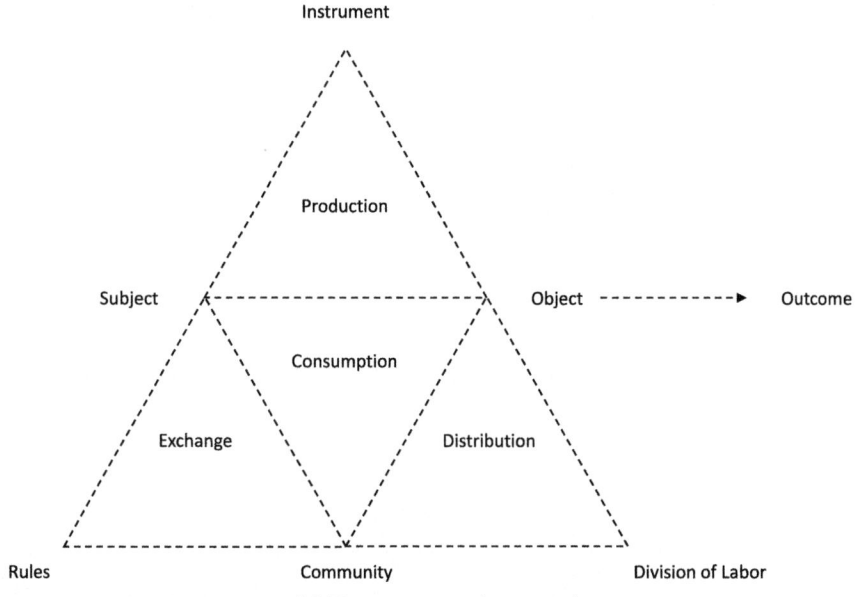

FIGURE 5.1 Activity system model (Engeström, 1987/2015, p. 63)

The activity system as a unit of analysis has proved to be useful in researching manifold and plural entities in which components of human functioning arise from several realms of social life and have their own histories. The approach has been found to provide researchers with a systemic view and approach to capture development of societal aspects of activities which evolve through conflicts and tensions in human interaction with the world. Modeling *activity* as a unit of analysis indicates the basic theoretical CHAT position that the 'mental' is not accomplished in the head of an individual person but is placed "in a space external to the individual—in a space of real interactions between the subject and the objective world around him" (Stetsenko, 2000, pp. 60–61). The principle of object-relatedness of mind has received in DWR/CL a special interpretation, which is inscribed in the commonly used phrase of *object-oriented activity*.

In CHAT research, the notion of 'object' has been a topic of disputes not least because of its effect on how to understand the notion of motive. Concerning Leontiev's theoretical claims about motive, the literature includes disagreements of what is viewed as individual and subjective and what objective or collective in his concept of activity. On the one hand, Leontiev has sought to put in place a foundation in which activities are carried out by concrete individuals, and analyses are predominantly dealing with units within the life of individuals (i.e., "individual's activity") (Kaptelin, 2005; Kramer, 2021). This view has been summarized by Nissen (2011) as follows: subjectively, we have activity, motive and sense (personal), and on the objective side, then, there are action, goal, and meaning (social meaning). On the other hand, using the theoretical idea of hierarchical organization of motives according to the three levels of human functioning (Leontiev, 1978), Engeström (1987/2015) has pointed to the motive of collective activity in order to argue for the unit of activity system. In the graphical model of activity system "each corner of the triangle would thus have three qualitatively different levels": that of the overall collective activity/motive, that of individual actions/goals, and that of operations/conditions (pp. 153–154). In the activity system, the object as motive of activity embodies the socio-historical experience of mankind, being "the vehicle" of this collective experience (see Stetsenko, 2000). The essence of an object is then constituted "by the specific connections and relations that become known in the process of collective activity, i.e., by the aggregate activity underlying the object," or "with which it may be said to be invested" (p. 59).

The question, posed in early years of DWR, concerned the methodological issue of how to relate the activity to mental processes, acknowledging, that these processes are "specific components of the activity structure and promote the realization of other components" (Davydov, 1999, p. 45). The DWR projects tended to respond to the question by emphasizing the model of activity system, which was collective and proved to be constructive in actual research practice, not only as a theory-grounded tool in intervention research with work communities, but also for conceiving learning in the participating communities as an object-oriented collective activity (represented by the cycle of expansive learning). The impressive and needed move from individual approaches to collective units in human sciences did not put pressure to elaborate the role of mental processes in human practice. As steering the research interest more toward subjectification, partly resonating growing general interest and discourse in social and human sciences, the investigations of DWR/CL have started to include more discussion on the mutual dependencies and interrelationships of the mind and activity–subject and object. I propose in this chapter that this move requires, in the framework of DWR/CL research, a more detailed and theoretically solid notion of objectification, which is, following Stetsenko (2000), a two-fold process. First, there is *objectification* of ideas that stimulate and regulate the activity of the subject in the form of externally sensuously perceived objects; and second, there is the process of *de-objectification*, the passage of an object into its subjective form, into an image whereupon an activity can be assimilated to the properties, connections, and relations of the objective world and acquire objective determination (p. 59).

Object formation brings about intermediary artifacts, or "special objects" (Ilyenkov, 1977, p. 280) which are used to alter the sensuously perceived objective world. For example, Foucault (1976, pp. X–XI) approaches the object formation in the context of modern medicine by a question "how to transform the region of 'subjective symptoms' that defines–for the doctor–not the mode of knowledge but the world of objects to be known." He explicates further that this does not lead to make "an 'objectal' choice in favor of objectivity itself" but that *"the fantasy link* between knowledge and pain" becomes reinforced "by a more complex means" in which the articulation of medical language and its object appear "as a single figure" (emphasis added). This provides a doctor with a possibility to "hold a scientifically structured discourse about an individual" (p. XIV), known in research as the biomedical view of the sick person. The twofold process of objectification indicates the active role of individual. As known, Vygotsky (1978) emphasized the real tie between the artificial means (sign and tool) and, hence, the real tie of their development in phylo- and ontogenesis. The essential issue here points to Vygotsky's claim about changes of all psychological operations as the use of tools broadens the range of activities "within which the new psychological functions may operate." For the research methodology, the point addresses the *diverging lines* (sign and tool) of mediated activities. They are according to Vygotsky "so different from each other that the nature of the means they use cannot be the same" (ibid.).

To understand better the sign-mediated line of activity as resting upon the foundation in which the human mind and the world are ontologically inseparable, Arievitch and Stetsenko (2014, p. 222) investigate how signs get into individual's thought and what they do there. Using the method of cultural mediation, they examined how cultural mediation itself "emerges and develops in ontogeny from its early roots in infancy." Their discovery was the growing complexity of a developmental continuum of emerging mediational means from operational meanings to object meanings and finally to verbal meanings (pp. 235–237). The developmental progression challenges 'the mental' as sets of semantic-referential meanings that affect activities "from outside as extraneous adds-ons." Arievitch and Stetsenko (2014) suggest that in the same way as one sees in joint infant-adult activity, "any joint activity draws its participants together by creating a joint space—the space of human meanings" (p. 230).

2 Means of Sign–A Dimension of Dialogue[1]

Marková (2012) whose thoughts, along with Bakhtin's, have influenced my stance on dialogue, argues that in humanities and social sciences objectification is linked to a new notion of subjectivity (see also e.g., Edwards, 2012). In this notion, "in and through language, objects enter into the scope of human vision, that is, they become things only in so far as they *undergo* human activity, and it is then that they obtain their designation, their names" (pp. 209–210). Individually, humans choose aspects of things that are relevant for them emotionally, cognitively, or otherwise. In these mediating processes objects become constructed into human products that originate from using cultural means and systematic practices to render something an intelligible "thing" to work on. In relating dialogicality to the concept of intersubjectivity, Marková (2003) makes the distinction between *'I and Other(s)'* and *'Ego and Alter.'* She argues that intersubjectivity expresses the idea of a distance between *I* and *Other(s)* and of closing this gap, i.e., it is theoretically working on the sphere of 'in-between.' Whereas, if our aim is to constitute the concept of *subjectivity*, Marková's claim is that we miss, in focusing on *'I and Other(s),'* the possibility of accounting "for innovation, creativity and for change in individuals" (p. 257)—a developmental aspect of the mind.

Marková's (2003) methodological contribution is to address *historical epistemology* and sociocultural change in defining dialogicality. She regards that the mainstream conception of cognition and language in research is based largely on static epistemologies, which also indicates that social change in language is extremely difficult to conceptualize. Drawing upon the work of Bakhtin, she argues "there is no communication unless the self lives through active understanding of the strange, of *Alter*" (p. 257) There would be no dialogue if participants were not opposed to one another through mutually experienced *strangeness*, which creates tension between them. *Ego–Alter* exists only within the realm of communication but is understood as standing for the self, groups, sub-groups, communities, societies, and cultures. Taking a cultural view in analysis means that prior meanings encounter historically new (unknown) elements of meaning that come, in real-life practice, into our social interest and interrogate previous ones with tension (Volosinov, 1973).

The epistemological view grounding in history becomes analytically more concrete with different processes of communication which Markova proposes (2004) (referring to the theory of social representations by Moscovici), namely, *anchoring* and *objectification*. Anchoring is an inner-directed process that relies primarily on the individual's prior experience and memory in classifying and naming newly experienced phenomena. It functions as a stabilizing process that orientates the mind toward remaining in the existing state of knowledge. Objectification (as a process of communication) is an other- and outer-directed process dealing with a vague and unfamiliar idea. It is primarily a meaning-making activity in which the individual, because of his or her interpretation of events, reconstructs the existing contents of representations, creates new ones, and gives meanings to these new contents. Methodologically, it is important to pay attention to Marková's (2004) claim that we cannot predict how communication might turn out, and quite certainly, we cannot assume that communicative forces will resolve themselves in some kind of integration and progress (see more Engeström, 2014).

3   Methodology as a Mode of Perception in Research

Research work is particular, as Knorr-Cetina (2001) notices, in that the definition of things (the consciousness of problems) is deliberately looped through 'objects' and the reaction occasioned by them in order to proceed in the research. This condition creates dissociation between the self (researcher) and the object, especially when the complexity of the studied phenomena grows. Knorr-Cetina suggests that a challenge of research methodology is to approach research through practice "in a way that accommodates this dissociation" (p. 175). This stance also indicates that a research methodology is a researcher's deliberate way to imaginatively construct the link between the world of phenomena and research practice—a way of "seeing" on which to focus in research (Gutiérrez, 2016). The typical way to approach any research field in DWR/CL is to use the activity system model as a unit of analysis to construct a historical and situational understanding (consciousness) of the research object. The unit conceptualizes studied phenomena into elements of activity system and makes possible to use *the method of identifying contradictions* evolving in the system over a longer period of time. Empirically, the focus is put on *disturbances* in everyday life of practices for producing situated knowledge about contradictions in the systemic whole of one or interacting activity systems. In formative methodology the research proceeds through phases of expansive learning in which practitioners and researchers collaborate in producing the data and analyses and searching for solutions to the contradictions of the studied activity system; this joint undertaking intends to result in a new conceptual understanding of the activity and entailing pilots of applications in practice.

A rarely addressed issue in the publications of DWR/CL studies is the question: What does a *unit of analysis* mean in research practice? Does the unit imply the methodology in which the data are analyzed in a way that returns the observations to the elements of the activity system. An extended way to reflect this *praxis of method* is to focus on the components of the unit of analysis and how these have been theoretically introduced or reflected and practically used in the context of individual investigations. Some interesting initiatives can already be found. For example, Spinuzzi (2011, 2017) focuses on the 'object' of the activity system and has seen it an adequate tool of research as long as the object has been bounded enough to define the activity under investigation. He has remarked about a methodological problem while the object has been expanding all the time in research and the DWR framework is being applied to cases of ever broader scope and is becoming analytically more multidimensional. Looking at the object, he has been searching for a way to get back into a bounded context of the unit.

Langemeyer (2017), in turn, gives her attention to the element of 'tool' at the top of the triangle ("Engeström's triangular model"). She argues that instead of Vygotsky's design "to understand the important role of cultural development as it takes place on the psychological plane of internalized mediating activities," the triangular model (of Engeström) provides the view in which "the activity as a *system* acts independently from the concrete human subjects and their consciousness" (p. 55). Langemeyer sees the model as highly problematic and too simple if Vygotsky's method of "the double stimulation" is used as a tool for constructing "transformative agency." She has an opinion that transformative agency should be related to differences in societal structures entangled in people's way of life. Her claim is based on her reading the model in the way that 'tool' should remind us of the artifact in Vygotsky's 'mediating activity,' but in fact, it represents a 'mediated activity' that signifies "the subject's acting upon an object by using a tool (e.g., the axe to chop a tree)" (p. 55) (see also Silvonen, 2011).

I have regarded the 'subject' of the triangle as problematic while being marked to signify a group, collective or an individual without informing what 'individual' might mean as a subject of the activity system which is defined as collective in nature and carries longitudinal-historical aspects of practice (Engeström, 2009). The problem is not only logical but rather theoretical because individuals as an agentive and inherently necessary moment within unfolding activity processes are positioned to be involved in multiple activities simultaneously (Daniels, 2001). For an individual, object-relatedness of mind shows up as *'inter-object'* which allows to make subjective connections between people, objects, and phenomena that surround a person in the time and space (Bratus, 2005). From this view, individual participants in a joint activity share the process of engagement but simultaneously are constructing their *subjectively unique understandings* of issues associated with ongoing activities (see Valsiner, 2001). Human consciousness is said to be oriented to link and connect—in creative and sometimes the most unexpected fashion.

In the next section, I enter the field of subjectification with two examples taken from the research practice. My starting point is that the activity system model is valuable for the projects: it provides the project participants with a shared analytical tool, it guides data collection in different ways and extensively on the elements of activities, and it helps to discern contexts (activities) from each other (Engeström et al., 2003). Besides, the DWR/CL approach makes possible to gain access to different sites and communities and use multi-voiced data collecting methods. At the same time, the constant interaction in data gathering, mostly in natural settings, with people whose actions are video recorded, who are interviewed, and who participate in interventions provides the researcher with a possibility to encounter a rich space of human meanings which shows how people, individually, choose, experience and foreground aspects of things that are relevant for them. In listening people and reading data sets, for years, have surprised me how active people are in trying to understand and make sense of ongoing events and things around them and in themselves. A quest to understand, as a researcher, this world of phenomena in interaction with theories has pushed me to go beyond the epistemological boundaries of the activity system in scientific knowledge production and consider meaning making as an activity through subjective processes being actualized in object-oriented activity. From this follows that I am interested in developing methods to investigate means of sign 'indirectly' as specific components of collective activities having socio-historically construed motives. Special attention is paid here to a unit of analysis for semiotic mediation. Due to the limits of space, I share information about the projects only briefly. The examples have been taken from the projects of health care and school education; both areas being studied in several projects in which I have also acted as a researcher.

4 Semiotic Mediation and Objectification

4.1 *New Forms of Cognitive Functioning in Health Care*

First DWR/CL studies in Finland have taken place in the field of health care. The core of the clinical practice is seen, in these projects, to be in doctor-patient consultations, which have been visualized with the help of two activity systems sharing an object: one of the patient and one of the doctor (for the illustration, see, e.g., Engeström, 2017, p. 55). Following the object (a patient in the consultation/s), we gathered data by videotaping consultations, adding to them stimulated recall interviews conducted by viewing the videotape with the patient and doctor (separately) or viewing only by the researchers for selecting pieces for CL sessions in order to trigger a joint discussion between the CL participants including the patient. These sets of data form a part of the projects' whole data set also including ethnography and interviews.

In our first studies we distinguished two different views to artifacts: the system view and the personal view (Engeström, 1990). Nevertheless, the study of the personal view focused on the tool use within the activity system in which the tools were given (at the top of triangle). For example, while the doctors were using medical records – documented in computerized systems and considered as their tools – they were asked in interviews 'what is essential in the medical records in your work?' and 'how do you use the information contained in medical records?' We may ask, following Daniels (2001, p. 19), whether we can assume that "mediation through activity in and of itself" implies a semiotic mediation or that "engagement in activity implies direct psychological engagement with the objective environment?" Indicating a lack of method for differentiating tool-mediated and sign-mediated activities, the questions led us to explore the tradition based on the work of Bakhtin. As his starting point, Bakhtin (1987, p. 70) remarks that "speech" is terminologically "imprecise" word and leads in linguistical thinking to methodological confusion. He proposed a unit of speech communication which denotes *the context* in which "the situation enters into the utterance as a necessary constitutive element of its semantic structure" (Todorov, 1984, p. 41). In this unit linguistic matter is only one part of semantics, another part is nonverbal and "corresponds to the context of the enunciation," i.e., requires active construction of context in action (Todorov, 1984; Volosinov, 1973). The unit of analysis, called *utterance*, is then composed of the actor, the means, and the object. In communication, the object has two directions: the one of a listener (or potential interlocutor) and the other of content in the sense of possibilities of human activity (the world) (Engeström, 1995).

The unit helped us to approach semiotic mediation from the point of view of object-relatedness of mind. The approach differed from the way and methods of theoretical discourse and conversation analyses used for studying doctor-patient consultations. Instead of representing an autonomous realm of 'discourse' or 'talk-in-interaction,' the dialogic framework addressed cultural dynamics of mediation, which was connected to language in its intensive social and historical life—"in its heteroglot development" (Bakhtin, 1981, p. 356). Bakhtin's unit assisted us to elaborate 'a method of voices' for investigating the talk of medical encounters. The logic of the method based on identifying both the doctor's and the patient's *individual voices as mediating means* in the processes of meaning making. The notion of voice (in Bakhtin's sense) was defined in the study as "a speaking subject's perspective, conceptual horizon, intention, and world view" (Wertsch, 1991, p. 51).

The voices were made empirically observable with the help of nine "social languages" (Bakhtin, 1981) which were not taken as fixed cultural embodiments of language (and thus closed categories of the analysis) but as being shaped in social processes of object formation.[2] The systematic analysis of joint meaning-making episodes showed how the speakers made choices between the languages and were creative in using and producing meanings through their own voices (though, simultaneously, mainly accomplishing a historically constituted 'social order' of a medical encounter; see Goffman, 1964). The main finding here is that the voices, particularly the ones of the patients, were *intersecting* everyday and medical languages on the somatic. The excerpt (below) offers an example of the patients' talk, which is voiced through medicine in the start of consultation.

Doctor: What is it that brings you to see me?
Patient: Right now I have the problem that last night I had a terrible pain in the throat, just like I thought I had a *strep throat* or something. Once it happened that I had a *strep throat* for a week and I did not know anything about it. I don't necessarily get fever ...

In intersecting languages, diagnoses and medical interpretations were not simply borrowed from medicine by the patients but, essentially, were reworked with experiences of the significance of these judgments in biographical context and situation, and these interpretations were accommodated to the circumstances of daily life of the patients. Experiencing illnesses emerged as a continuing process of activity in which tentative ideas were built upon and elaborated (cf. Jornet, Roth, & Krange, 2016). The findings of the study showed that the patient's knowledge which was constructed from different sources compared to medicine, and which was connecting matters to each other in a unique way, proved to be relevant in clinical problem solving.[3] This understanding of communication was important when our projects moved from primary care to complex networks of health care systems, especially in boundaries between primary and specialized health care of patients with multiple problems in a system of ongoing specialization in medical knowledge (Engeström et al., 2003; Kerosuo, 2006). In the next example, taken from the Change Laboratory -project, a person who had diagnoses of diabetes, coronary heart disease and heart failure told in the interview his worries about breathing difficulties during the night while sleeping. He was worried how it could be related to his overall wellbeing and in the future to his heart surgery. When he was recently hospitalized in the department of cardiology, he acted there to find out new possibilities of getting more oxygen during night.

Patient: During the night I tried one of these oxygen masks which they have there for a patient with heart disease. And it clearly helped.

I was able to sleep even on my back for several hours with the mask.
Researcher: Did you try by yourself or was a nurse involved?
Patient: It was my own experiment.

After this experiment, the patient's breathing problem was taken into consideration (being previously disregarded by cardiologists) and he was referred to the department of lung diseases for examinations in the hospital. By crossing the boundary, the problem was found and given a medical name for planning the care.

The broader meaning of the findings is that they reveal the initial epistemological categorization between 'subjective' (lifeworld/everyday) and 'objective' (medicine) as *a problematic fabrication of social sciences*. In addition, the findings led investigators to question the common (sociological) frame of reference of *medicalization* of people and turn their view to cultural-historical change of language in the health care. The findings suggest not only that what we know has a history, or that there is a historical development of ideas and theories, but that the nature of knowing, of cognitive acquisition itself and *how we construct processes of knowledge production changes also historically* (Wartofsky, 1979, p. XIII). The findings shed light on the change of cultural mediation and new forms of mental functioning.

4.2 New Constitution of 'Individual' in School Education

Research on education pays today increasingly attention to alternative understanding of learning and school knowledge with pedagogical strategies of participating in cultural practices and networks of learning around real-world (outside school) phenomena. In contextualizing knowledge, skills, and attitudes for preparing students for 'real-life,' Säljö (2003) underlines that education is not identical with performing a 'real-life' action, rather, education is a valuable and rewarding activity in its own right. My second research example is taken from the research of entrepreneurship education, broadly promoted in European (EU) education policy documents and many national policies in Europe, including in Finland, through the whole educational system (European Commission, 2012). The policies and entrepreneurship education research have challenged the economic-based traditional (disciplinary) content of entrepreneurship education and replaced it conceptually with "entrepreneurial learning" which focuses on "the human and social dynamics of entrepreneurship" (Rae & Wang, 2015). This view argues for conceiving an entrepreneur as an ideal of a new kind of agency which is creative in initiating new activities.

The DWR project started with an interest in having a practical view of entrepreneurship education and its developmental challenges in the studied school (Käyhkö, 2015). The school had already created a course of entrepreneurship education which was carried out as a project with the concrete target of planning and putting into practice a communal fair as a business enterprise shared between the school and local association of entrepreneurs. The fair had a history of being organized yearly by the municipalities jointly with entrepreneurs as the event, which was expected to serve local entrepreneurs in businesses and be a paid-admission entertainment event for the public. The data gathering covered the whole course period and included different types of materials, such as video recorded planning meetings of the students, and meetings between the course teachers and students, video recorded fair including on-line interviews, interviews with an appointment, students' written reports and a transcript of the video recorded intervention which used findings from the preliminary analysis of the data as a mirror in the joint meeting called 'future forum.'

The course was conceptualized in the project with the help of the activity system model as *a tool* of the specific (entrepreneurial) school activity. A data-based study revealed that this new learning had implications that went beyond the contents of known subjects and epistemological (truth-based) practices historically used in schools. In addition, in the course, the students were not anymore expected to be seen as objects to be molded and disciplined but were provided with possibilities for being subjects of action through their active engagement with society, i.e., with the practices constituting social realities. Being mainly oriented to how to investigate and promote entrepreneurship in schools at the individual level, entrepreneurship education research focused less on the question of how this opening toward society may add complexity to *the learning object* – the issues that are expected to be learned.

The study became refocused by viewing 'the tool' (the course of entrepreneurship education) as a process of *unfolding activity* working on an open object and having a collaborative subject of actors across inside and outside the school (Engeström & Käyhkö, 2021). This methodological move needed a theoretically constructed unit of analysis that considers transactions between object-oriented activity and semiotic mediation in the context of actualizing entrepreneurship in practice as a recently invented (partly unknown) subject of comprehensive schooling. We relied on the notion of *boundary object* as a unit that maintains continuity of actions across social worlds without necessarily having an object which is shared (Star, 1989). Empirically, we focused on the internal dynamic of boundary object of which materiality derives from action and becomes constructed by means of meaning making for functioning in collaboration (see Star, 2010, p. 603). For the analysis of meaning making as an activity, which reconciles meanings drawn from different activities and negotiates new ones, we constructed an analytical tool of four-field matrix (with the dimensions of collaboration and dialogicality). The study showed how *different meaning systems* (as mediating means) evolved in the fair course when the students were engaged in practices of organizing regionally meaningful activity outside the school and positioned themselves into these processes of learning. The central finding was that the meaning system, which took a dominant role in providing a common ground for doing entrepreneurship and had a practical relevance in making decisions (Edwards, 2010), was constructed socially by using concepts, such as *money* and *profit* and with a relative content of making money. The excerpt (below) taken from the students' meeting illustrates 'money-making meaning system.'

Student 1: Well, we could keep the program cheaper and save money. But I don't know which one is better. If we invite a more expensive performer, so would it bring more money?
Student 2: Who will take that kind of risk? It would be easier to do in the same way as before [previous courses].
Student 3: Yes, I agree
Student 2: Then we are sure that we will get money
Student 3: The limits of budget have to be taken into account also
Student 2: That's it. But if we think that we have to make profit, one way is to save on everything in which we find it possible to do so.

Many actions and interactions of making the fair required issues of money to be considered, as in the example the students had to get acquainted with risk taking and choosing between alternatives. The use of the kind of "functional concepts" (addressing the situated nature of concepts) "contributes to the way participants organize their understanding of what they are doing" (Greeno, 2012, p. 311). Our study showed that the used concepts provided the students with a common ground for understanding entrepreneurship in and for doing it. Dissociating entrepreneurship from applying economics and marketing disciplines, as it is becoming part of the educational system, conflicts with the means of making the activity meaningful for themselves by the students who are engaged in acting with society.[4]

Entrepreneurship education research (made public and discussed, for the most part, in the educational journals associated with business and management research interests and theories) has responded to educational change by drawing upon the dualistic ontology and epistemology and, thus, by treating connections between persons and their practical and social contexts as two different, self-contained elements. In this view, change takes place as a shift from "transferring knowledge and fostering thinking" characteristic of traditional schooling to "fostering and changing attitudes and motives" (Berglund & Holmgren, 2013, p. 10) or to "personality-developing educational objectives" (Holmgren & From, 2005, p. 385). Leaving societal aspects of entrepreneurship education outside epistemic activity, the ideal of entrepreneurship education ("enterprising mind-set") looks 'neutral' and politically 'free' in the context of historically constituted epistemological and evaluative practices of education.

From the perspective of non-dualist approach, the study turned the attention to new forms of subjectivity of a student. The change raises the question about the quality of motive that is educationally produced with the means of experiencing an agency as a way of becoming engaged in society. The motive and drive of activity relying on money making brings about a question how 'the epistemic' meets 'the political' in school activity. Critical scholars point to this motive (money-making) as the reason for dissociating the economics from entrepreneurial ideals (Holmgren & From, 2005; Mononen-Batista Costa & Brunila, 2016). These ideals are seen implying the neoliberal view of economics and society and cultivating processes of neoliberal subjectification of the individual as new objectives of schooling.

5 The Relation of 'the Self' and Society

The above reflections on DWR projects call for a complex interplay between mental (psychological) and socio-historical processes and turn attention to changes in the dialectical person–environment relation concerning people being investigated, as well people who do research. The environment of the globalized world of the 21st century, and the co-evolution between science and society, on the one hand, and technology, on the other, accelerates these changes. The ensuing knowledge society means not only radical new social forms (of globalization) but also possibilities of new forms of self-creation and *self-definition of individuals*. Such a change in the relation of 'the self' and society challenges DWR/CHAT methodology and requests to advance kinds of analysis which allow to conceive the individual as a historical subject (Daniels, 2008; Saxe & Esmonde, 2005)–making to see society itself as a *human product* which involves the contexts of ideology, worldviews and value systems, i.e., "that social human world in which perception has its genesis, and in which it functions" (Wartofsky, 1979, p. 210).

My motive to bring a dialogical approach into the DWR framework is that it conceptualizes the capacity of human mind to conceive, create and communicate about social reality in terms of the 'Alter' (strangeness), i.e., being open to the not-yet-known (of itself and the other), and open toward emergent possibilities of thought and "being where being includes all beings, human, animal and earth" (Davies, 2010). The role of knowing and how we construct its unfolding and practically intertwining processes have become not only more central but also more forceful with words and concepts which change their social meaning over time in relation to changing social, economic and political pressures (Engeström, 2014). The extended spaces to operate on imaginative nature of the means of sign have not only afforded more possibilities but also brought about mutually conflicting epistemologies and consequences or justifying actions of the delivered views, concepts and values. These means have taken the significant place in policy making and rhetoric in many domains, particularly also in education. While addressing the notion of "situated imagination" in reconsidering the feminist standpoint theory, Stoetzler and Yuval-Davis (2002, p. 324) remark that we cannot take the imagination of people *as such* a faculty, which is creative but rather that the one, which allows for "emancipation and border crossing," is the same one that "constructs and fixes the borders." In both instances the imagination is 'creative' (or 'innovative').

'Subjectification' cannot either be taken as free from power of others, as separated from social and cognitive history (for "individualized subject-of-will," see Davies, 2010). The social meaning space is a political arena (e.g., neoliberal market society) where one of its persuasive powers lies in *apparent non-ideological* character and matter-of-fact, common sense status of words which prioritize certain actions and activities (e.g., values of economics and competition) and subordinate others (e.g., values of humanities and social equality) (Holborow, 2015). In education, we cannot expect that it relies 'as such' on values, which promote social justice and equality but rather, following Biesta (2013, p. 8), "freedom cannot 'be produced' educationally but can only be achieved politically." The culture and community are a specific historical medium, i.e., "the history of the group into which one is born and the activities that characterize their society" (Cole, 2005, p. 169; see also Daniels, 2001, pp. 21–22). Hence, we have to recognize, as to DWR/CL studies, that the health care and school education settings were parts of Nordic welfare society, of a special form of capitalism, traditionally characterized by institutional and social trust and universal public services provided by the state. Medical doctors were in most part provided with education in and by society, which appreciated public health care and a preventive and epidemiological view to the health of population—a meaningful practice that itself was an outcome of political struggle. Also, in schools the topic of money was not, traditionally, included in education, curriculum, or teachers' professional views in the system of free and unified education from preschool to university.[5]

Therefore, should we see also DWR/CL projects as part of the culture of aiming to improve quality of public services and their economic efficacy for 'public good'? The culture involving the political contexts of value systems arguably then offered 'a springboard' to a way of seeing and interacting with environment (Wartofsky, 1979, p. 210). As mediational medium with and through which ideas are developed, society enabled the use of the means (drawing upon CHAT and related theoretical work, like the theory of expansive learning) which brought about the idea of making science and society more integrated as achievements of members of work communities and through their agency of expansive learning. The outcomes of the projects would not then function as evidence of a general capability of the conceptual model of activity system (the unit of analysis) to deal with and find solutions to contradictions of capitalism (to "primary contradiction") but rather as evidence to judge the DWR methodology as a consequential artifact of human and social sciences in the context of its production and formation of concepts.

Acknowledging the mediating role of culture and society in DWR does not mean wiping away its significant invention of bringing together the practice-driven approach and the idea-driven construction of the future, and its research on developing practical and conceptual tools (including the activity system model) for serving this idea, also in societies outside Nordic welfare societies (see on discussion, Engeström et al., 2014). The rising complexities of human conduct and society have already more broadly indicated a strong pressure for science to move from a 'segregated' model of disciplinary interaction to one in which science becomes more 'integrated' with its social and societal contexts (Nowotny et al., 2001). A blend between different contexts changes the *epistemological core of science* toward heterogeneity of meaning systems entailing the complex dynamics of human development and historical change itself and its relation to the conceptual activities of individuals, as the example studies also indicate.

In present time of pluralism of meaning systems of which processes are simultaneous and multidirectional, and also potentially have been distracting traditional meaning communities (like professions), the challenges of advancing the CHAT methodology are related to strengthening understanding of the space of human meanings. As shown and problematized in a range of research, digital technology is embedded in human activities as a knowledge foundation which brings about the new underlying communication system and re-mediation of individual socio-cognitive processes. The knowledge-based capability of the system to function as independent makes the system, as Rückriem (2009, p. 92) points out, smart "by a self-increasing recursiveness in using and generating knowledge." The complexity of today's scientific practice gives rise to meta-level problems in advancing through its own sign systems and conceptualizations which cannot be taken for granted. Hence, I have taken a critical view to the theory-historical aspect of DWR/CL, which is in the form of a unit of analysis. The unit directs to see the processes of mediated activity through the relations and interactions of the components of activity system. Conceptualizing cultural 'tools' as a specific resource and considering this component as a wholeness in mediated activity, justifies the meaning of object-oriented activity from the perspective of 'use-value' in relation to significances of reality and its generalized reflections. This shortcoming[6] bears the risk that use-value presents itself as 'neutral' and politically 'free,' as an outcome of developmental trajectory and resolution of contradictory forces into progressive unity, leaving political and ideological aspects of culture outside knowledge production, i.e., without explicating their role in this production. The analyses of the theoretical components of activity system brought into foreground a human being as the meaning-maker, not only of personal lives of the participants, but also in a role of historical subject of societal reality.

The future challenges are related to more complex means of science to reinforce the link between science and values, standpoints and worldviews anchoring on the politics of humanities.

6   How Does the Chapter Address the Challenges of a Non-Dualist Methodology?

The author contributes to non-dualist or dialectical methodology by discussing, first, the concept of consciousness in research. She states that in approaching human activity, developmental methodologies treat consciousness in movement and conceive consciousness as being in a dialectic with social practices. Consciousness plays a role in producing future-oriented thinking, visions, and new practices and, conversely, contributing to this process of knowledge production can generate consciousness. This implies that CHAT's research settings are directly situated within social practice, where human development is generated. She develops specifically on two empirical studies that use Developmental Work Research (DWR) and Change Laboratory (CL) as a method for integrating science in relation with two specific social contexts: health care and school entrepreneurship education. In her chapter, she emphasizes one lesser-developed aspect of DWR, namely the dialogical aspect of activity in the relation between the subject and others as well as between the subject and their environment. As she mentions, "the typical way to approach any research field in DWR is to use the activity system model as a unit of analysis to construct a historical and situational understanding (consciousness) of the research object." But this model can neglect how every subject can contribute to creating new meaning and understandings by their participation in object-oriented unfolding activity. She uses the dialogical concept of objectification to conceptualize how the subject in the dialectical relation to the environment reconstructs the existing contents of representations (discussed, notably, in collective activity during DWR); creates new ones; and gives meanings to these new contents. As stated by the author, one important contribution of the dialogical perspective is to conceptualize the role of the cultural dynamics of mediation, which is connected to language in its intensive social and historical life. This mediation supports the human mind in conceiving, creating and communicating about social reality by being open to the not-yet-known (of itself and the other), and in opening to emergent possibilities of thought, feeling and being. The concept of voices is aptly used to demonstrate how the voice of patients—whose interpretations are grounded in their biographical context and daily life—a concept newly used in one DWR study to develop a treatment plan that was not considered before. In the author's words, "both the doctor's and the patient's individual voices [serve] as mediating means in the processes of meaning making." The shared dialogical conception of students and discussion over the concept of monetary profit, and the meaning of their engagement in a communal fair, generate progressively new forms of functioning in school and a new conception of students' agency. The students "were provided with possibilities for being subjects of action through their active engagement with society, i.e., with the practices constituting social realities." The chapter concludes by pointing out that the cultural dynamics of mediation and development cannot be conceived as free from power relations existing within the activity system or separated from social and biographical history. This suggests a need for CHAT research to address the link between political and ideological aspects of culture and their role in knowledge production within specific social settings.

Notes

1 The term 'dialogue' has several conceptual forms (Linell, 2009). Bakhtin used the term 'dialogism' to refer to the epistemology of human sciences. Marková prefers the term 'dialogicality' in the sense of the cultural theory of knowledge (Marková, 2003). I draw upon these terms in the text. Both differentiate from the other approaches studying conversation and dialogue.
2 Social languages were constructed by the researcher as combinations of object's conceptual history in object-oriented activity (bio-somatic/psychological/social) and its activity contexts of language use (health care, everyday, administrative).

3 The findings of conflicts and ruptures between the voices of the doctor and patient were foregrounded in the developmental project.
4 A teacher recounted in the interview that in the beginning of the program they had faced difficulties "to *talk about money*" in teaching because it had not traditionally been included in pedagogy. After coming up with an idea that the students can use the money for funding their international fieldtrip, the teachers had started to feel more comfortable in combining entrepreneurial phenomena with pedagogy.
5 Being achieved politically, public services in education and health care are objects of continuous political struggle in welfare societies. The ideals (e.g., 'freedom of choice') underlying a worldview of market-driven society sustain tensions between the relationship of the individual to communities, public values, and the public good. In critical studies, the ideals are claimed to be coming from the (neoliberal) political view in which the individual ("internal") is "at the center of social life and economic activity" and which makes her "responsible for the economic conditions of her existence in society" (Foucault, 2008; see Holborow, 2015, p. 94).
6 Rückriem (2009) considers the origin of the problem in the conceptual solution of the unit of analysis in which the collective activity system includes the categories of Marx' political economy (production, consumption, and distribution) as components of a psychologically oriented structural scheme of collective activity.

References

Arievitch, I., & Stetsenko, A. (2014). The "magic of signs." In R. Yasnitsky, R. Van der Veer, & M. Ferrari (Eds.), *The Cambridge handbook of cultural-historical psychology* (pp. 217–244). Cambridge University Press.

Bakhtin, M. M. (1981). *The dialogical imagination: Four essays by M. M. Bakhtin* (M. Holquist Ed.). University of Texas Press.

Bakhtin, M. M. (1986). *Speech genres and other late essays* (V. McGee, C. Emerson, & M. Holquist, Trans.). University of Texas Press.

Berglund, K., & Holmgren, C. (2013). Entrepreneurship education in policy and practice. *International Journal of Entrepreneurial Venturing*, *5*(1), 9–27. doi:10.1504/IJEV.2013.051669

Biesta, G. J. J. (2013). *The beautiful risk of education*. Paradigm Publishers.

Bratus, B. S. (2005). Personal sense according to A.N. Leontiev and the problem of a vertical axis of consciousness. *Journal of Russian & East European Psychology*, *43*(6), 32–44. doi:10.1080/10610405.2005.11059271

Cole, M. (1996). *A once and future discipline*. Harvard University Press.

Cole, M. (2005). Introduction. *Mind, Culture, and Activity*, *12*(3–4), 169–170. doi:10.1080/10749039.2005.9677809

Daniels, H. (2001). *Vygotsky and pedagogy*. RoutledgeFalmer.

Daniels, H. (2008). *Vygotsky and research*. Routledge.

Davies, B. (2010). The implications for qualitative research methodology of the struggle between the individualized subject of phenomenology and the emergent multiplicities of the poststructuralist subject: The problem of agency. *Reconceptualizing Educational Research Methodology, 1*(1), 54–68.

Davydov, V. (1999). The content and unresolved problems of activity theory. In Y. Engeström, R. Miettinen, & R-L. Punamäki (Eds.), *Perspectives on activity theory* (pp. 39–52). Cambridge University Press.

Edwards, A. (2010). *Being an expert professional practitioner: The relational turn in expertise.* Springer.

Edwards, A. (2012). The role of common knowledge in achieving collaboration across practices. *Learning, Culture and Social Interaction, 1*(1), 22–32. doi:10.1016/j.lcsi.2012.03.003

Emerson, C. (1986). The outer word and inner speech: Bakhtin, Vygotsky, and the internalization of language. In G. S. Morson (Ed.), *Bakhtin: Essays and dialogues on his work* (pp. 21–40). The University of Chicago Press.

Engeström, R. (1995). Voice as communicative action. Mind, *Culture, and Activity, 2*(3), 192–215. doi:10.1080/10749039509524699

Engeström, R. (2009). Who is acting in an activity system? In A. Sannino, H. Daniels, & K. D. Gutiérrez (Eds.), *Learning and expanding with activity theory* (pp. 257–273). Cambridge University Press.

Engeström, R. (2014). The interplay of developmental and dialogical epistemologies. *Outlines: Critical Practice Studies, 15*(2), 119–138.

Engestrom, R., Hakkarainen, K., & Miettinen, R. (2014). Intercultural collaboration: A response to Serpell's commentary. *Mind, Culture, and Activity, 21*(3), 264–267. doi:10.1080/10749039.2014.922585

Engeström, R., & Käyhkö, L. (2021). A critical search for the learning object across school and out-of-school contexts. *Journal of the Learning Sciences, 30*(3), 401–432.

Engeström, Y. (1990). *Learning, working and imagining: Twelve studies in activity theory.* Orienta-Konsultit.

Engeström, Y. (2001). Expansive learning at work: Toward an activity-theoretical re-conceptualization. *Journal of Education and Work, 14*(1), 133–156.

Engeström, Y. (2009). The future of activity theory: A rough draft. In A. Sannino, H. Daniels, & K. Gutierrez (Eds.), *Learning and expanding with activity theory* (pp. 303–328). Cambridge University Press.

Engeström, Y. (2015). *Learning by expanding: An activity theoretical approach to developmental research* (2nd ed.). Cambridge University Press. (Original work published 1987)

Engeström, Y. (2017). *Expertise in transition: Expansive learning in medical work.* Cambridge University Press.

Engeström, Y., Engeström, R., & Kerosuo, H. (2003). The discursive construction of collaborative care. *Applied Linguistics, 24*(3), 286–315.

European Commission. (2012). *Entrepreneurship education at school in Europe. National strategies, curricula and learning outcomes.* https://op.europa.eu/en/publication-detail/-/publication/74a7d356-dc53-11e5-8fea-01aa75ed71a1

Foucault, M. (1976). *The birth of medicine: An archaeology of medical perception.* Tavistock Publications.

Foucault, M. (2008). *The birth of biopolitics: Lectures at the Collège de France, 1978–1979.* Palgrave Macmillan.

Goffman, E. (1964). *Behavior in public process: Notes on the social organization of gatherings.* Free Press.

Gutiérrez, K. D. (2016). Designing resilient ecologies: Social design experiments and a new social imagination. *Educational Researcher, 45*(3), 187–196.

Holborrow, M. (2015). *Language and neoliberalism.* Routledge.

Holmgren, C., & From, J. (2005). Taylorism of the mind: Entrepreneurship education from a perspective of educational research. *European Educational Research Journal, 4*(4), 382–390.

Ilyenkov, E. V. (1977). *Dialectical logic: Essays on its history and theory.* Progress Publishers.

Jornet, A., Roth, W.-M., & Krange, I. (2016). A transactional approach to transfer episodes. *Journal of the Learning Sciences, 25*(2), 285–330. doi:10.1080/10508406.2016.1147449

Kaptelin, V. (2005). The object of activity: Making sense of the sense-maker. *Mind, Culture, and Activity, 12*(1), 4–18. doi:10.1207/s15327884mca1201_2

Käyhkö, L. (2015). *Kivi kengässä'-opettajat yrittäjyyskasvatuksen kentällä. Tutkimus koulun ja paikallisyhteisön kumppanuudesta* [Teachers in the field of entrepreneurship education: A study about partnership between school and local community] [Doctoral dissertation]. University of Helsinki.

Kerosuo, H. (2006). *Boundaries in action. An activity-theoretical study of development, learning and change in health care for patients with multiple and chronic illnesses.* Helsinki University Press.

Knorr-Cetina, K. (2001). Objectual practice. In T. R. Schatzki, K. Knorr-Cetina, & E. Savigny (Eds.), *The practice turn in contemporary theory* (pp. 175–188). Routledge.

Kramer, M. (2021). *Teachers' agency in school development. A journey of expansive learning* [Doctoral dissertation]. University of Helsinki.

Langemeyer, I. (2017). Methodological challenges of investigating intellectual cooperation, relational expertise, and transformative agency. *Nordic Journal of Vocational Education and Training, 7*(2), 39–62. doi:10.3384/njvet.2242-458X.177239

Leontiev, A. N. (1978). *Activity, consciousness, and personality.* Prentice Hall.

Marková, I. (2003). Constitution of the self: Intersubjectivity and dialogicality. *Culture & Psychology, 9*(3), 249–259.

Marková, I. (2004). Dialogicality of anchoring and objectification. In C. Soares & L. Amâncio (Eds.), *Em torno da Psicologia* (pp. 75–82). Livros Horizonte.
Marková, I. (2012). Objectification in common sense thinking. *Mind, Culture, and Activity, 19*(3), 207–221. doi:10.1080/10749039.2012.688178
Mononen-Batista Costa, S., & Brunila, K. (2016). Becoming entrepreneurial: Transitions and education of unemployed youth. *Power and Education, 8*(1), 19–34.
Nissen, M. (2011). Activity theory: Legacies, standpoints, and hopes: A discussion of Andy Blunden's *An interdisciplinary theory of activity*. *Mind, Culture, and Activity, 18*(4), 374–384. doi:10.1080/10749039.2011.595037
Nowotny, H., Scott, P., & Gibbons, M. (2001). *Re-thinking science*. Polity.
Rae, D., & Wang, C. L. (Eds.). (2015). *Entrepreneurial learning: New perspectives in research, education and practice*. Routledge.
Rückriem, G. (2009). Digital technology and mediation: A challenge to activity theory. In A. Sannino, H. Daniels, & K. D. Gutiérrez (Eds.), *Learning and expanding with activity theory* (pp. 257–273). Cambridge University Press.
Säljö, R. (2003). Epilogue: From transfer to boundary crossing. In T. Tuomi-Grön & Y. Engeström (Eds.), *Between school and work: New perspectives on transfer and boundary crossing* (pp. 311–321). Pergamon Press.
Saxe, G. B., & Esmonde, I. (2005). Studying cognition in flux: A historical treatment of Fu in the shifting structure of Oksapmin mathematics. *Mind, Culture, and Activity, 12*(3–4), 171–225. doi:10.1080/10749039.2005.9677810
Silvonen, J. (2011). Vygotky's plural discourse on the human mind. In P. Aunio, M. Jahnukainen, M. Kalland, & J. Silvonen (Eds.), *Piaget is dead, Vygotsky is still alive, or?* (pp. 33–59). Finnish Educational Research Association.
Spinuzzi, C. (2011). Losing by expanding: Corralling the runaway object. *Journal of Business and Technical Communication, 25*(4), 449–486. doi:10.1177/1050651911411040
Spinuzzi, C. (2017). "I think you should explore the kinky market": How entrepreneurs develop value propositions as emergent objects of activity networks. *Mind, Culture, and Activity, 24*(3), 258–272. doi:10.1080/10749039.2017.1294606
Star, S. L. (2010). This is not a boundary object: Reflections on the origin of a concept. *Science, Technology, & Human Values, 35*(5), 601–617. doi:10.1177/0162243910377624
Star, S. L., & Griesemer, J. R. (1989). Institutional ecology, "translations" and boundary objects: Amateurs and professionals in Berkeley's museum of vertebrate zoology 1907–1939. *Social Studies of Science, 19*(3), 387–420.
Stetsenko, A. (2000). The role of the principle of object-relatedness in the theory of activity. In V. V. Davydov & D. A. Leont'ev (Eds.), *The activity approach to psychology: Problems and perspectives* (pp. 54–69). USSR Academy of Pedagogical Sciences.
Stetsenko, A. (2017). *The transformative mind: Expanding Vygotsy's approach to development and education*. Cambridge University Press.
Stetsenko, A., & Arievitch, I. (2004). The self in cultural-historical activity theory. *Theory & Psychology, 14*(4), 475–503. doi:10.1177/0959354304044921

Stoetzler, M., & Yuval-Davis, N. (2002). Standpoint theory, situated knowledge and the situated imagination. *Feminist Theory*, *3*(3), 315–333.

Todorov, T. (1984). *Mikhail Bakhtin: The dialogical principle*. Manchester University Press.

Valsiner, J. (2001). Process structure of semiotic mediation in human development. *Human Development*, *44*(2–3), 84–97. doi:10.1159/000057048

Virkkunen, J., & Newnham, D. (2013). *The change laboratory: A tool for collaborative development of work and education*. Sense Publishers.

Volosinov, V. N. (1973). *Marxism and the philosophy of language*. Seminar Press.

Vygotsky, L. S. (1978). *Mind in society: The development of higher psychological processes*. Harvard University Press.

Wartofsky, M. W. (1979). *Models: Representation and scientific understanding*. Reidel.

Wertsch, J. V. (1991). *Voices of the mind: A sociocultural approach to mediated action*. Harvester Wheatsheaf.

CHAPTER 6

Dialectical Analysis of Learning and Development through Career Counselling Groups

The Challenge of Emotions

Patricia Dionne

Abstract

In CHAT, one of the methodological challenges is to consider the dialectical movement between cultural-historical development and the subjective development of individuals who gain consciousness through their contribution in collective activity. In our research practice, this challenge is particularly salient when we pursue a dialectical analysis of how a subject progressively gains consciousness of her or his emotion during activity and how this consciousness affects in return the development of this activity. Very frequently, emotions are considered as individual attributes of a subject separate from material activities (Dionne & Jornet, 2019). According to Vygotsky (1987), the materiality of activity is inherently connected to the motive sphere of consciousness, which includes the emotions. Humans become particularly conscious and free with the mediation of scientific knowledge or concepts (as historical products). In our research setting, group career counselling, the meaning of emotions become often an object of learning. Facing long-term unemployment, some participants may interpret this social situation as a personal responsibility (Blustein, 2006). This can cause sadness, anger, and shame that can hinder actions toward social and professional integration (SPI) (Dionne et al., 2017). The present analysis puts emphasis on a methodology that permits to trace the discursive manifestations of systematic instruments that participants learn (in group) for attributing meaning to and managing emotions. We discuss principally how those systematic instruments serve two complementary purposes: as concepts of analysis and as tools for development in praxis. The results show that the systematic instruments, transmitted and learned in the collective activity, contribute to more control and to a greater consciousness of the relation to self, to others and to the world, which further promotes actions toward their SPI.

Keywords

emotion – cultural-historical activity theory – group career counseling – dialectical methodology – consciousness

∴

Emotions constitute a central dimension of human development and activity (Vygotsky, 1986) that is dialectally linked with thinking and acting. Despite this centrality, the consideration of emotions in cultural-historical activity theory (CHAT) analysis is deserving of greater consideration (Fleer et al., 2017). For Vygotsky (1987), the dimension of the motivating sphere of consciousness—which includes inclinations, needs, interests, impulses, affects and emotions—is conceived in a dialectical relationship with concrete material collective activity. In his view, "There exists a meaningful system that constitutes the *unity of affective and intellectual processes*" (Vygotsky, 1987, p. 50). At the end of his life, Vygotsky used the concept of *perezhivanie* as a unit of analysis of personal and environmental characteristics. Importantly, this concept implies that affective dimensions of social and subjective life have to be taken into account and analyzed in dialectical relation (Jornet & Roth, 2016). A *perezhivanie* is therefore inclusive of situational characteristics, how these characteristics affect (are perceived and felt by) the individual, and how this individual addresses her or his emotions (Blunden, 2016). In much current research, emotions are considered individual attributes of a subject separate from his or her material activities (Dionne & Jornet, 2019). On the contrary, according to Vygotsky (1987), the motive sphere of consciousness is inherently connected to the materiality of activity. This motivating sphere of consciousness affects the collective and subjective planes of activity through volition and affective investment. Moreover, social activity, interactions, tools and instruments culturally and historically developed are understood to be at genetic origins of human consciousness and development. As I will elaborate on further in this chapter, humans become particularly conscious and free with the mediation of scientific knowledge and concepts (as historical products). This outlook suggests the primacy of the social over the individual.

Along these lines, Roth and Jornet (2017) emphasize the dialectical relationship between the subjective development of each human and practical activities. "In the practical activities that contribute to generalize production of need and need satisfaction the individual becomes human" (p. 6). As Stetsenko (2016) points out, in reference notably to Marx, as they contribute to social transformative practice, humans transform their world and themselves. She deepens her argument by noting that human subjectivity and mind gain ontological status through their role within these transformative practices. Indeed, from a CHAT perspective, one methodological challenge is to take into account the dialectical movement between cultural-historical development and the subjective development of individuals who gain consciousness through their contribution to collective and social activity (Davydov, 2005). This challenge is particularly salient in the context of dialectical analysis of how a subject—through and with instrumental mediation—progressively become aware of her or his emotion during social and collective activity and how this consciousness influences the development of this transformative activity. Even if on an epistemological level of analysis one takes into account the dialectical relationship between the subject and her or his environment, how to conceive of her or his subjectivity and how to trace back the movement within this relationship still remains a methodological challenge.

In the research setting under study in this chapter—i.e., career counselling groups with long-term unemployed adults—the meaning of emotions often becomes an object of learning. Counsellors transmit linguistic instruments that help participants to conceive of and progressively master their emotions, notably those which are linked with work's exclusion (Dionne et al., 2017). In their situation of facing long-term unemployment, certain participants may interpret their social situation as one for which they are personally responsible (Blustein, 2006). This situation of long-term unemployment is unevenly distributed in different social groups, which may experience a sense of having lost their power to act. Indeed, in the current context of a competitive and globalized labour market, some individuals or social groups face discrimination or injustice when it comes to their vocational opportunities and access to work. Some groups (Aboriginals, youths, ethnic and racial minorities, women, LGBTQ2 members, etc.) are still underrepresented in the labour market (Flores, 2009; Langlois & Villotti, 2022). Long-term unemployment is therefore a situation of concern from a social justice and equity perspective, and more particularly in terms of the risks of marginalization and the detrimental effects on physical and mental health (Paul & Moser, 2009) for people facing this exclusion and poverty. The situation can cause sadness, anger, shame, or powerlessness that can hinder actions towards social and professional integration (SPI) (Dionne, 2015). The shame they feel about their situation can also cause people to isolate themselves socially. They can then lose the driving force that social contradictions constitute for learning and development (Dionne & Bourdon, 2018). Indeed, as Duboscq and Clot (2010) illustrate, from a dialectical perspective, the state of social conflictuality shapes individuals' level of internal conflictuality, and accordingly, psychic functioning shrinks and can even be extinguished when society no longer offers the individual external conflictuality. This conflictuality can affect the emotional dimension of subjective activity. In a situation where a person is isolated and lacks social interaction, the ability to affect others and to be affected by others can be lost in her or his activity's habits. Echoing Spinoza, Roche (2016) notes, "It is precisely through their power to affect others and to be affected by them (*potestas*) that individuals increase their power to act (*potentia*)" (p. 108). This development of the power to act is a key concept in our analysis. It is linked to the power to act voluntarily and freely in and on the world in the Spinozian sense, with an awareness of what determines my behaviors and the capacity to bend them to my will (Saussez, 2017). This power to act implies the mobilization of a plurality of capacities to act, in other words, the possibility of mobilizing a set of effective means of action in a specific situation (Dionne et al., 2017).

The present analysis emphasizes a methodology that allows for tracing back the discursive manifestations of systematic instruments that participants learn in groups in order to assign meaning to and manage emotions. As we will see, these systematic instruments serve two complementary purposes: as concepts of analysis and as tools for development in praxis. The text examines how the systematic instruments conveyed and learned in the collective activity of the group can contribute to greater consciousness of and mastery over the individuals' relation to self, to others and to the world, which further promotes actions towards their SPI.

1   Consciousness and Emotions

In his conception of emotions, Vygotsky (2003) envisions a complex relationship between emotions and consciousness. Because human consciousness is developed during social interactions, the social element comes first and foremost. Thus, Magiolino and Smolka (2013) base themselves on Vygotsky to assert that, like other higher psychic functions, the emotional psychic functions are first social, then subjective. Their development is mediated by psychological linguistic instruments and by emotional signs of expression (Holodynski, 2013). As such, according to Magiolino and Smolka (2013), "We do not simply 'feel,' but we 'feel' with sense and meaning. We become emotioned within a web of interpersonal relations—immersed in a social-individual history of relationships where people affect each other" (p. 106). This dialectical relation between the social/historical environment and the emotion lived by a person is at the root of the concept of *perezhivanie* (Jornet & Roth, 2016). When feeling an emotion, the child first progressively learns in social interactions to take a distance from the emotion through the mediation of words through his or her inner language. The child first experiences the emotions physically and psychologically, then manages to put them at a distance to gain consciousness of the emotion and learn to control it. Children thus learn to control their behavior especially by giving meaning to feelings or emotion that affect their activity. On the path to adulthood, a child progressively learns mechanisms for analyzing the social behaviors of others, and in turn this enables them to gain a distance from their own experience. Indeed, for Vygotsky (1997b) "Consciousness is in a way a social contact with oneself" (p. 91). Moreover, "The personality becomes for itself what it is in itself through what it is for others" (p. 105).

Nevertheless, this consciousness does not shed light on the entire psyche, a part of which remains unconscious (Vygotsky, 1997a). Vygotsky defines the unconscious as what is potentially conscious, or, in other words, potentially accessible. In his actions and development, "Man is every minute full of unrealised possibilities" (Vygotsky, 1997a, p. 70) of which he is not conscious. Even for adults, emotions can be embedded in or dominated by a concrete situation. Therefore, adults can be affected, for example by their unemployment, without understanding their emotions. For Vygotsky, the process of learning systematic (scientific) instruments helps to progressively gain the requisite mastery and consciousness to act voluntarily in a situation. For this author, verbal thought is originally engendered by sense and motive. In certain situation, the emotion is thus put at a distance by the individual and, through the mediation of the meaning of words, becomes an object of thought. Vygotsky (1986) underscores the importance of words as a reflection of consciousness: "The meaningful word is a microcosm of human consciousness" (p. 255). Thus, words spoken for oneself or for others can be understood as a reflection but also the instrument of human consciousness, which is mediated by the cultural and historical meaning of words. In relation to emotions, Vygosky provides a framework for understanding the role of language in the emotional consciousness that a career group intervention aims to elicit. For adults, sometimes the emotions linked to significant professional and personal experiences, especially linked to work and education, remain unrealized. As stated earlier, these emotions of helplessness and fear can paralyze the participants in connection with SPI. Being conscious of the "paralyzing role" of their emotions can help create a movement to restore the power to act (Dionne, 2015). Furthermore, Vygotsky demonstrates that each conscious moment of emotion is accessible only to the person herself or himself, who can then share it through the mediation of verbal thought (oral or written) (Vygotsky, 1987). This mediation and this indirect contact with others' consciousness is very important from the standpoint of a cultural-historical methodological approach. It implies that as researchers, we cannot directly access participants experience by observing it. Our methodological approach must be indirect.

2 Methodology: The Dual Function of Emotions

Our research was conducted over an 18-month community group intervention entitled People and Communities in Motion (PCM), which is aimed at fostering the social and professional integration (SPI) of long-term unemployed adults (Michaud et al., 2012). The intervention, which took place in an employability organization, was based on a contextual and systemic approach (Patton & McMahon, 2014) and included the introduction of systematic instruments to address and develop the power to act in order to surmount structural barriers in the community, such as discrimination against long-term unemployment, and thus facilitate the welfare-to-work transition. In this setting, the object of activity is to enable participants to develop a greater consciousness of their relation to self, to others and to the world, with the aim of stimulating their actions towards SPI. One key aspect of the group is a collective project that the participants planned and carried out to transform and positively influence their community. As such, this group is conceived, according to the definition of Stetsenko (2016), to stimulate each member's contribution to a transformative collective practice and to stress the role of present actions in creating the future. The program also provides flexible pathways to employment, namely through volunteer work, internships, jobs, or school integration. Concerning this pathway, the counsellors and the employability organization assert their feminist position and place special emphasis on helping women go back to school to earn a degree. The aim is to enable each woman and her family to escape poverty and make a decent living.

The program also included written and spoken exercises aimed, among other things, at raising consciousness of emotions. Systematic concepts are conveyed to help the participants learn the meaning of emotion and become progressively more conscious of the emotions they are feeling, especially during collective activity. Action systems[1] are conveyed to help the individuals step back from their emotions and gain progressive mastery over what they are feeling. Therefore, in our analysis, emotions have a dual function and futurity. They serve two complementary purposes: as concepts of analysis and as instrument for learning and development in praxis.

The group under analysis was held in the downtown of a large suburban city in Québec (Canada). The participants were 15 Caucasian women, over 25 years old. Half of them had an initial high school diploma or certificate. They had been in a situation of long-term unemployment for more than 2 years, and were mostly single with young children. Most of them were survivors of domestic violence. At the beginning of the PCM program, many participants expressed doubts and fears about their ability to return to school or integrate the job market. Many of them were experiencing strong emotions that impeded their actions towards SPI. During the PCM program, they contributed to two collective projects they had decided to organize in order to respond to some community needs they had identified.

During the PCM program, a close bond was forged between the research team, the counsellors and the participants. As a researcher on that team, I also accepted to be affected by them and to affect them. In line with Honneth's model of recognition (2002), our involvement was for example to take every opportunity (formal and informal) to provide social recognition and social esteem to support the collective and subjective transformative actions of the participants. Like Elias (1993), I posit the impossibility of complete neutrality with regard to the object of research and consider that there is no break, but rather a continuum, between commitment and distancing in research. Elias (1993) puts it well: "Scientists seek to solve human problems by a detour, that of distancing" (p. 14). This detour does not mean that scientists are not part of the social realities they seek to describe or are not driven by values that influence their relationship to their research. Indeed, the values of justice and social recognition—as well as the aspiration to better understand what might contribute, in the interventions, to the social and professional integration of long-term unemployed—are all fundamental to my interest in this object of research.

The data collected came from four sources: semi-structured interviews, non-participant observation (70 hours) with notes in a field journal, employment counsellors' weekly journals, and various documents pertaining to the program. During the non-participant observation (Lui & Maitis, 2010), the observers remained clear of the action, but could interact with participants and counsellors during lunches and other breaks. These observations were valuable in better understanding of how concepts and systems or actions were conveyed and learned. The counsellors' daily journals were used to document the tasks completed during the intervention, the instruments they used, and the perceived effects of their intervention. The written artefacts were collected throughout the program and were used to describe and keep track of the concepts and action systems conveyed. They give access to the reading and writing exercises handed out by the counsellors. The semi-structured interviews were conducted with 5 of the participants (2 interviews each), the 2 counsellors (2 interviews each), and 10 key community actors closely involved in the intervention (1 interview each). The interviews, lasting between 35 and 150 minutes, focused on the interventions, the changes experienced by the individuals, and the group and the community.

With the collected material, I began with a procedural and longitudinal analysis that involved tracing back the elements learned by the participants. As Vygotsky (1986) points out, learning does not coincide with development. Rather, learning awakens, stimulates and guides the development process. Therefore, if we want to understand a subject's development during their contribution in a group, we must trace back what was conveyed and learned during the group that helped the participant develop their capacity to progressively gain mastery and consciousness to act voluntarily in a situation. As we have shown previously (Dionne & Bourdon, 2018), many contradictions are identified during such a group activity. Numerous counsellors take these contradictions as occasions to introduce systematic instruments linked with emotions. Therefore, the analysis traced back the discursive manifestations of contradictions and resolutions that involved emotions during collective activity. The typology proposed by Engeström and Sannino (2011) serves as a framework for analyzing collective contradictions, under the categories of double-bind, conflict, critical-conflict and dilemma. Emphasis was also placed on participants' contributions and the introduction and learning of scientific concepts and action systems that can serve as thinking instruments for emotions (Vygotsky, 1997b). On a subjective level, I drew on our different data sources to determine if the instruments used during the collective activity were subsequently mobilized by a subject to gradually gain more control and a greater consciousness of the relationship to self, to others and to the world. To trace back this movement, I used the NVivo 10 framework matrix tool to condense the data. In the resulting matrix frame, lines are used to represent contradictions, their resolutions, and the conveyed concepts and action systems, in this case, those linked with emotions. Columns are used to represent each week of collected data. This makes it possible to follow the participants' discourse and specifically their appropriation of the concepts and action systems which allow for understanding and managing emotions. This help to retrace their actions towards social and professional integration.

3 Results

3.1 Transmission and Learning of Systematic Instruments Linked with Emotions

The affective dimension that was omnipresent in the career counselling group under study. Emotions are an object of systematic learning. Counsellors on many occasions conveyed conceptual instruments to help give meaning to specific emotions such as stress, anger, pride or shame. For example, during one workshop, counsellors distinguished between anxiety disorders and stress, and discussed how both are linked to fear. Theoretical explanations were given to the participants, who, in defining stress, differentiated chronic stress from acute stress, examining the components as intensity, duration, and absorption. As part of the career counselling group, participants gradually learn how to use systematized emotional instruments that are conveyed to them by the counsellors and the other participants. Each situation, whether *in situ* or encountered in the lives of the participants, can serve as an occasion to systematize emotions. Many written documents were also used to raise the women's consciousness and to give them the opportunity to write about concepts such as their interests, aspirations, needs, values, competencies and so on. Besides learning systematic instruments linked with career counselling, another aim of this group work was to nurture participants' pride in themselves. Véronique, a participant, remarked how working on competencies stimulated her emotion of pride in relation to herself.

Véronique: The way I saw the program, it motivates me to focus more on my life project. When you're alone, it's easier to stay at home to let yourself be driven by life. This whole process of writing down my competencies was good.

Interviewer: Having to write your competencies, did you find that helpful?

Véronique: Yes. But, it's always a little harder to talk about yourself positively. Working on it, it makes you feel good and proud.

Interviewer: It made you feel good, it makes you see what competencies you have.

Véronique: Yes, that's it. In fact, well I may have more than I think. I esteem myself more.

Furthermore, many action systems are conveyed to help participants master their emotions in their relation to themselves, to others and to the world. For example, to learn to bring stress and related emotions such as anger under control, the participants learned relaxation and breathing methods. They also learned to take a pause, to think about their experience as an object of reflection, and to notice when they are stressed before interacting with others. In the following excerpt, the counsellor emphasizes this method that was taught during the program. After leaving the premises of the group due to her strong anger about the progress of administrative procedures for her return to school, one participant asked to speak to the counsellor:

Véronique (participant): I apologize, I am stressed out and I've gotten upset
Claire (counsellor): I accept your apologies, Véronique. You know, I love you and I know you're a good person, but a person who has trouble controlling her emotions. However, can you understand that someone you would answer by yelling and losing your temper like that might respond in the same way? You must breathe, Véronique, you must learn to take a step back."

Progressively this participant learned to master her stress and to acknowledge her need for help without getting angry with others. Indeed, many spontaneous concepts are used as instruments by the counsellors and by the group. They tend to be primarily applicable during an immediate situation. In the next excerpt, one participant was putting off actions she needed to take linked with her return to school. After many empathetic interventions by the group and by the counsellor, she said that she was totally "frozen" by her fear. The counsellor reported the conversation she had with this woman in her journal.

> We'll be able to move on and work on what gets your two feet on the ground!! Manon, if you knew ... all the girls in the group are creeped out, you wouldn't be normal if you were not afraid. Going back to school is a big decision, it's an important change in your life, BUT it is a change that is achievable IF[2] we prepare well together. Go talk to the girls and ask them if they're afraid, you'll be surprised at their answers. (Claire, counsellor to Manon, participant)

Manon then went to see three other participants who confirmed that they were creeped out, but also eager to start school. After this situation and many months of being paralyzed by her emotions, the participant started to take multiple actions to prepare for returning to school.

3.2 *Learning During and Through the Resolution of Contradictions*

The group participants faced many contradictions during their participation. These contradictions engendered various emotions, such as anger, sadness and fear that often gave rise to a discussion and led to new actions by the participants, or by the group. During the third week of the program, when two participants visited a food bank to collect information for the group, the receptionist at first thought that they were there for food. Her attitude softened when she realized that they had come for information. As the counsellor reported in her diary, the participants shared their indignation and anger with the group:

"They told us that they found it hurtful. They were the same people, but the look of the other [the receptionist] had changed when she realized they were not coming begging" (Claire, counsellor). After the participants shared their emotions with the group, this contradiction sparked a discussion about "how to change things." The beginning of the reflection leading to the collective project can be traced back to this moment. This resolution was stimulated by the participants' motivation to collectively take action for the benefit of other single mothers in situations of poverty and precariousness. This inspired their collective contribution to creating a directory of community organizations.

During the collective project, the division of labour was another source of contradiction. One collective norm was mutual help between participants and teams. A critical conflict occurred close to the deadline with the editors, when a participant noticed the absence of several other participants on her team and found herself overwhelmed by the tasks to be completed to resolve the situation. In tears, she expressed her anger as follows:

> I find it crappy to see the others with all this time on their hands while in our team we're rushing about like crazy. Others are totally uninterested in the directory; they do not care at all! It is nice to be independent but I felt lonely sometimes, while you and Julie spent your time settling conflicts and helping the other teams. (Marie-Hélène, participant)

To resolve this critical conflict, a listening session was offered and a discussion took place. The anger and sadness were shared with the others and the norm of mutual help was reaffirmed. The same day, four other individuals were called upon to help the participants with the directory. The counsellor wrote in her diary that when they finished their day, "They were more light-hearted and smiling." The following week, the entire team that handled the directory was present and a counsellor accompanied the participants during the last stages with the printer. The participants who were involved in the critical conflict said they were relieved and they felt they were no longer alone in taking care of the project.

The participants' relations with administrative documents was also in some cases affected negatively by a deep sense of injustice and powerlessness. In many cases, the group and the counsellors came to the defence of a particular participant and her family's rights. This was the case, for instance, when a participant's family was endangered by the presence of a former violent spouse in their home, or by an unsanitary home. During the group, one double bind (contradiction) faced by a participant concerned her living situation. She was at first trying, unsuccessfully, to secure decent housing. She was paralyzed when she learned about the presence of a rat in her apartment where she lived with her 10 children. She uttered a discursive manifestation of powerlessness: "What can I do? My landlord doesn't want to do anything!" As seen in one counsellor (Julie's) journal, "The group helped Carole. Marie-Hélène [who volunteers on a tenant committee] gave instructions on how to write a letter to the owner. The counsellors helped them 'take action' and obtain legal explanations from the various authorities." With the help of the group, the participant was able to share her emotion with others and to be supported in her situation.

Another double-bind situation was encountered when one officer at the government employment agency (Emploi-Québec, EQ[3]), offered what seemed to be unjust help to one participant in comparison to the others. Indeed, Louise at first had to produce more evidence than the other participants to obtain access to full-time day care service (week 3); she had to deal with a delay in one month's payment for this service (week 6) and struggled together with Claire (her counsellor) to get the money she owed. In her relationship with her EQ officer, Louise was initially so helpless and stressed that she thought of abandoning the project:

> My officer still does not believe in me and from the beginning she did not want me to participate in this project. She said it would not take me anywhere and I would not do anything. Then anyway, she did not want to pay me anymore. But she will not accept for me to stay on welfare. It's very, very contradictory. I had many, many, many difficulties with her along the way. Cheques she did not send me, I had to argue a lot with her to pay me …. (Louise, participant)

Louise nevertheless emphasized that Claire helped her become conscious of her emotions of fear and anger, as well as her sense of paralysis in the situation. In the beginning she was undergoing the situation and her emotions. With the counsellor's assistance, she learned two action systems, one to manage her emotions and a second to know how to defend and assert herself, specifically when she was facing a double bind. At the outset of the program, Louise said that she would have lost her temper in this situation and it would not have helped. But after learning this action system, Louise scheduled an appointment with her officer to explain the importance of EQ in her success in the program. She reminded the officer of the difficulty for a single-parent woman to pay childcare costs. She told her, "I have three children and I am alone at home. Getting back on the job market is not easy" (Louise, participant). She stated that one of the most important elements to support her in her SPI was the financial support to cover childcare expenses. Normally, these fees are covered with participation in the PCM program, but Louise said, "If I have to run after my cheques to get paid for my daycare, it's very difficult. Because I'm the one who's late on daycare. Then, they threaten to expel your child" (Louise, participant). This assertion and the reaffirmation of her goal of integrating into the labour market, according to her, slightly improved the collaboration with the EQ officer.

Louise also had to leave her apartment following several episodes of violence because of her former spouse who was harassing her. She was afraid and mad about the situation, and about the complexity of the administrative procedures to be able to leave. But, with the help of the counsellors and the other participants, she did not suffer her emotions, but rather was able to leverage them as a driving force for her actions. She took steps to arrange for her relocation to be paid for by a victim assistance organization (week 27). In explaining her refusal to request support from her former spouse, she was required to prove that the ex-spouse was violent. In this situation, the counsellor supported the participant with advocacy. The following excerpt shows how she had appropriated an action system to assert, fight for and enforce her rights in such a double-bind situation:

> Louise posted the letter to her owner, citing why she needs to move quickly. We sent both mover bids to [name of victims' advocacy organization]. She will complete the forms for the office of the prosecutor's surrogates [to be sure that her owner respects her right]. (Claire, counsellor)

At week 29, Louise managed to prove her point to the owner. He cancelled her lease. At week 43, Louise's return to school resulted in the loss of free childcare for one of her children since she was no longer benefiting from welfare. When, in the summer of the following year, she had to find affordable daycare centers, they had no spots for the children of mothers in school. Her initial reaction was one of discouragement and anger. However, she was able to step back from her emotions and use them to take action. She had taken steps to promote to decision-makers the importance of supporting her situation and obtaining the service she needed. Thus, despite the refusals she met with at first (week 50), Louise persevered and made further steps to assert her point of view on her situation. At week 53, she finally managed to find a low-cost day camp for her children so she could continue her studies during the summer. Thus, Louise learned instruments allowing her to positively manage her emotions and to assert herself and stand up for her rights, to persevere despite the many obstacles in the way of SPI, and to overcome the powerlessness caused by double-bind situations. As the two following examples illustrate, progressively over the course of the program, participants learned to think of their emotions as an object while addressing administrative documents and to use these emotions to stimulate actions to defend their rights.

3.3 Empathetic Support: A Social Condition for Learning and Development in the Career Counselling Group

The counsellors introduced emotional concepts and action systems to the participants, in addition to offering emotional support and empathetic guidance regarding the emotions experienced. The participants likewise offered each other such support. During a workshop on competencies, one participant showed the resume that she had to submit for a job application:

Claire (counsellor): If you were on the board of the organization, what would you like to see in a resume?
Marie-Hélène (participant): [*crying softly*] It's coming back all the time! It seems that every time I have to write my qualities, it looks bad, I find it hard to talk about my skills. Writing them down is hard! In the interview it's OK!
Claire: Do you want us to take the time right now?
Marie-Hélène: Yes, it would help lower my stress.

As this excerpt shows, emotionally speaking, writing may represent an additional challenge, and self-writing in particular. Recognizing their own skills during the program was a key assignment for the participants. As we can see in the following excerpt, acknowledging their skills was a task fraught with many emotions for the participants. The bond and sense of trust developed among the members and with the counsellors has constituted an essential condition for affective guidance in this context. A degree of emotional security is necessary to be able to work on emotions as an object of learning. In their interviews, all of the participants said they felt loved by the counsellors.

> I felt the counsellors were close to us, listening to our needs. The program allowed us to be understood in terms of the realities we face. Of course, in the beginning, the girls found it difficult with child care, but we had Claire, who deserves a trophy. It's … excuse me [*emotional, voice trembling*] … I don't know if you could have found someone better than her, but she gave herself more than if you had put anyone in there. I felt that it was really important to her. I'm sure that when she comes home at night, she was still thinking about that. That girl, she ran so much, she

loved us and wanted so much for us. It makes a huge difference to me. Of course you don't want to disappoint someone who is so giving of herself. [...] When I had doubts about college, Claire seemed to believe in it. Then finally, I got letters of recommendation to go back to university from the people in the community who had worked with me [in the collective project and her volunteering]. This made me feel more confident about it all. (Marie-Hélène, participant)

Moreover, being able to help other participants, by mobilizing instruments they had learned in the program, was also a source of pride in many discursive manifestations. The women had also created a Facebook page to support others with going back to school. The counsellor reported, in the following excerpts from her diaries, the solidarity created in the group and the pride that the participants felt about their accomplishments (both in the collective project and in their individual endeavours).

At our Christmas dinner, we were all talking together about the progress each girl had made. They were astounded and proud to see everything they had been able to do in eight months. I told them how extraordinary they were and how they defied the dropout statistics. (Claire, counsellor)

Manon was telling me after Christmas that all the girls had sent her e-mails or Facebook messages to say, "Congratulations, I heard you passed your French class" [this class was a prerequisite to begin her professional course]. (Claire, counsellor)

For Manon—and for many others—the group's support was important to maintaining the project of returning to school; indeed, Manon was proud to receive positive feedback from her peers after having doubted so much in her ability to achieve this goal. In summary, in this group, working on and with emotion was an important part of the career counselling group process. Among other things, during the group, the participants challenged their emotions and thoughts about their capacity to return to school and to work. At the end of the program, 13 out of the 15 participants successfully returned to school. Two of them also worked concurrently in their field of study. In the excerpts below, the discursive manifestations of development via the program can be traced.

If you'd told me, a year ago, "Marie-Hélène, you're going to go to school and you're going to work," I would have told you: "Are you crazy?!" But gradually, well, the program always allowed me to do a little bit more, to be more structured and more able to do it [to work and to study at the university], and to be proud to do so without letting go. (Marie-Hélène, participant)

I felt like I do much and I had the famous blockage, "I have three children, I'm a single parent, I'm at home, I can't do anything." I realised that it was not the end of the world to go and take them to daycare, to go and bring them to school. [...] I realised that yes, we can go to work and be a single mother. When I go take my kids to daycare and I tell them, "I'm going to work," they are all like, "Oh wow! My mom works and she's going to school!" They are proud and so am I. I understood here [at PCM] that it makes a difference in your life when someone believes in you. (Louise, participant)

4 Discussion: The Dual Destiny of Emotions

The procedural and longitudinal analysis proposed in this chapter allows us to trace back the dialectical movement of emotions during group career counselling. In this field, even if the importance of emotions is widely recognized (Puffer, 2015) and is sometimes linked with culture and concepts (Meijers, 2002), the development of emotional consciousness during the group is often measured using pre- and post-testing. This type of measurement is done without accounting for how the group's activity stimulated or created the social conditions for this development (Dupuis et al., 2022). Indeed, the methodological relation between cultural/social concrete activity and emotion in a career group counselling, as well as subjective learning and development, would require greater exploration.

In the present analysis, the first "destiny" of emotion has been as an object of analysis. By using a framework matrix, I traced back, over time and based on discursive manifestations, what contradictions arose in the group, how they were resolved, and what kinds of instruments—specifically linked to emotions—were conveyed in the group. I was able to follow the social and emotional conditions that affected the group, the participants and the counsellors. The results support Blunden's definition (2016) of *perezhivanie* as unit of analysis. It was purposeful to analyze dialectically social and affective conditions with how they are perceived, affected, and managed by the subject. A second framework serves to trace back how these conditions, contradictions, resolutions, and conveyed conceptual instruments linked with emotions, are apprehended by the participants and subsequently used voluntarily to contribute to more control and to a greater consciousness of their relation to self, to others, and to the world. This second framework also helps trace back the participants' movement in action towards SPI. In this text, these two framework matrices have been consistently analyzed in relation to each other.

In my analytical experience, it was useful, as Gale et al. (2013) suggest, to start by coding the different sources of data before charting it in the framework matrix. But, in contrast with these authors, my coding involved directly applying an analytical framework that I developed using a tree node structure in NVivo10 qualitative data software. As stated by these authors, this method and these tools help with summarizing longitudinal data and "encouraging thick description that pays attention to complex layers of meaning and understanding" (p. 5). This was certainly the case with my analysis of the movement of emotion and more broadly of group participants' consciousness of their relation to self, to others and to the world.

The second "destiny" of emotion in the present research has been as an object of learning and development in the career counselling activity. My results show, as Vygotsky insightfully proposed, the importance of instrumental mediation in relation to the consciousness of emotion. The results relating to the transmission of the scientific concepts and action systems associated with emotions support the disclosure of one's emotional experience and the eventual appropriation of the meaning and signs of emotions. In fact, during this career counselling group, a specific space was reserved for expressing and developing consciousness and control of emotions on two planes: firstly the interpsychic plane during the collective activity, then the intrapsychic plane during subjective activity. In the course of collective activity, various interacting situations gave rise to relatively intense emotions that were used to raise consciousness and eventually enable the participants to gain a greater understanding and control of the emotions they felt. This resulted in a new capacity to act voluntarily through a consciousness of their emotional experience. Accordingly, as many examples illustrate, by integrating various cultural instruments, a collective activity can open up an affective zone of proximal development (Levykh, 2008). The caring support and bond of trust offered by counsellors and peers open a zone that seems to facilitate learning, and, eventually, the development of the power to act voluntarily and freely in and on the world. As adults, several participants expressed the need to conceptualize the emotions associated with significant experiences from their professional and personal backgrounds, sometimes even unconscious or unrealized experiences. This space, marked in particular by the empathy of the peers and the counsellors, also made it possible to express confidences, in particular about experiences considered to be taboo such as physical or sexual violence. These results echo those observed in career counselling interviews that are conducive to trust (Orly-Louis, 2015).

As shown in particular with the example concerning administrative documents and governmental institutions, the participants are more conscious of their emotion and they have a knowledge of what determines their behaviors and their capacity to bend them to their will (Saussez, 2017). When faced with injustices, many participants undertook new actions—notably with the help of the action systems they had learned—to defend their rights and better explain their respective situations. Many examples have also been given where emotions—of joy, anger, pain and love—were elicited through contradictions during the collective activity and during shared moments of joy and laughter when personal ties were created through group activities and tasks, etc. Some participants, in the course of collective activity and with the help of other members, reuse scientific concepts and action systems allowing them to gain some distance from their emotional experience and become more conscious in their relation to self, to others and to the world. They are now able to control their emotions and use them as resources to empower their situation. The results demonstrate the importance of considering that emotions can spur or impede goal-oriented actions and operations, as already demonstrated by Roth (2009) and Roche (2016) have previously demonstrated. Along these lines, Levykh (2008) emphasizes the two central neo-formations in Vygotsky's conception of human development: consciousness and voluntary action. In addition to the capacity to act voluntarily, the motivating sphere of consciousness, which includes emotions, plays an important role in actions, both on a subjective plane and in terms of the individual's contributive actions during collective activity. Given the hoped-for results of the group with respect to SPI, this dimension appears to be essential to consider in analysis and in praxis in order to identify the obstacles and the dynamogenic elements that shape participants' actions.

It also seems that contributing to a collective transformative activity can restore participants' emotional vitality and sense. Sometimes this vitality was dormant or impeded by negative emotional experiences or by social isolation. Contributing to a collective transformative activity would appear to restore some positive social conflictuality (Duboscq & Clot, 2010). A sense of shared pride in collective success, especially in overcoming a challenge, resolving a contradiction, successfully completing a mock interview perceived as difficult, or being accepted into an educational program, sometimes provoked loud exclamations. These situations allowed the participants to come into contact with each other and to live positive and collectively intense emotional experiences. The participants' recognition, through their awareness of the reliable, secure and unconditional affective bonds created through collective activity, also created a feeling of belonging and security which, as (Michaud et al., 2012) have suggested, may be associated with the love sphere of Honneth's model of social recognition (2002):

> The intersubjective experience of love opens the individual to this fundamental space of emotional security that allows a person not only to experience, but also to quietly manifest his needs and feelings, thus ensuring the psychic condition of the development of all other attitudes of self-respect. (p. 131)

In keeping with Holodynski (2013), this emotional security and space to express needs and feelings seems to have stimulated subjective readiness to take action towards SPI.

5 Conclusion

In the present chapter, I have emphasized the centrality of emotion during activity and as a source and object of learning that can lead to development. The proposed methodological strategy serves to trace back the functions and movement of emotions—and their links with linguistic instruments—on the social and collective as well as subjective planes of activity. This proposition permits to address the challenge of conceiving the subject and her or his emotional activity in relation to concrete collective material activity in accordance with the CHAT dialectical perspective. It also reaffirms the unity of affective and intellectual processes as stressed by Vygotsky (1987) and González Rey (2016). Furthermore, it shows the importance of collective activity and the positive role of contradiction in opening an affective zone of proximal development for participants that dynamizes actions towards social and professional integration. Furthermore, in relation with freedom and social justice, the results show that consciousness and progressive mastery of emotions seems to create a movement from an initial sense of powerlessness to engagement and a progressive power to act. Participants notably carry out certain actions to defend their rights and overcome structural barriers. This research—involving deep engagement with a career group intervention—seems to respond to a central aim of CHAT research, which is "to understand how to create conditions for full human development" (Chaiklin, 2012, p. 33). The participants act in the present to create a future (Stetsenko, 2016) marked by greater justice and that will be more meaningful in term of what they want for themselves, their families and their communities.

6 How Does the Chapter Address the Challenges of a Non-Dualist Methodology?

The author addresses the dialectical perspective of CHAT methodology and living praxis to conceptualize the inextricable relation between emotions, thought, and actions in the course of human development and activity. Building on the work of Vygotsky, Dionne focuses on the dimension of the motivating sphere of consciousness, which is conceived in a dialectical relation with concrete material collective activity, notably through the mediation of linguistic systematic instruments. Regarding the dialectical link with social activity, the author discusses the relation between emotions and consciousness by discussing the affective dimension of the concept of zone of proximal development. This chapter is anchored in the analysis of a group intervention aimed at the social and occupational integration of women survivors of domestic violence in situations of long-term unemployment. In this context, the meaning of emotion is an object of learning. Before they participate in the program, adults can be affected negatively, for example by their unemployment, without being conscious of their emotions. As such, counsellors, with the help of other participants, contribute generating spaces and linguistic instruments that help participants to conceive of and gradually master their emotions, and especially the ones linked with their biographical experience of exclusion from the labor market. These linguistic instruments are both concepts and action systems, both theoretical and practical, which help participants raise their consciousness of emotions embedded in collective and subjective actions. Indeed, being conscious of the paralyzing role of their emotions can help to create a movement to restore the power to act. The results also show another dialectical relation between emotions and collective activity in the social and professional integration (SPI) group. Taking part in a collective transformative activity, more specifically during a collective community project, can restore participants' emotional vitality and sense. A sense of shared pride in collective and subjective success, for instance in overcoming contradictions, allows participants to live positive and collectively intense emotional experiences. Those emotions are linked together in purposeful actions toward SPI. This chapter reaffirms one important CHAT underpinning: the unity of affective and intellectual processes during collective and subjective activity. Furthermore, it shows the importance of engagement in collective activity and the positive role of contradiction in stimulating actions toward social and professional integration. The researcher discusses how this living praxis of CHAT has generated many emotions for her and how they can be useful for the research process, when their sense is analyzed. All of this entails that one must accept to be affected by emotions and, in turn, to affect them through our research practices.

Acknowledgments

The author offers her most sincere thanks to the participants and advisors involved in this research. She is deeply grateful for the discussions with Frédéric Saussez, Sylvain Bourdon and Guylaine Michaud that have enriched this work.

Notes

1 We define an action system as follows: "A conceptual and therefore systematic organisation of actions linked together by a principle of intelligibility, which connects the actions to be taken according to already established knowledge (Barbier, 2000), here the knowledge associated with SPI situations. The intelligibility principle that underlies the system allows individuals to develop a more conscious and voluntary relationship to their actions and to understand the effectiveness of these actions in a given social context" (Dionne et al., 2017).
2 Capitalized in the journal.
3 Now Services Québec.

References

Blunden, A. (2016). Translating perezhivania into English. *Mind, Culture, and Activity, 23*(4), 3–12. doi:10.1080/10749039.2016.1186193

Blustein, D. L. (2006). *The psychology of working: A new perspective for career development, counseling, and public policy.* Lawrence Erlbaum.

Chaiklin, S. (2012). Dialectics, politics and contemporary cultural-historical research, exemplified through Marx and Vygotski. In H. Daniels (Ed.), *Vygotsky and sociology* (pp. 24–43). Routledge.

Davydov, V. V. (2005). The content and unsolved problems of activity theory. In Y. Engeström, R. Miettinen, & R.-L. Punamäki (Eds.), *Perspectives on activity theory* (pp. 39–51). Cambridge University Press.

Dionne, P. (2015). *Le groupe d'insertion sociale et professionnelle : apprentissages et développement au cœur de l'activité collective des personnes en situation de chômage de longue durée* [Doctoral dissertation]. Université de Sherbrooke.

Dionne, P., & Bourdon, S. (2018). Contradictions as the driving force of collective and subjective development group employment programmes. *Journal of Education and Work, 31*(3), 277–290. doi:10.1080/13639080.2018.1468071

Dionne, P., & Jornet, A. (2019). Conceiving work as (an) activity: Epistemological underpinnings from a cultural-historical perspective. In P. F. Bendassolli (Ed.), *Culture, work and psychology: Invitations to dialogue* (pp. 37–57). Information Age Publishing.

Dionne, P., Saussez, F., & Bourdon, S. (2017). Reconversion et développement du pouvoir d'agir par l'apprentissage de systèmes d'action en groupe de réinsertion sociale et professionnelle. *L'Orientation scolaire et professionnelle, 46*(3). doi:10.4000/osp.5475

Duboscq, J., & Clot, Y. (2010). L'autoconfrontation croisée comme instrument d'action au travers du dialogue : objets, adresses et gestes renouvelés. *Revue d'anthropologie des connaissances, 4*(2), 255–286. doi:10.3917/rac.010.0255

Dupuis, A., Dionne, P., & Saussez, F. (2021). L'intervention groupale pour la prévention de l'anxiété en milieu scolaire : une analyse critique des écrits. *Canadian Journal of Career Development, 20*(2), 40–58. https://doi.org/10.53379/cjcd.2021.96

Elias, N. (1993). *Engagement et distanciation*. Presses Universitaires de France.

Engeström, Y., & Sannino, A. (2011). Discursive manifestations of contradictions in organizational change efforts: A methodological framework. *Journal of Organizational Change Management, 24*(3), 368–387. doi:10.1108/09534811111132758

Fleer, M., González Rey, F., & Veresov, N. (2017). Perezhivanie, emotions and subjectivity: Setting the stage. In M. Fleer, F. González Rey, & N. Veresov (Eds.), *Perezhivanie, emotions and subjectivity: Advancing Vygotsky's legacy* (pp. 1–15). Springer.

Flores, L. Y. (2009). Empowering life choice: Career counseling in the context of race and class. In N. C. Gysbers, M. J. Heppner, & J. A. Johnston (Eds.), *Career counseling: Contexts, processes, and techniques* (pp. 49–74). American Counseling Association.

Gale, N., Heath, G., Cameron, E., Rashid, S., & Redwood, S. (2013). Using the framework method for the analysis of qualitative data in multi-disciplinary health research. *BMC Medical Research Methodology, 12*(117). doi:10.1186/1471-2288-13-117

González Rey, F. (2016). Advancing the topics of social reality, culture, and subjectivity from a cultural-historical standpoint: Moments, paths, and contradictions. *Journal of Theoretical and Philosophical Psychology, 36*(3), 175–189. doi:10.1037/teo0000045

Holodynski, M. (2013). The internalization theory of emotions: A cultural historical approach to the development of emotions. *Mind, Culture, and Activity, 20*(1), 4–38. doi:10.1080/10749039.2012.745571

Honneth, A. (2002). *La lutte pour la reconnaissance*. Édition du Cerf.

Jornet, A., & Roth, W.-M. (2016). Perezhivanie—a monist concept for a monist theory. *Mind, Culture, and Activity, 23*(4), 353–355. doi:10.1080/10749039.2016.1199703

Langlois, I., & Villotti, P. (2022). Oppressions et barrières systémiques en relation d'aide pour les populations marginalisées : Une revue de la portée. *Canadian Journal of Career Development, 21*(1), 20–39. https://doi.org/10.53379/cjcd.2022.227

Levykh, M. (2008). The affective establishment and maintenance of Vygotsky's zone of proximal development. *Educational Theory, 58*(1), 83–101. doi:10.1111/j.1741-5446.2007.00277.x

Lui, F., & Maitis, S. (2010). Non participant observation. In J. Albert, G. Durepos, & E. Weibe (Eds.), *Encyclopedia of case study research, Vol. 2*. Sage.

Magiolino, L. L. S., & Smolka, A. L. B. (2013). How do emotions signify? Social relations and psychological functions in the dramatic constitution of subjects. *Mind, Culture, and Activity, 20*(1), 96–112. doi:10.1080/10749039.2012.743155

Meijers, F. (2002). Career learning in a changing world: The role of emotions. *International Journal for the Advancement of Counselling, 24*(3), 149–167. doi:10.1023/A:1022970404517

Michaud, G., Bélisle, R., Garon, S., Bourdon, S., & Dionne, P. (2012). *Développement d'une approche visant à mobiliser la clientèle dite éloignée du marché du travail*. http://erta.ca/sites/default/files/2017-04/michaud-belisle-garon-bourdon-dionne-rapportsynthesepcm2012.pdf

Orly-Louis, I. (2015). Activité dialogique et micro-improvisations en entretien de conseil en orientation. *Activités, 12*(1), 3–23. doi:10.4000/activites.973

Patton, W., & McMahon, M. (2014). *Career development and systems theory: Connecting theory and practice* (3rd ed.). Sense Publishers.

Paul, K. I., & Moser, K. (2009). Unemployment impairs mental health: Metaanalyses. *Journal of Vocational Behavior, 74*(3), 264–282. doi:10.1016/j.jvb.2009.01.001

Puffer, K. A. (2015). Facilitating emotional awareness in a career counseling context. *Journal of Career Assessment, 23*(2), 265–280. doi:10.1177/1069072714535027

Roche, P. (2016). *La puissance d'agir au travail*. Éres.

Roth, W.-M. (2009). On the inclusion of emotions, identity, and ethico-moral dimensions of actions. In A. Sannino, H. Daniels, & K. D. Gutiérrez (Eds.), *Learning and expanding with activity theory* (pp. 53–71). Cambridge University Press.

Roth, W.-M., & Jornet, A. (2017). *Understanding educational psychology: A late Vygotskian, Spinozist approach*. Springer.

Saussez, F. (2017). La zone de développement la plus proche : une contribution de Vygotski à l'approche par l'activité ? In J.-M. Barbier & M. Durand (Eds.), *Encyclopédie d'analyse des activités* (pp. 911–920). Presses Universitaires de France.

Stetsenko, A. (2016). *The transformative mind: Expanding Vygotsky's approach to development and education*. Cambridge University Press.

Vygotsky, L. S. (1986). *Thought and language*. MIT Press.

Vygotsky, L. S. (1987). *The collected works of L. S. Vygotsky: Vol. 1. Problems of general psychology*. Springer.

Vygotsky, L. S. (1997a). *The collected works of L.S. Vygotsky: Vol. 3. Problems of the theory and history of psychology*. Plenum Press.

Vygotsky, L. S. (1997b). *The collected works of L.S. Vygotsky: Vol. 4. The history of the development of higher mental functions*. Plenum Press.

Vygotsky, L. S. (2003). Psychisme, conscience et inconscient. In Y. Clot (Ed.), *Conscience, inconscient et émotions* (pp. 95–121). La Dispute.

CHAPTER 7

Decision-Forming Processes Leading to Peer Mentorship

Sylvie Barma, Marie-Caroline Vincent and Samantha Voyer

Abstract

The purpose of this study illustrates the relevance of giving voice to emotions when teachers expand their professional development and become mentors. We share our analysis of a long-time span study in the field to understand how events are worked over when conflicting emotions emerge. Members of a research team question and make sense of new educational policies, co-design and implement curricular artefacts engaging in expansive resolution of conflicts of motives. The results show that teachers redefine the borders of their praxis as new contexts and broader layers of influence are reached. The experiential trajectory is reconstructed through the dialectical analysis of their discourse. Giving voice to the emotional experience brought to light the relation between perezhivanie and the social situation of their professional development. The emotional experience or the act of experiencing is related not only to the personal characteristics of the individual but also to the environment. The results press that individual and collective process is characterized by revolutionary leaps. An interesting potential for research in education is to document how teachers work over conflicts of motives to engage in building second stimuli to create new ideas, to produce artefacts, and new teaching strategies to transcend paralyzing situations. In complex research settings where boundaries between researchers and participants get blurred, CHAT is fruitful as a developmental methodology when pinpointing the anchors of agency at the core of resolution of conflicts of motives.

Keywords

agency – conflicts of motives – double stimulation – expansive learning – perezhivanie

1 Some Elements of Context: *Building Site 7*

As researchers doing CHAT in the field and engaging in collaborative endeavors with teachers who voice a need for professional development despite a busy and sometimes difficult teaching practice, we face challenging theoretical and methodological issues witnessing how emotions are key to their practice. One of those challenges is to understand the complexity of teachers' practice and their motivation to engage into change (Barma et al., 2015). Teachers' practice is a controversial issue at the heart of societal debates in Quebec (Conseil supérieur de l'Éducation, 2014). Audio and videotaped one year after the beginning of our collaboration with two teachers, this excerpt gives voice to one of the participant's motivation to collaborate with us. The discourse of the participant teachers was analyzed using a French-language adaptation of the methodological framework for analyzing discursive manifestations of contradictions that highlight teachers' resistance to change (conflicts, critical conflicts, double binds and dilemmas), and also the formation of agency (Engeström & Sannino, 2011).

> I find teaching science is difficult. I have never fully got used to working with young people who are sometimes ungrateful, and other times very thankful. I came to the conclusion that, if I could not get used to it after all these years, I had to change my practice so they would react differently. (Simon, Teacher 1, March 2011)

Interestingly enough, Simon (Teacher 1) expresses a dilemma and a double-bind. His only way out is to engage into change. This discussion took place three years after the implementation of a challenging educational reform in 2006 in science and technology (ST) and led to some resistance on the part of the teachers (Barma, 2011). In the aftermath of the curricular implementation, the leading researcher engaged in a school-university partnership from 2010 to 2017 with a small group of ST teachers who co-produced curricular materials they shared with their peers through eight teacher professional education workshops. The funds originated from the Ministry of Education and the funding program was designated *Chantier 7*, a French metaphor that we take the liberty to translate as *Building site 7*. *Building site 7* was aimed at universities interested in developing and implementing continuing education projects for school personnel (teaching staff, school principals, professional staff and counselors and preschool educators) in primary or secondary education. Competing academics who were granted money were to support the design, the deployment and the evaluation of teacher-training projects based on a strong partnership with the school community (project MEESR, 2015). These projects could take the form of action research and collaborative research with the goal to understand, explain, modify or improve the professional practice of the school community and support the school personnel involved.

2   A Necessary Detour toward the Quebec Science and Technology Program

In 2006, the prescriptions of the Quebec Science and Technology programme challenged science teachers. Having been educated and trained at universities to teach disciplinary content, the new programme merged six "traditional disciplinary science fields" into one high school teaching subject.[1] Biology, chemistry, physics, physical geography, astronomy and technological design were now part of the same teaching content, namely Science and technology (Ministère de l'Éducation du Loisir et du Sport, 2007). Science teachers were now asked to integrate technological design process methods during class-workshops to support the appropriation of scientific concepts through the development of three disciplinary competencies.

> The first competency focuses on the methodology used to solve scientific and technological problems. The students become familiar with concepts and strategies in a hands-on approach [...]. The second competency focuses on the students' ability to conceptualize and apply what they have learned in science and in technology, especially when dealing with everyday issues [...] The third competency involves the different types of languages used in science and technology, which are essential for sharing information as well as interpreting and producing scientific or technological messages. (Ministère de l'Éducation du Loisir et du Sport, 2007, pp. 3–4)

A good majority of ST teachers did not have any training on machine tools or much knowledge of technological techniques like graphical language and manufacturing (Conseil supérieur de l'Éducation, 2013). In the ministerial textbooks they were handed, they learned that technological processes were the means and method used to perform a task or obtain a concrete result like a technical object, a system, a product or a manufacturing process. The technological design process was to be used by students when a need was identified. Once it was done, students had to take into account any conditions and constraints in the specifications with the goal of "finding solutions to operational and construction problems, defining shapes, determining the necessary materials, and designing parts" (Ministère de l'Éducation du Loisir et du Sport, 2007, p. 16). A rapid and top-down implementation destabilized a lot of science teachers (Conseil supérieur de l'Éducation, 2013). The Ministry of Education missed out on providing teacher training sessions: from teaching ecology, biology or physical sciences, their teacher's identity would be referred to as Science and Technology teachers. Technology was viewed as a means to support the learning of science concepts. This chapter does not document how teachers view the status of technology as a discipline when teaching science through technological design. The Quebec Education Programme (QEP) positioned itself by stating that Science and Technology were two different theoretical and practical domains although technology provided a fruitful context for the appropriation of scientific concepts.[2]

In this context, we established a partnership with a school district in Quebec for seven years (2010–2017) and with the agreement of their principals and the director responsible for their respective school district, two ST teachers and a pedagogical counselor joined our research team. By doing so, they accepted to adopt new roles on a daily basis: they became curriculum material developers, not only for their own interests with their students but to model teacher-training workshops once or twice a year. Fifty percent of the money granted to the leading researcher was used to unburden their teaching load. Approximately twenty percent of their teaching task was dedicated to the design and the production of technical objects[3] that would meet the curricular demands as well as learning and evaluation situations[4] (LES) to support the learning of concepts and the development of disciplinary competencies. The prototypes produced (wooden microscopes, wind turbines, colorimeters, electronic devises) and their corresponding LES were tested and validated by the participant teachers with their high school students.

Over the seven years, sharing and giving visibility to their work motivated them to 'think outside the box.' The first phase of *Building site 7* (2010–2012) consisted in co-modeling and implementing seven days of continuous training addressed to teachers in the school district. Simon and Jane (teacher 2) and the pedagogical counselor (Francis) worked an average of eight hours a week with the research team in the preparation of three training sessions. It brought together 92 teachers, six pedagogical counselors and 11 lab technicians. More than 1000 high school students benefited from the follow up provided by the research team. The teachers started to be known by their peers and their competency in helping others was recognized. In view of the very encouraging results obtained during the first phase of the project, Simon, Jane and Francis made available to their colleagues the resources presented during the training sessions.[5] Forty-one science teachers implemented the projects in their classroom and allowed the research team to gather data (qualitative and quantitative). In that light, the second phase (2012–2014) focused on sharing and following up the projects as well as co-modeling a new training workshop. Visibility was gained as the participants co-presented at a scientific conference with the research team. The third phase (2015–2017) aimed at continuity, reinvestment and sharing of the best practices developed in order to decrease professional isolation and better support science teachers. School principals tagged along and a community of practice was identified as an important center for sharing and discussing the issue of teachers' professional development.

Below, is an excerpt transcribed from a videotaped session at the end of the research project. This excerpt is an example of the expansion of the activity in which the participants got involved: Francis, the pedagogical counselor, discusses with the leading researcher and one of the participant teachers. He reflects on what *he considers* is their great accomplishments.

> What is great, is that they [the two teachers] came to the AESTQ[6] conference with me. It's not only that they did something in their classes: they became multipliers. It's rewarding for them because there is not much valorization at the school level. Participating in conferences is good and they have become role models in their community. Other teachers from the school district see their names in the conference program and they think: 'I, too, would like to do that' […] We have built a small community at the school district level, together, quietly, not going too fast. (Francis, Pedagogical counselor, June 2017)

As Francis expresses it, over the seven years, the participant teachers became 'mentors' to their peers in their respective school communities and across Quebec. They even went as far as being invited in November 2017, by the Minister of Education who had heard about them because of the visibility they were giving to their school, to discuss their vision of professional development in science education. Interestingly enough, the initial research project supposedly situated at the local level in Quebec City overflowed to the Provincial level in every geographic direction as the demand for professional development for ST teachers increased (see the circle and the black lines in Figure 7.1).

The members of the research team collaborated closely with the two teachers and the pedagogical counselor as they questioned and made sense of the new educational policies, co-designed and implemented curricular materials (artifacts and teaching strategies). More than 170 teachers, lab technicians and pedagogical counselors coming from 15 school districts benefited from five

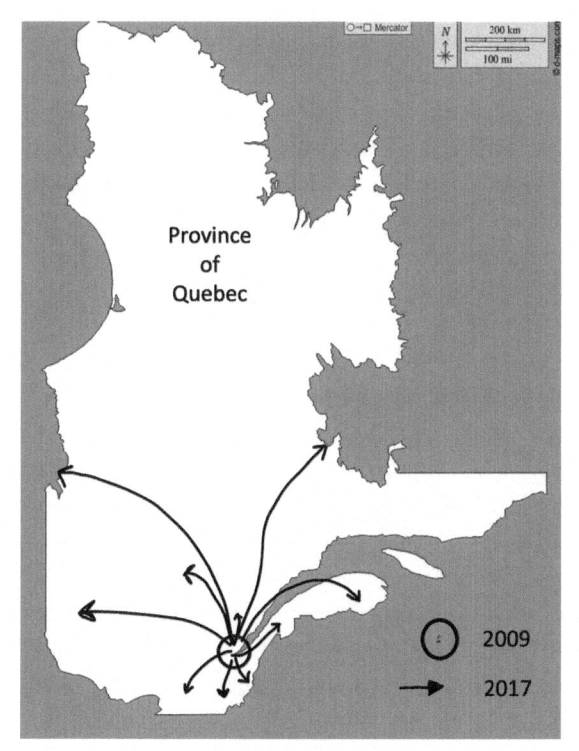

FIGURE 7.1   The geographic expansion of *Building site 7*, a 'collaborative action' research project (2010–2017)

continuous education workshops co-produced by the participants for their peers' benefit. They created websites to gather twenty-two lessons accompanied by tutorials, videos and other useful documents, including shopping lists to help their peers.[7]

3   Focus and Approach of the Chapter

The complexity of the development of *Building site 7* challenged us as a research team. Documenting the emergence of agency in a multilayered individual|collective activity is daunting. How is a research team to address possible fruitful methodological issues to close the gap between the praxis and the theoretical discussions that inform it? This chapter presents how we documented and analyzed the decision-forming process of three participants who engaged in mentorship with their peers and how they reflected on it. The result section reconstructs the narrative of Simon and Jane's experience of mentorship and the meaning they attributed to it as they managed to resolve conflicting motives related to contextual events or interpersonal situations at work. It revealed a lot of emotional hardships and it led us to investigate more into the identification of their emotional experiences in the form of tensions, especially conflicts of motives. This is why we dedicate sections to agency, perezhivanie, and analytical issues related to the development of their mentoring activity. The analysis of the ethnographic data revealed how crucial the emotional experience is when teachers overcome tensions in the form of conflicts of motives to engage into professional development.

4   Developmental Work Research and Double Stimulation to Address Complexity in Praxis

With the announcement of the grant proposal, the Ministry of Education defined the type of research that was to be conducted: collaborative action-research. However, over the course of the seven years, our actions went beyond collaborating and agreeing on what was happening in the field. We intervened regularly and the development of the participants' agency was closely related to our inputs. The methodological approach adopted was in sympathy with Development Work Research (DWR), an interventionist research method consistent with double stimulation to allow participants to move away from an "every day" vision of their work practice and into a "scientific" vision by which they can gain an understanding of what they are doing in their usual activities at work (Engeström & Sannino, 2011; Vygotsky, 1986). DWR suggests the need for collaborative work between the interventionist research team and the participants to identify and address problems encountered in their work environment and create new tools or signs to solve them. CHAT stresses the need to view social activity as a series of interrelated events having to be described as such in order to appropriately reflect the reality at hand. Sannino, Daniels, and Gutiérrez (2009) point out that

> The 'second series stimuli' offered in DWR are the conceptual tools of activity theory provided by the workshop facilitators to enable participants to analyze and make sense of their practices, the objects of those practices, and the organizational features that shape them. (pp. 204–205)

DWR focuses primarily on collective transformation and work development to design a new form of activity with a focus on the object and the motive of the activity (Engeström, 1987/2015).

Vygotsky's principle of double stimulation, an epistemological principal in 3rd generation activity theory, is fruitful to understand how agency emerges when an individual constructs a second stimulus in response to a problem involving a conflict of motives (Barma et al., 2015). Double stimulation refers to the mechanism with which human beings break out of difficult situations and transform them (Sannino & Laitinen, 2015). This principle "refers to the mechanism whereby human beings can intentionally emerge from a conflict situation and change the circumstances in which they find themselves or solve problems" (Engeström & Sannino, 2013, p. 6, author's translation). A researcher can also make use of double stimulation as a means to elicit agency with participants (Virkkunen & Newnham, 2013).

In Vygotsky's theory, an initial stimulus situation involves a conflict of motives (Vygotsky, 1997). The conflict is resolved by invoking a neutral artifact as a second stimulus which is turned into a mediating sign by investing it with meaning. Overall, we can say that the challenges addressed by Simon, Jane and Francis ensured that highschool science students would integrate technological design processes; contextualizing the appropriation of concepts despite pressure to perform during the exam sessions (problem situation). For example, the neutral artifact acting as a second stimulus like a prototype (wooden microscope, wind turbine) makes it possible for teachers to give meaning to the problem they face and engage in agentive actions to prepare teachers' professional workshops. The wooden microscope conceived by the Simon, Francis and Jane appeared to be a great way to integrate woodwork and technical skill to the appropriation of scientific concepts like lenses and the observation of unicellulars. Simon's engagement in the *Building site 7* project gave him the space and the time to model new teaching strategies, test them with his students and share his work with his peers and the research team. The three of them were convinced of the relevance of their work, but were concerned about how they could engage their peers in order to exploit the prototypes produced in their respective classrooms.

In order to address this question, we draw from Vygotsky's premises (1987) who maintains that emotions are the traits that characterize how individuals perceive life. Vygotsky's premises also offer a framework for transformative social activity, the expansive resolution of conflicts of motives (Barma et al., 2015), and the principle of double stimulation (Sannino, 2015). We will illustrate some key moments in the decision forming process of Simon, Jane and Francis over the years that led to transformative, agentive actions.

5 Agency and Teacher's Practice

An increasing body of studies have recently focused on how teachers engage in transformative agency to envision and bring about new forms of curricular materials. "Transformative agency may be defined as breaking away from the given frame of action and taking the initiative to transform it" (Engeström, 1987/2015, p. XXIII). Severance et al. (2016) have documented that more democratic forms of participation are necessary for teachers to co-design curricular artefacts and demonstrate agency. In their study, CHAT is used as a theory and a methodology to organize and lever the expertise of teachers as they face an educational reform. The authors investigate how tools and activities their team designed, could help teachers break away from their current practice. These artifacts were used as a first stimulus to trigger teachers' agency.

Teaching practice is complex and it is unlikely that a teacher will manage to break away from a challenging situation in a single attempt. Beijaard et al. (2004) suggest four features for the redefinition of teacher's professional identity development: (1) professional identity is an ongoing process of interpretation and re-interpretation of experiences; (2) professional identity implies both person and context; (3) teacher's professional identity consists of sub-identities that more or less harmonize—the notion of sub-identities relates to teachers' pedagogies according to different contexts and relationships; and (4) agency is an important element of professional identity, meaning that teachers have to be active in the process of professional development. The boundaries between these four features can reveal blurry and closely intertwine when examining the previous excerpts who give good indications of dual elements, opposing forces, clashing contextual elements in the emotional experience of Simon and Francis.

Building on Leontiev's (2005) reflections on conflicts of motives, Sannino (2015) brings to our attention that engaging into volitional actions is more than just about "choice and decision making" (p. 15). Making a choice supposes that "duality is at the very foundation of the volitional act, and this duality becomes especially prominent and vivid whenever several motives, several opposing strivings, clash in our consciousness" (Vygotsky, 1997, pp. 167–168). Conflicts of motives are important components in Vygotsky's principle of double stimulation and key elements to trigger agency. They act as first stimulus to begin the process of will formation (Barma et al., 2015; Sannino, 2015).

Konopasky and Sheridan (2016) offer another point of view in a study focused on how teachers' agency is often limited when a new curriculum is implemented. The teachers do not always feel able to control, or even want to define or reshape, the educational policies. The implementation of a new educational curriculum often means making sure members of a school community adhere to the proposed changes and are ready to invest time in developing new teaching practices: two potential obstacles to innovation according to Brandt-Pomares et al. (2008). It is not easy to engage in professional development or new forms of collaboration when new conceptual resources or tools are made available to practitioners (Edwards, 2010). Barma et al. (2015) document how two science teachers hesitated during eighteen months before accepting to change their pedagogical strategy in class just for a short period of time (5 weeks) and take agentive actions to implement a novel instructional strategy to address the issue of climate change. Interestingly enough, even if the teachers' initial conflicts of motives were resolved, unexpected ones emerged and reached another level of the school community. Barma (2008, 2011); Barma et al. (2015) document that a strong motive orienting the activity of science teachers' practices lies in increasing the students' interest in science.

Tensions play an important role when teachers are striving to change and express a desire to transcend them. Below, Simon and Francis are reflecting on the pertinence of using a project based teaching strategy to engage students in the appropriation of the new curricular prescriptions. Their discussion turns out to be emotional and reveals conflictual elements in their discourse, even to the point of almost reaching a critical conflict. If the reader recalls, the first excerpt at the beginning of the chapter clearly indicated that Simon had to change his teaching strategies in order to cope with his unsatisfactory professional situation. He felt ashamed of teaching science badly. The government and the school board seemed to negatively affect his intentions through their emphasis of the importance of students' results to ministerial tests. After three years of involvement in the research project, Simon expressed a feeling of powerlessness in that situation. There was an important clash between his expectations in terms of teaching activities and the actual topics evaluated in the Provincial tests.

Simon: The question I asked myself when I teach science to align with the new curricular policies is: To what extent can my projects benefit young people? [hesitation] ... I ended up not doing any projects at first because I focused on the theoretical aspects of the new science program I had to teach.

Researcher: I see ...

Simon: The students, didn't like it. So, I thought to myself: I'm not good at this, I teach science badly. Even now, you know ... there are limits ... and I hit a wall because I know that the main goal of the government *is to find out if you are good or not good when students' results to tests are published and schools publicly ranked in the newspapers every year.* If I shared this with anyone who does not teach science, they would see that there is a gap between one of the projects I would like to share with my students, and the ministerial evaluation task expected to be answered on paper in June.

Researcher: So, what do you do to face the pressure that is put on your performance when it comes to your students' grades?
Francis: I started to network with teachers on the ground. Those who put the most sticks in my wheels, it was those who were furthest from the class.
Simon: Yes, it takes intermediaries to help, because it's not the school board that is going to help you (May 8th, 2012).

In this example, the conflicting issue linked to assessment ended up being transcended by demonstrating relational agency with colleagues "on the ground." It is interesting to document how the participants reflect on their teaching practices. Hartley (2009) has argued that it is hard for teachers to change their routine, especially since organizational structures and pedagogical processes have proved resistant to change; the excerpts illustrate the double bind in which the teacher and the pedagogical counselor were embedded.

These reflections bring to the surface the existence of a basic inner contradiction in the teacher and pedagogical counselor object-oriented-activity between two competing teaching strategies for the production of a new form of school activity: teaching to prepare students for the test *versus* teaching in accordance to one's personal conviction or motivation for the benefit of the student. The activity of the science teachers is still defined by their ability to have students perform at provincial standardized tests and assess disciplinary content (Barma, Power, & Daniel, 2010). Nevertheless, teachers are expected to act as professionals which means they have the capacity to reflect on their practice (Guo, 2008). If they do so, they open a space for questioning the emphasis put on assessment and consider modelling new forms of teaching activities. Barma et al. (2015) document how agency emerges when teachers feel trapped or when they feel resistance in their practice and demonstrate a will to gain control over them.

6   Perezhivanie as a Way to 'Work Over' Conflicts of Motives

Vygotsky thought that emotion was a function of the personality; a function of the subject and not an instrument. He considered that emotions and human development are mutually connected to each other and that "thinking and action" are not different things that interact (Jornet & Roth, 2016, p. 353). Jornet and Roth underline the contribution of Vygotsky's late work on the relation between perezhivanie and the social situation of children development. The development is more characterized by "revolutionary leaps" that going in circle and in line with Vygotsky's dialectical premises. The individual formulates and interprets his experiences through emotional and cognitive means which in turn, lead to new experiences (meta-experiences). Vasilyuk (1988) describes perezhivanie as the act of "experiencing." We are very much in sympathy with the latter and it orients our understanding of teacher engaging in professional development. Even if Vygotsky worked with children, the concept of perezhivanie seems fruitful with adults too: emotions dominate aspects of an individual's life. The emotional experience or the "act of experiencing" is related not only to the personal characteristics of the individual but also to his/her environment. In engaging into agentive actions, individuals bring to their environment different meanings and roles that will change the relationship they maintain. An interesting potential for research in science education is to document how teachers work over conflicts of motives to engage in building second stimuli to create new ideas, to produce artifacts, new teaching strategies so they transcend their initial paralyzing situations. It is potentially an example of "the inseparable integration of thinking, emotions, imagination, and fantasy, which express the history of the individual [...] perezhivanie as the aggregate of all the characteristics of the personality with all the characteristics of the environment" (González Rey, 2016, p. 5). González Rey (2016) refers to it as a concept of the "social situation of development" and a new way of defining motivation.

Clarà (2016) brings more depth to the concept of perezhivanie by stipulating that its' definition is the fact of experiencing struggles, more precisely the action taken by an individual when facing an unmanageable situation in order to regain his psychological balance. Going back to the focus of our study, these are strong premises to consider the participant's development of workshops for their peers as a creative performance and a transformative process. González Rey (2016) mentions that perezhivanie brings a new definition to motivation where the motive is the emotional and intellectual organization of a psychic function used to engage the individual in. Why couldn't the "performance" be the co-modelling of technical objects, websites go beyond the "encapsulated" form of traditional learning common in our schools? However, this definition does not seem to be complete because Vygotsky states that perezhivanie is mediated by meanings. The situation becomes critical for an individual only when he perceives it as such as in the case for Simon: that is the contradiction he feels between wanting to teach for the benefit of the students instead of teaching to the test. The influence of an environment is therefore not objective but rather centered on the meaning attributed and formed by the individual. In the context of this chapter, we approached perezhivanie as an act of experiencing the resolution of conflicts of motives and engage in the production of concrete artifacts shared with peers during and after professional development workshops.

7   Data Collection

Ethnographic data was collected over the seven years in the form of audio-video recordings of teacher training sessions, photographs during co-teaching lessons in the classroom, and artefacts produced by the team (teaching documents, YouTube videos, prototypes, websites, administrative documents, transcripts of interviews with the principals and the follow-up of thousands of emails). Table 7.1 presents the ethnographic data and artefacts produced, analyzed and used to prepare the sessions with the two participant teachers and the pedagogical counselor.

Over the seven years, the DWR research sessions were led by the main researcher or co-led with members of the research team (master or doctoral students).[8] The sessions were in alternance with eight professional development workshops and followed-up with classrooms. Online questionnaire were sent and used as mirror data to inform us on the repercussions of the professional workshops with attending teachers and the students who had experienced the design and analysis of some of the prototypes. Figure 7.2 presents an overview of the DWR of *Building site 7*.

In total, twenty DWR sessions were conducted:
- seven with 52 high-school students who had experimented the technological desing of the prototypes (modelled by the participant teachers, the pedagogical counselor and the research team);
- three sessions with eight pre-service teachers;
- ten with the participant teachers and the pedagogical counselor (Simon, Francis, Jane, the main researcher and five graduate students).

Six online questionnaires were completed by a total of 777 highschool students. Following each professional development workshops, an online questionnaire was sent to the 99 high-school ST teachers who had attended the training workshops: 39 responded. The questions in the questionnaire were targeted to gather information about:
- their opinion of the new curricular prescriptions asking them to make us of technological design to teach science;
- its impact on their work environment, their teaching strategies;
- their need to collaborate with colleagues;
- the time spent to prepare their lessons in the science class given the new curricular prescriptions.

TABLE 7.1 Ethnographic data analyzed and used to prepare the sessions with teachers (2010–2017)

Type of data	School years					
	2010–2011	2011–2012	2012–2013	2013–2014	2016–2017
Questionnaires	Online questionnaires: teacher (14) Questionnaires: students (77)	Online questionnaires: teacher (19)		Online questionnaires: teacher (27) Online questionnaires: students (299) Online questionnaires related to training sessions: students microscope (132) electronic (78) colorimeter (35) wind turbine (73)	Online questionnaires: teacher (39) Online questionnaires: students (304) Online questionnaires related to training sessions: students microscope (148) electronic (79) colorimeter (84) wind turbine (149) iPad (13)
Sessions (audio and videotaped)	Researcher—Teacher (7) Researcher—Students (7)	Researchers—Teachers—Pedagogical counselor (1)	Researchers—Teachers (2) Researchers—Pedagogical counselor (1) Researchers—Professor (1)		Researchers—Teachers (2) Researchers—Pedagogical counselor (2) Researcher—Students (4) Researcher—University Students (3)
Ethnographic notes	22	6	14	18	10
Photos and videos	52		120		10 audio, video recordings 30 photos

(cont.)

TABLE 7.1 Ethnographic data analyzed and used to prepare the sessions with teachers (2010–2017) *(cont.)*

School years

Type of data	2010–2011	2011–2012	2012–2013	2013–2014	2016–2017
Teaching documents co-produced by the research team	Wind turbine: 27 Electronic: 55	Microscope: 35	Colorimeter: 34		iPad: 5
Web site	Wind turbine on Pistes.org	Microscope on Pistes.org	Colorimeter on Pistes.org	5 LES on netsciences.ca	22 LES on netsciences.ca
Administrative documents	Wind turbine: 13 Electronic: 7 E-mails: ≈15/week	Microscope: 4 Meetings reports: 2 E-mails: ≈15/week	Colorimeter: 5 Meetings reports: 4 E-mails: ≈15/week	Follow up documents: 2 Consents form: 6 Recruitments letters: 2 E-mails: ≈15/week	Meetings reports: 2
Speaking Turn	316: researchers 107: teachers 237: students	192: researchers 246: teachers 157: Pedagogical counselor	349: researchers 204: teachers 73: Pedagogical counselor		153: researchers 110: teachers 36: Pedagogical counselor 68: school principal 53: technician

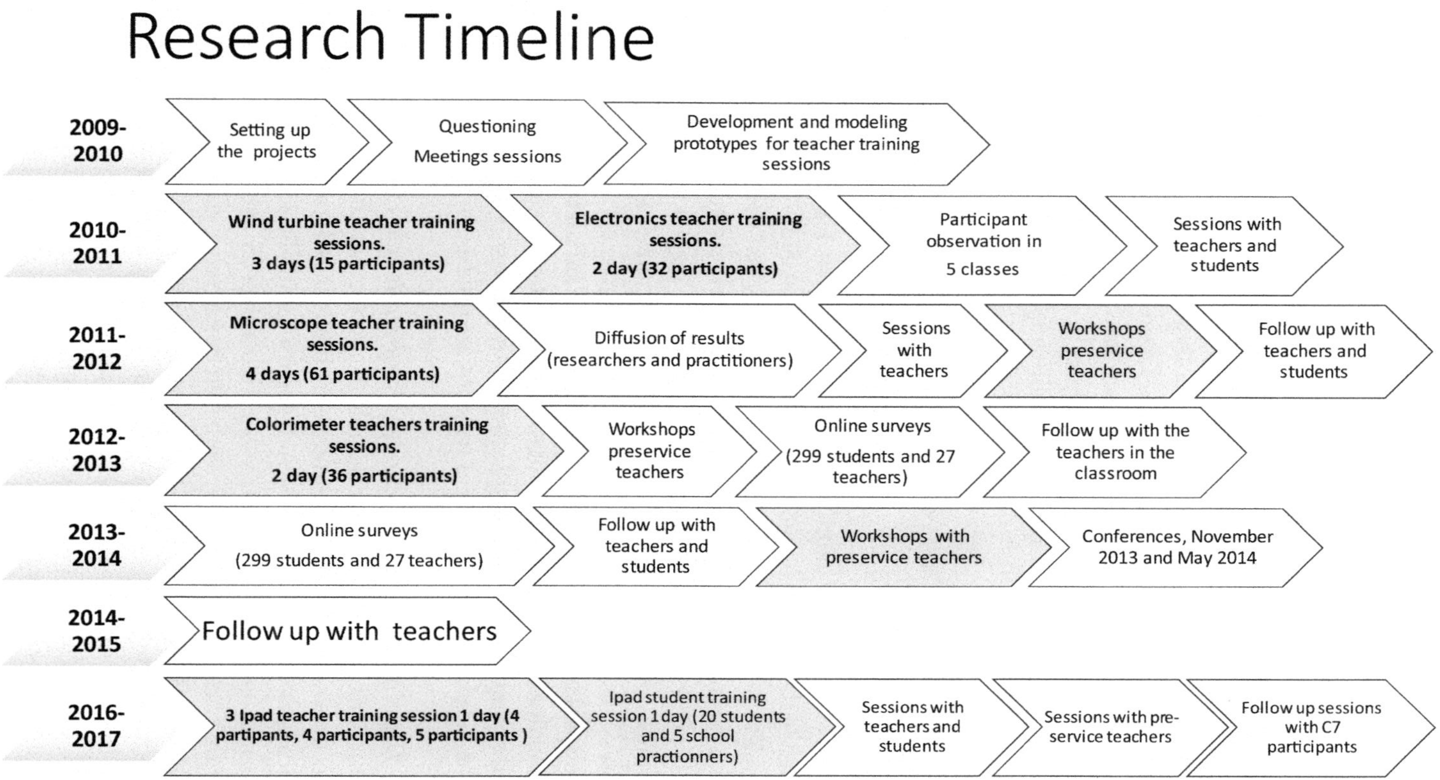

DECISION-FORMING PROCESSES LEADING TO PEER MENTORSHIP 165

Research Timeline

2009–2010: Setting up the projects → Questioning Meetings sessions → Development and modeling prototypes for teacher training sessions

2010–2011: Wind turbine teacher training sessions. 3 days (15 participants) → Electronics teacher training sessions. 2 day (32 participants) → Participant observation in 5 classes → Sessions with teachers and students

2011–2012: Microscope teacher training sessions. 4 days (61 participants) → Diffusion of results (researchers and practitioners) → Sessions with teachers → Workshops preservice teachers → Follow up with teachers and students

2012–2013: Colorimeter teachers training sessions. 2 day (36 participants) → Workshops preservice teachers → Online surveys (299 students and 27 teachers) → Follow up with the teachers in the classroom

2013–2014: Online surveys (299 students and 27 teachers) → Follow up with teachers and students → Workshops with preservice teachers → Conferences, November 2013 and May 2014

2014–2015: Follow up with teachers

2016–2017: 3 Ipad teacher training session 1 day (4 partipants, 4 participants, 5 participants) → Ipad student training session 1 day (20 students and 5 school practitionners) → Sessions with teachers and students → Sessions with pre-service teachers → Follow up sessions with C7 participants

FIGURE 7.2 *Building site 7 (2009–2017): an overview of the DWR and the iterative research interventions (qualitative and quantitative) between teacher professional development workshops (gray) and research activities (white)*

Many formal and informal meetings were also held with the school principals over the seven years.

All the sessions were transcribed and analyzed. The sessions were also key to build mirror data in order to orient the development of the teacher's professional workshops and follow up on the implementation of the LES in the classrooms. They were also key to understand the way the participant teachers collaborated to design the workshops and their repercussions on the colleagues who attended the professional development days.

Table 7.2 presents an overview of the workshops developed over the years and reached more than 170 peers coming from 15 school districts (2010–2017).

Figure 7.3 shows a bricolage of some photographs of the workshops.

8 Discursive Analysis: Two Frameworks to Document the Act of 'Experiencing'

To identify conflicts of motives and document the formation of agency expressed in the discourse, 1756 speaking turns of ten audio-recorded sessions were analyzed. Table 7.3 presents the speaking turns that were analyzed twice. The members of the research team triangulated their categorization by crossing their analysis with a minimum of two others members. Two analytical frameworks were used: dialectical analysis (Engeström & Sannino, 2011) and the expressions of transformative agency (Haapasaari et al., 2016). The analysis of these speaking turns orients the way the results are presented: (1) the dialectical analysis sheds light on the more specific types of tensions expressed by the participants; and (2) the identification of transformative actions helps pinpoint the development of agency as tensions are resolved or remain unsolved.

8.1 *Dialectical Analysis: Discursive Manifestations of Contradictions*

Contradictions are not directly accessible to a researcher: they become visible when recurrent tensions in the discourse are brought to the surface by way of a dialectical analysis (see Figure 7.7). A dialectical contradiction refers to a unity of opposites, opposing forces, or trends within a given evolving system, a point of view that has informed the way verbatim transcripts were examined. Identifying discursive manifestations on the basis of dialectical criteria supposes an attentive reading of the verbatim and the spotting of elements that are, at one and the same time, indissociable and antagonistic (Engeström & Sannino, 2011). Our criteria to select the units of meaning were the presence of opposing forces potentially revealing conflicts of motives in the speaking turn: struggles,

DECISION-FORMING PROCESSES LEADING TO PEER MENTORSHIP 167

TABLE 7.2 Professional development teacher training workshops: 170 peers from 15 school districts (2010–2017)

Participants attending	Wind turbine 2010 October (25–27)	Electronics 2011 January (26–27)	Microscope 2011–2012 November (3–4) January (26–27)	Colorimeter 2012 December (6–7)	IPad 2016 September (30) October (12 & 18)	Total
High-school science teachers	9	19	35	20	16	99
University pre-service teachers	2	0	1	0	5	8
Pedagogical counselors	2	4	7	2	3	18
Civil servant from the Ministry of Education	0	0	0	1	0	1
Lab technicians	2	9	18	13	0	42
Student researchers	0	0	0	0	2	2
Total	15	32	61	36	26	170
Some example of artefacts produced and shared with high-school teachers who attended the workshops						

FIGURE 7.3　The first professional training day begins in Simon's classroom in front of his peers. The main researcher participates the entire day and intervenes to support Simon. Jane and Francis are present to help with the hands-on activities happening in the afternoon (2011)

FIGURE 7.4　Two years later, a new workshop for Simon: the colorimeter. Jane and the leading researcher are also participating (2013)

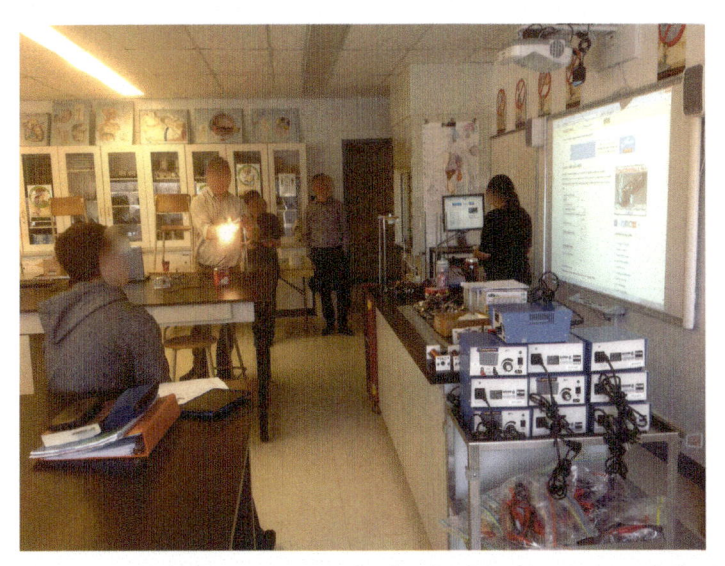

FIGURE 7.5 Intervening in a science and technology classroom outside the Quebec region: Jane, Francis, the research leader and a ST teacher welcoming us in his classroom with students to learn how to optimize the use of and ipad when teaching electromagnetism

FIGURE 7.6 Testing a prototype in robotics with a ST teacher who had attended the professional workshops in 2011. He eventually became a mentor himself and is preparing a workhop at AESTQ for peers. Philip (joins the team of *Building site* 7 in 2017), Francis and the main researcher (2017)

TABLE 7.3 Speaking turns analyzed

Date	Duration	Participants	Speaking turns (Participation %)
09-02-2011	00:02:57	Researcher A Jane	5 (71.43%) 2 (28.57%)
		Total	7
24-02-2011	00:12:45	Researcher A Jane	18 (51.43%) 17 (48.57%)
		Total	35
28-03-2011	00:38:42	Researcher A Simon Researcher B	58 (50%) 57 (49.14%) 1 (0.86%)
		Total	116
08-05-2012	02:10:30	Researcher A Researcher C Jane Simon Francis	177 (29.75%) 15 (2.52%) 92 (15.46%) 154 (25.88%) 157 (26.39%)
		Total	595
15-05-2013	00:37:28	Researcher C Researcher D Jane	89 (44.5%) 15 (7.5%) 96 (48%)
		Total	200

(*cont.*)

TABLE 7.3　Speaking turns analyzed (*cont.*)

Date	Duration	Participants	Speaking turns (Participation %)
15-05-2013	01:10:57	Researcher C	68 (44.16%)
		Researcher D	13 (8.44%)
		Francis	73 (47.40%)
		Total	154
17-05-2013	01:13:04	Researcher D	89 (38.86%)
		Researcher C	32 (13.97%)
		Simon	108 (47.16%)
		Total	229
07-06-2017	00:42:00	Researcher A	19 (31,67%)
		Francis	25 (41,67%)
		Jane	16 (26,67%)
		Total	60
16-06-2017	01:05:00	Francis	11 (18,64%)
		Philip	26 (43,33%)
		Researcher A	22 (37,73%)
		Total	59
21-12-2017	00:33:25	Principal	68 (22,59%)
		Jane	68 (22,59%)
		Lab technician	53 (17,61%)
		Researcher A	112 (31,21%)
		Total	301
Grand total			1756

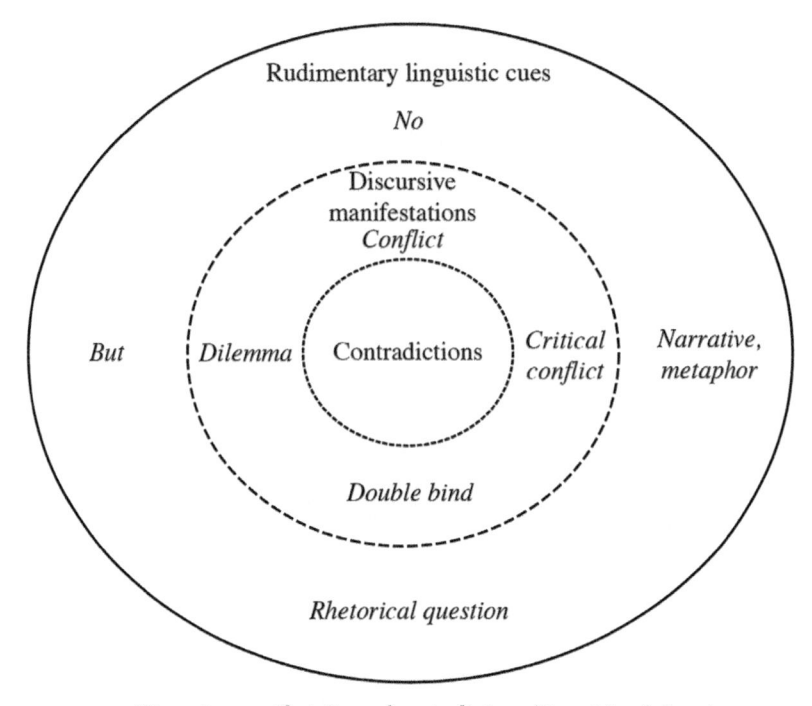

FIGURE 7.7   Discursive manifestations of contradictions (Engeström & Sannino, 2011, p. 375)

obstacles, tensions and clashes (Barma et al., 2015; Engeström & Sannino, 2011). Not all speaking turns were related to expressed tensions: some expressed the transformative agency actions that led to their resolution or to the decision process. An important challenge we faced was to take into account the overlap of the present, the past and the future in the teachers' narration as we reconstructed the narrative (Virkkunen & Newnham, 2013). Periodically, we were able to identify recurrent tensions encountered and how they were resolved. It allowed for a 'reconstruction' of the experiential narrative over the seven years by selecting some excerpts that are presented in the result section to highlight the teachers' recollection of their experience as mentors for their peers.

The discourse of participants was analyzed using a French-language adaptation of the methodological onion of Engeström and Sannino (2011) in order to identify in dilemmas, conflicts, critical conflicts and double binds. To identify the emotional content in the narration, wherein individuals may express their doubts and hesitations, sentences such as "I realize that," "I must," "It had to," etc. give good indications of a discursive manifestation of contradiction. Sometimes, the participant's discourse revealed frustrations in the form of disappointment. In some case there was a high degree of emotionality in their discourse linked to primary contradictions in the object of their mentorship activity related to modelling new tools, proposing new rules and forms of division of labour and how the workshops would end up being implemented in their school district.

Table 7.4 presents an adaptation of Engeström and Sannino (2011) the research team translated to French but is presented in English here.

TABLE 7.4   Discursive manifestations of contradictions: analytical criteria (Engeström & Sannino, 2011)

	Manifestations	Characteristics	Linguistic cues
Linguistic criteria	Double bind	Facing pressing and equally unacceptable alternatives in an activity system. *Resolution*: practical transformation (going beyond words).	Had we known; we could have; that way; we have to; we must.
	Critical conflict	Facing contradictory motives in social interaction, feeling violated or guilty, emotionality. *Resolution*: finding new personal sense and negotiating a new meaning.	I now realize that; put in those terms; admittedly.
	Conflict	Arguing, criticizing. *Resolution*: finding a compromise, submitting to authority or majority.	I disagree; this is not true, no, etc.
	Dilemma	Expression or exchange of incompatible evaluations. *Resolution*: denial, reformulation.	Well; as you like; so saying; I wasn't sure; I didn't know for certain; I didn't mean; what I meant is; on the one hand on the other hand; yes, but.

8.2 Analysis of Expressions of Transformative Agency

To identify the development of agency and help us reconstruct the decision forming process leading to mentoring peers, we adopted Engeström and Sannino (2013) and Haapasaari et al. (2016) categorization of six main forms of participants' emerging agentive actions:

1. criticizing the existing activity: resistance may take the form of questioning, criticism, opposition or rejection in relation to the propositions made by the participants;
2. questioning and resisting suggestions or decisions from the interventionist or the management,
3. explicating new possibilities or potentials in the activity,
4. envisioning new patterns or models for the activity,
5. committing to concrete actions aimed at changing the activity, and;
6. taking consequential actions to change the activity.

The same verbatim were re-examined a second time but focusing on the types of expressions of transformative agency.

9 The Decision-Forming Process of Simon's Experience of Mentoring: Reinvesting His Expertise in Professional Training for the Benefit of Students

Simon joined the research team in 2009. He was the first participant teacher to be recruited in *Building site 7*. Simon became a teacher by accident: he had previously been an electronic technician and had lost his job after the company he worked for reorganized its workforce. Here is how he recalls the first days of his teaching career:

> Unfortunately, my first career ended with the crash of telecoms. So, I found myself in a dark period. I was a peer professional trainer for my company and fell back to be a technican. Although the salary and the conditions remained interesting, I fell to the bottom of the ladder [...]. So, this is when I decided to move on and start from scratch at the end of my thirties. I applied to the school and was hired ... I have been here since 2002. I initially taught a course which eventually disappeared. It was called Initiation to Technology and after a year of uncertainty where I wondered if I would not become a substitute forever, I was integrated in a new department, the science department where I teach now. (Simon, Teacher 1, March 28th, 2011)

Although Simon has a college diploma in electrical engineering and a certificate in vocational education, an important charasteristic of Simon is that he did not consider himself a good teacher, although he was definitely focused on the student's well-being (see the first part of the chapter). Nevertheless, he and Francis had been working together for three years at the same school and they had both been proactive in creating windturbine prototypes on week-ends and evenings at home.[9] Their goal was to make sense of teaching electrical concepts while engaging students in hands-on approaches in the labs. Both of them were keen on developing new teaching lessons and testing them with students in their classrooms. With the help of Jane, they produced a fair number of teaching documents to meet the integration of technological design into science teaching. Jane built on Simon's work to incorporate the evaluation aspect of the learning situation.

In March 2011, after one year of collaboration with the research team, he reflects on his contribution to the team and he is proud of his contribution:

> I am a good participant for the research group. I try to offer my help as much as I can. When it is time to prepare the workshops, I know I have a facility with the practical aspect of things. I joined the team because I see my role as a useful one. I have a sense of belonging to the group and the desire to contribute. (Simon, Teacher 1, March 28th, 2011)

After the first year of designing and testing many prototypes for the wind turbine and electronics workshops, some tensions rose at Simon's school: conflicts emerged between him, his lab technician and other ST teachers. Simon felt that he was not understood by his closest peers. In the next excerpt, he feels let down by his colleagues at school: "Well, the day the lab technician and the principal understand that when you work for *Building site 7*, you work for the student in the class, they will support us" [conflict] (Simon, Teacher 1, May 8th, 2012). Despite this tension, his confidence in his capacity to create workshops and collaborate with Francis and Jane, and be accepted by peers outside his close school community, remained intact. Another year went by and more prototypes, websites, technical drawings were produced. Everything was ready for the upcoming professional training workshop on the wooden microscope in 2011. Only two days had been reserved for the professional training on the wooden microscope but the success was great and it created a need among the other ST teachers who wanted to attend too. The second workshop was offered at the beginning of 2012 to meet the demand: it was another success and the repercussions were felt in the rest of the Province.

Nevertheless, Simon still faces adversity in its own school environment: "I even told my school principal this year: you have to better explain *Building site 7* to the lab technicians and to the colleagues because they do not understand what our real intention is" (Simon, Teacher 1, May 8th, 2012). Simon faces adversity and deep down, he expressed his fear of failure:

> The fear of failure ... It's clear. I would not go for a project that I did not master personally, for which I did not have the ability to retroact quickly with a student who raises his hand and who says to me: "Sir, I have a question." I would never dare present it to the students. It would be nice if I did not feel it was risky. If it was too risky, I would not do it [conflict, double bind]. (Simon, Teacher 1, May 17th, 2013)

A more critical conflict was expressed by Simon. His first interest remained the success of his students when it came to the ministerial exams. For two years, he had decided to engage in a project based approach in his classes to adopt the prescriptions of the new curriculum. The students liked it but their marks didn't follow:

> Well, I gave the students no choice: if they do not master the prototype they like to build, well it will not work. I told myself: inevitably, they will become good at it ... But that was not the case. I helped them, but then it got worse for me, they did not really perform [at the exam]. (Simon, Teacher 1, May 17th, 2013)

In the same DWR session, Simon is close to a critical conflict and the discussion between the researcher and him becomes quite emotional as he confides that he has overheard that some colleagues were stabbing him in the back during a school meeting: "teachers, who are teaching 11th grade science started to verbalize that I, the teacher creating the workshops, am looking down on them. The colleague ST teachers don't feel comfortable with integrating my prototypes in their classroom with students." Simon adds: "That's what I hear from others" (Teacher 1, May 17th, 2013). Simon feels distressed and isolated. To overcome that conflict, he found a way out by reaching out to and engaging the support of his provincial member of parliament. The results were very satisfaying for Simon: he managed to obtain gouverment funding and was able to improve the equipment in his classroom (robots, 3D printers, software). Between 2014 an 2016, Simon's teaching and extracurricular activities started to be conducted parallel to *Building site 7* and, during that time, his collaboration with us decreased. The actions Simon took are in keeping with Engeström and Sannino (2013) who point out that it is hard to address a critical conflict alone. The money granted by *Building site 7* could not fill his growing needs. His motive is now to expand to the provincial level where he feels he is appreciated and has more impact than in his own school environment. Reflecting on the first four years of developing new prototypes and their corresponding LES, Simon expresses the fact that he is more appreciated outside his own school district than at the local level:

> In retrospective, I would say that participation in the workshops of ST teachers coming from a fair distance showed more interests in the prototypes I presented. So I get the impression that the project is spreading by word of mouth and is doing its job of dissemination. It's not just a local anymore, it's scaled up. I would say that this is the effect of the change that I perceived the most. (Simon, Teacher 1, May 17th, 2013)

Despite his past experience in professional development, Simon's conflicting motives were mostly related to: (1) his relationship with his colleagues at work; (2) his fear of failure and; (3) his disappointment in the face of his students' performance at the provincial test. As we pointed out previously, 2014–2015 were years where Simon isolated himself from the rest of the research team. He became active again in 2016 as he had shifted from woodwork to electronics, robotics and 3D printing. He felt more at ease with everything related to electronics in harmony with his previous interests during his first job.

Figure 7.8 presents the analysis of Simon's expressions of transformative agency. The results highlight that even if he commited to actions (as documented in the ethnographic data) and contributed significantly to put together the professional development workshops, his discourse still indicates a need to criticize and explain his actions. Interestingly enough, the identification of transformative actions in Simon's discourse does not reflect the success we witnessed as he became a mentor and leader. He received recognition in the local media for his accomplishments in robotics with his students. He was engaged more into acting than discursing, but when given the chance to reflect on his emotional experience, his criticisms in 2013 were even more numerous than in 2010. As researchers, it is interesting to see here a limit of the discursive analysis. Figure 7.8 highlights a lot of criticizing and explicating on his part, with far less committing to action. In fact, our ethnographic notes and observations illustrate that Simon engaged in an important number of curricular and extracurricular activities. The expertise he gained was shared broadly by means of five participations in teacher professional development conferences at the Provincial level.

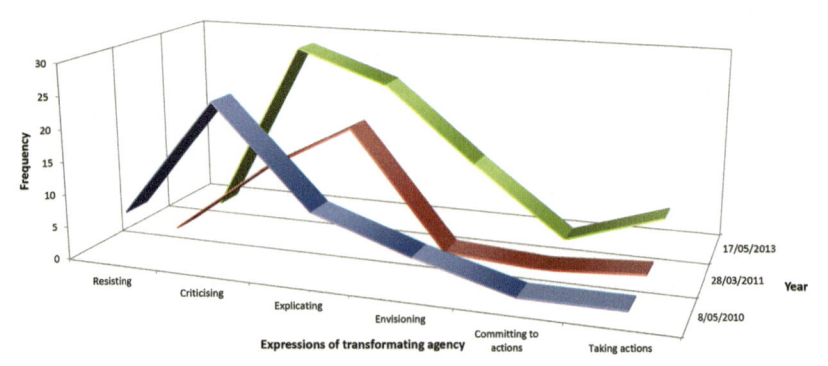

Expressions of transformative agency over seven years for Simon

	Resisting	Criticising	Explicating	Envisioning	Committing to actions	Taking actions
8/05/2010	7	25	10	5	1	1
28/03/2011	0	11	19	1	0	1
17/05/2013	0	28	23	11	0	5

FIGURE 7.8   Expressions of transformative agency over seven years for Simon

Using dialectical analysis to identify the types of tensions (manifestations of discursive contradictions) for Simon points to an increase in units of meaning related to conflicts and critical conflicts. The expansive resolution of conflicts of motives in his case has led to new ones as we explained earlier. Figure 7.9 needs to be put in perspective with Figure 7.8: more double binds and critical conflicts below, and their manifestations in terms of transformative action above.[10]

In his own school environment, Simon put together an extracurricular group of students in robotics. The back of his classroom was now filled with pieces,

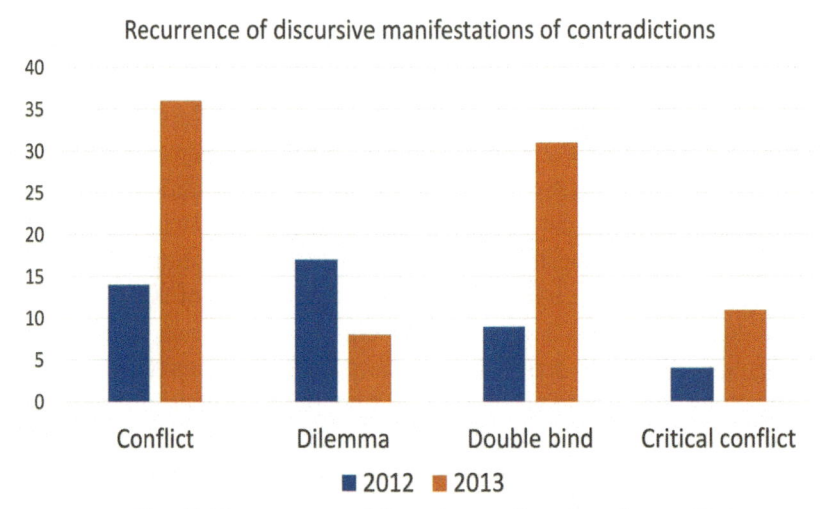

FIGURE 7.9   Trend in the recurrence of discursive manifestations of contradictions

FIGURE 7.10 Students working on their robot

robots and electronic parts and he needed more money and more space (see Figure 7.10).

Simon expressed his need for equipment and space to the Minister of Education in November 2017: with the end of *Building site 7* funding, he is now left with many more students interested in technology but feels financially let down. In putting together that group in robotics he has reconciled himself with the contradiction of preparing students for testing versus teaching in accordance to his personal convictions of engaging students in scientific and technological activities. By engaging in expansive resolution of conflicts of motives reaching out to other levels of activities like political contacts, Simon constructed second stimuli that gave new meaning and broader recognition to his mentoring activities.

10 The Decision-Forming Process of Jane's Experience of Mentoring: Sharing Her Expertise with Colleagues to Make More Sense of Hands-on Approaches

Jane's deep motivation was to help her colleagues. "I like to share my ideas, … already there are teachers who write to me to have information to know how to make the wind turbine. And it gives me pleasure to help them" (Teacher 2, February 24th, 2011). She had been a science teacher for 14 years when she joined *Building site 7*. Her motivation to teach science was linked to her love of biology:

> I liked biology a lot, so I studied biology at University, I enrolled a semester, but I realized that the work of a biologist researcher was not what I thought it would be. I still wanted to keep in touch with science, so I thought to myself, I'll go teaching, that way, I'll do both. So it was not a place ... a vocation for me to be a teacher ... I developed my professional identity over the years ... now I could not do without it. (Jane, Teacher 2, February 24th, 2011)

As she expresses during a DWR session, her initial teaching strategies did not include technological design process. The new prescriptions pushed her to better understand how to integrate her expertise in assessing the development of competencies when it came to hands-on approach in the workshops.

> In fact, I did not understand anything about reform when it happened. And then, I was a bit lacking, I chose to do a technlogical project and get help [from Francis]at the same time ... to be able to know how to work with machine tools. (Jane, Teacher 2, February 24th, 2011)

In 2017, reflecting on the team accomplishment, she describes how she experienced the development of *Building site 7* team's trajectory:

> At first we went blind. The wind turbine we created was the first project and almost the only project that existed in the province [right after the implementation of the curriculum]. We did our best to try to understand how to work in a workshop and how to integrate the evaluation aspects at the same time. I was working a little bit with my hands but not much, I was not competent with woodwork and nul with electronics, I liked teaching theory. We work more the same way now. It has changed so much over the years. Now it's more electronic, computer, 3D printer, it's beyond what we did at first. We pushed it so hard, we took at a lot of different paths. We had to adapt. Our first workshops seem outdated now: it is more computer based than hands-on using machines and tools. (Jane, Teacher 2, June 7th, 2017)

The double-bind identified in the excerpt reveals that, on one hand she likes theory and feels competent but on the other hand, she felt incompetent when it came to addressing more hands-on approaches. This paragraph is a good example of Jane expressing the unfolding of transformative actions: accepting to take risks (*we went blind*) and getting over the conflict of motive related to her resistance and fear of hands on approaches. She explicates that they did their best to envision and commit to actions. Reflecting on her contribution and the members of the team's accomplishments, it is interesting that she verbalized that they pushed *"very hard"* and were able to create something different. Form *"machines and tools"* they moved to computer-based projects.

At the end of the school year 2011–2012, two professional teachers training workshops (for a total of 4 days) where 61 participants attended were offered to the extended ST teaching staff (outside the Quebec region). Jane built on Simon and Francis' technical drawings and technical specifications to produce open-accessed online documents. She chose to integrate biological concepts in the context of the design of the wooden microscope to give meaning to the teaching lessons: the microscope would be a pretext to raise awareness with her teanager students to the influence of energy drinks on their metabolism. Daphnies were to be put in different concentrations of diluted caffeine so the students would count up the heartbeats. With an enhancement of 100 times, the six-dollar wooden microscope was quite performant. It was so popular that participants left the professional training days with their prototypes. Even if this chapter does not focus on boundary objects, the artifacts produced by Jane and the rest of the team acted as such as they were shared by peers and triggered collective agency in the school district. Reflecting on 2011–2012, Jane questioned the impact of her contribution to Simon and Francis' work whom *she considered* are the real experts when it came to technological design to create prototypes.

> We (the three of us) talked a lot about the technological aspect of the microscope, but I would like to know also if what I do, if the teachers make good use of it. Because, *I too*, would like to know if I have to work differently. (Jane, Teacher 2, May 8th, 2012)

It is important for Jane to have a positive feedback from the teachers attending the team workshops.

The next year, a new prototype was in the process of being developed. The Centre for Pedagogical Development of the Ministry of Education, came up with a LES involving a technical object: a colorimeter. Quebec ST teachers did not respond to the invitation for the professional development offered. Simon and Francis decided to modify and adapt the technical plans so the prototype would be more efficient and easier to implement in a science class. Jane joined in and came up with the idea that her students would test the quality of the river near her school. "I know that Francis and Simon were working on a colorimeter, but it was useless! That's why I thought about my project and merged the two" (Jane, Teacher 2, May 15th, 2013). The professional workshop on the colorimeter was delivered (the representant of the Ministry of Education among the participants!) but it was probably the hardest teacher workshop to monitor because it included a lot of electronics and most participants had little knowledge related to that domain. In the end, few ST teachers implemented the lesson in their classes: Simon went as far as producing seven versions of the prototypes to accommodate his peers. Jane reflects on the experience at the end of the school year 2012–2013:

> I realize there are teachers who really need to be supervised like students. When we created the wind turbine, we even had to make a security protocol with machines and tools for the attending ST teachers: as for highschool students. As if they had never set foot in a workshop, as if the teachers were students … And I think that the more we progress in the development of professional teaching workshops, the more we are at ease. We let them come to us, and I think they need to be mentored. (Teacher 2, May 15th 2013)

In light of her teaching experience and the way she talked about her involvement in *Building site 7*, Jane was driven by the need to make sense herself of the integration of technological design to her teaching. She admitted having no knowledge about it at the beginning but took the risk to get involved and learn on the spot. She expanded her activity by means of resolving conflicts of motives related to her ability to do woodwork and later to integrate 3D modelling and printing. Funnily enough, she characterizes her peers as student like and declare "they need to be mentored." The analysis of the expressions of transformative agency reveals more units of meanings related to committing to actions in her discourse, in 2013, building on her ideas about the colorimeter she becomes very productive. She holds a great ability to explain thoroughly how she engaged into concrete actions like producing documents and testing prototypes.

When it comes to the recurrence of discursive manifestations of contradictions in Jane's discourse between 2012 and 2013, the percentage of conflicts and dilemmas decrease as the double-binds increase. In light of the analytical framework, double-binds can find their resolution in engaging in practical transformation, which is the case for Jane, not for Simon as we saw previously. Jane's conflicting motives were mostly related to: (1) her sentiment of incompetency with practical work, and (2) her impatience when it came to adapt Francis and Simon's prototypes and transpose them into a "viable" learning and evelution situation in the classroom that was coherent with the ministerial evaluation grids. Figure 7.11 illustrates that between 2013, we identified 12 concrete actions taken by her to resolve double-binds. That year was a turnpoint for Jane as the envisioned and took concrete actions to improve the teachers' workshops.

Expressions of transformative agency over seven years for Jane

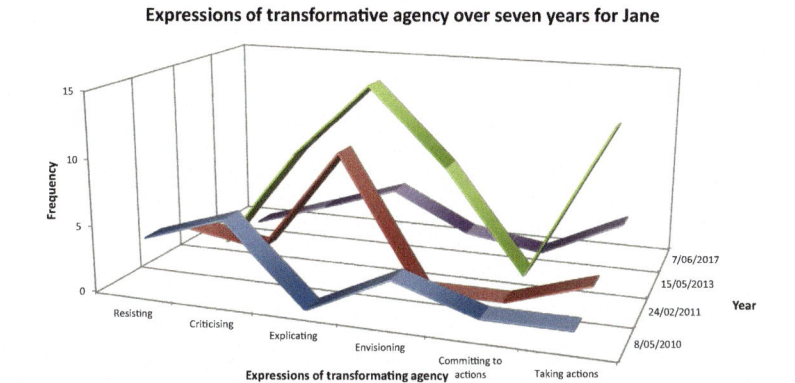

	Resisting	Criticising	Explicating	Envisioning	Committing to actions	Taking actions
8/05/2010	4	6	0	3	1	1
24/02/2011	3	2	10	0	0	2
15/05/2013	0	8	14	8	0	12
7/06/2017	0	2	4	1	0	3

FIGURE 7.11   Expressions of transformative agency over seven years for Jane

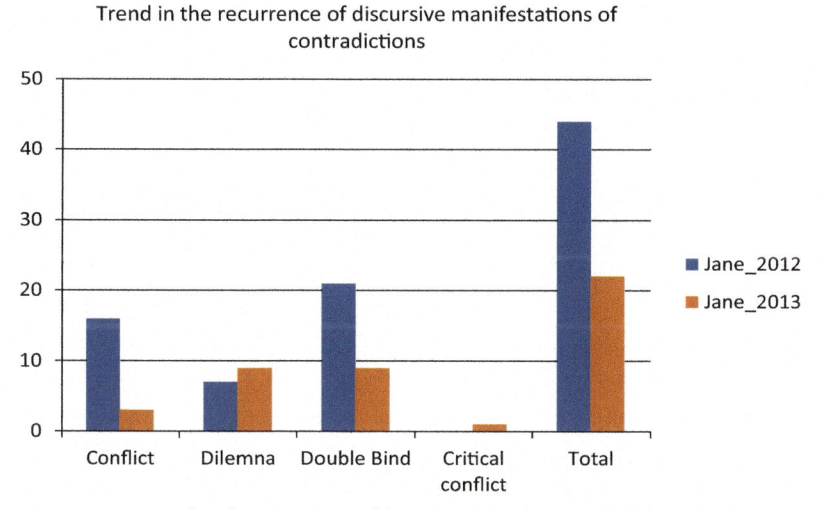

FIGURE 7.12   Trend in the recurrence of discursive manifestations of contradiction

11   Envisioning the Future: Francis and Jane Share Their Vision of a New 'Culture' of Collaboration between Science and Technology Teachers

The last DWR sessions were held in 2017. The next speaking turns between Jane, Francis and the researcher revealed a lot of satisfaction, hope for the future, but also lessons learned to push forward. Simon did not join in for the last sessions: he was still very much in contact with the research team but too busy in his school environment with robotics during lunchtime and after school hours. Jane expressed satisfaction and said that the workshops they created "taught them to work as a team" (Teacher 2, June 7th, 2017). Francis agreed with Jane about the fact that the projects had evolved over time and still would. But most important, both felt that their peers attitude had changed:

> At first there was more wood work and today there is more electronics. But what has changed is the attitude of some people. We put things together now. Many people in many schools have changed their attitudes and this is what is important to us ... as concrete results for *Building site 7*. It took time. There is a principal who recently told me that she did not understand our activity at the beginning of the professional teachers training workshops ... what *Building site 7* was useful for. This year, she told me that she understood its' pertinence and that, if we needed support, she we would support us. (Francis, Pedagogical counselor, June 7th, 2017)

The numerous resources produced by the members of the team are still available online on different websites. They are regularly consulted and the research team members still have to manage incoming emails coming from ST teachers from all over Quebec. The next speaking turns give a good idea of how the conversation went during the last DWR session and highlights the resolution of some of the conflicting motives we discussed.

Francis:	With the projects we did, I find that teachers visit the websites and try more hands-on projects to integrate the theory. So, I feel we did not waste our time, we worked differently, we managed to make sense of theoretical notions through technological design approach. Some of the participating teachers at the professional development training workshops even changed our projects for their own purposes with their students.
Researcher:	So there is a change in the culture at your school?
Jane:	Yes, really.
Francis:	A change in our culture at school.
Jane:	It is also true for the lab technicians.
Francis:	Nowadays, there is a critical mass of teachers who don't want to go back. I now try to have them collaborate with each other ... before, some teachers felt humiliated to ask for help (June 7th, 2017).

This conversation brings to light how learning together to prepare professional teacher training workshops can be satisfactory. It is also a way of "learning-in-practice, learning to talk about practice and learning by attempting to put theory (propositional knowledge) into practice" (Roth & Boyd, 1999, p. 53). Using double stimulation methodology in *Building site 7* has fostered a change in teachers' practices according to Simon, Jane and Francis. The interventions of the research team between or after the professional teaching days using mirror data made it possible for the participants to express how they were experiencing the development of artefacts and the planning of the training days. To the surprise of the research team, emotions were way more important than expected and led to investigate the meaning of the emotions expressed in the discourse. Discursive manifestations of identified contradictions spread from teachers' strategies integrating technical work into science teaching, to those assessing the performance of their students, organizing lab workshops at school, and collaborating with lab technicians or colleagues or the school principal. In light of our own experience in the field as a high school science teacher and later on as director of a teacher training program, we can say that teachers are not trained to consider emotion in their practice. Their formative years are more oriented toward making sure they control the class and their teaching strategies.

12 Expansive Resolution of Conflicts of Motives, Agency and Perezhivanie: A Challenge for a Research Team Doing CHAT in the Field

The seven years of praxis in the field were filled with unexpected and unpredictable events as well as intense moments of collaboration, discussions and problem solving. Hundreds of hours of ethnographic work in the schools with teachers and students blurred the boundaries between "us" and "them." Essentially linked to the contextual conditions in their schools, depending on Simon, Jane and Francis's capacity to resolve problematic situations and engage in creating prototypes along with the documents to support its' viability, we have followed a runaway object together during seven years. The shared object of "collaborating to engage in mentorship and support science teacher colleagues" kept being redefined and reconceptualized in order to expand. The analysis of the participants' reflections on their ongoing activity supports the premise that "turning toward oneself as a collaborative social quasi-partner in transformative activity" is fruitful to understand agency (Sawyer & Stetsenko, 2018, p. 10). Giving voice to the emotional experience of the participant teachers and the pedagogical counselor also brought to light the way they developed a "collective process of consciousness" as they confronted and overcame tensions along the way. We are in sympathy with Stetsenko (2016) who writes that "circumstances and conditions [...] are not so much given as taken up by people who actively grapple with them and, thus, realize and bring them forth in striving to change and transcend them" (p. 35).

As the participants reflected on their productions and experiences as mentors, their professional identities evolved and redefined the borders of their teaching activities: new contexts and broader layers of influence were reached through the various workshops they co-modelled. Using dialectical analysis and focusing on the transformative agentive actions over the seven years led us to identify three categories of conflicts of motives that were successfully resolved in order to expand the professional mentoring activity and make it a success: (1) critical contexts related to questioning and resisting change; (2) contexts of discovery leading to proposing new forms of learning and evaluation situation; and (3) social contexts of practice relevant to the broader science teaching community involving relational agency and broader expansion of the activity of mentorship (see Figure 7.1).

Simon, Francis and Jane's will to communicate and collaborate for learning and expanding their mentorship activity was traced back in their individual and collective agency as well as in the artifacts that acted as boundary crossing objects. For the research team, engaging in an interventionist methodology and doing CHAT in a complex educational setting challenged the way we evolved. As we pointed out previously, the boundaries between us and the field practitioners got thinner as we all engaged in giving meaning to a shared object: professional development by means of the co-modelling of workshops for peers. Proposing new teaching strategies to their peers allowed the participant teachers and the pedagogical counselor to resolve some tensions introduced by the new prescriptions related to the integration of technological design to science teaching.

The analysis of the sociomaterial production of the artifacts they produced allowed to understand how it gave new meaning to their teaching approaches and motivated them to engage in professional development. The windmill, wooden microscope and colorimeter acted as boundary objects and in the case of *Building site 7* were key in the development of the teacher training workshops. The variety of artifacts produced individually or collaboratively over the years triggered the participants' actions in their respective practice as they contributed to build second stimuli to resolve conflicts of motives. These mediating tools of agency are still shared between the participating schools and the websites constitute a testimony and a legacy for the science and technology teachers. One after the other, the prototypes produced and tested in the science classes gave meaning to the path that Simon and Jane chose as they engaged in overcoming difficulties and preparing the workshops for their peers. Both of them became mentors by accident. The implementation of the new curriculum did not make sense to them at first.

It was challenging to reconstruct the experiential mentorship trajectory of the participants through their discourse. CHAT, as a praxis, makes it possible to bring together and give life to the emotions that we document in the field. In this chapter, we have tried to better understand the concept of perezhivanie as an act of experiencing in praxis. The last DWR sessions reveal the nature of the change in their work environment and the hope to push forward. Identifying conflicts of motives in the discourse of the participants has proven fruitful: their resolution seems necessary to trigger agency and engage in taking decisions. The emotional experiential trajectory of Simon and Jane, as they collaborated to put together professional teaching workshops, supports Vygotsky's dialectical premise that making a choice supposes that "duality is at the very foundation of the volitional act, and this duality becomes especially prominent and vivid whenever several motives, several opposing strivings, clash in our consciousness" (1997, pp. 167–168). The analysis of the expansive resolution of conflicts of motives demonstrates that working over the conflicts of motives requires; (1) time before the participants reformulate a second stimulus to cope with the evolving conflicts; and (2) to reach another layer in the community (Barma et al., 2015). In this chapter, the expansive resolution of conflicting motives by the three participants led to new ones involving the broader school district when the workshops moved from one school to another: more than two principals and lab technicians joined the mentorship activity. The involvement of communities appears to be key for the expansion of the activity beyond individual practitioners.

Another interesting element we found is that Vygotsky states that perezhivanie is mediated by meanings and that a situation becomes critical when an individual perceives it as such. As Roth (2007) points out, "motive, emotion, and identity are important aspects of our being in the world, and mediate what we know and how we know it. Yet most cognition research still does not include affect" (p. 40). In this chapter, we have shared our analysis of seven years of research in the field hoping to understand how events or experiences are worked over (perizhivat in Russian). We have documented that individual critical situations in the form of conflicts of motives cannot be overcome without the support of others.

13 How Does the Chapter Address the Challenges of a Non-Dualist Methodology?

The authors discuss the dialogical concepts of perezhivanie and transformative agency in relation to a prolonged involvement (seven years) with the research teams of two teachers and one pedagogical counsellor in transforming current science and technology (ST) teaching activities intended for high school students in Québec. In the face of a major curriculum overhaul, longitudinal developmental Work Research (DWR) was implemented, with a pedagogical team, which has a mandate to create tools to help teachers in numerous school settings to review their teaching in light of this major change in their practices. The authors report how this prolonged CHAT living praxis, which involves an impressive number of hours of ethnographic data, generated many emotions during productive activities and blurred the "traditional" research boundaries between the research teams and the research participants. For the participants, the shared object of collaborating to engage in mentorship and support science-teacher colleagues gave rise to many conflicting motives and contradictions that were progressively addressed and resolved, particularly during the Change Laboratory meetings. In conceiving emotions and collective-subjective activity as being in an intertwined relationship, this DWR research setting and the Change lab methodology gave voice to the emotional experience of confronting. It also helped overcome contradictions linked to the production of ST prototypes and the workshop they co-modelled in order to help provide teaching activities (linked with those prototypes) to other ST teachers. These contradictions have historically been generated by the new prescriptions relating to the integration of technological design into science teaching in the governmental ST curricula.

Consistent with a non-dualist understanding of the relation between the subject and their environment, while they engage in transformative actions surrounding ST teaching, the participants transform themselves and stimulate their transformative agency. In the words of the authors, "as the participants reflected on their productions and experiences as mentors, their professional identities evolved and redefined the borders of their teaching activities: new contexts and broader layers of influence were reached through the various workshops they co-modelled." The collaborative engagement in creating and testing prototypes in the science classes, as well as their discussion about the challenge of the new role of mentor and about the ST curriculum, gave meaning to the participants' professional path and helped foster their transformative agency. With the concept of perezhivanie, the authors raise the importance in their conception of DWR research to consider.

Notes

1 The section of the Science and Technology component of the Québec Education Program (QEP) going under the heading of "Pedagogical Context" sets out a number of avenues for classroom practice that encourage teachers to move away from a strictly disciplinary approach to science teaching (Ministère de l'Éducation du Loisir et du Sport, 2007).
2 For more information on how science teachers apprehend the relationship between Science and technology, see Roth (2001): "Science educators have asked themselves for some time whether technology-centered activities afford a learning environment that scaffolds students" learning of science (e.g., Layton, 1994). The question of whether technology has a place in science education was probably framed most provocatively in the title of an article by Carlsen (1998): "Engineering design in the classroom: Is it good science education or is it revolting?" Carlsen answered his own question with a qualified "yes" an answer that required him to redefine science. Generally, some research shows that technology-related activities provide a rich ground for learning science when they focus on (a) designing and testing artifacts and (b) critical analysis and explaining performance failures of artifacts (Roth, Tobin, & Ritchie, 2001). Others, especially trained scientists, suggest that technology is merely an application of science. Technological (design) activities should therefore be used only *after* students have acquired "sound" scientific principles (Roth, 2001, p. 768).
3 "*A technical object* is a simple, practical object that has been manufactured, as opposed to an object found in nature (e.g. hammer, tweezers)" (Ministère de l'Éducation du Loisir et du Sport, 2007, p. 6).
4 "The learning and evaluation situations developed by the teacher should enable the teacher to judge the level of competency development at the end of each year in the cycle. To this end, they should vary in complexity from one year to the next, based on certain parameters" (Ministère de l'Éducation du Loisir et du Sport, 2007, p. 8).
5 https://www.pistes.fse.ulaval.ca/sae/?no_version=2741&no_recherche=1679867508957738524
6 Association pour l'enseignement de la science et de la technologie au Québec (Association for Science and Technology Education) is a non-profit organization open to science teachers and technicians from Quebec and to all persons or organizations interested in teaching science and technology It was born from the desire to contribute to the advancement and improvement of science and technology and brings together all levels of education (primary, secondary, college and university) and all disciplines (physics, chemistry, biology, geology, environmental sciences, astronomy and others).
7 A French web site where teachers can find all of our activities: http://netsciences.ca/moodle/course/index.php?categoryid=3
8 The main researcher had over 20 years of experience in science teaching as well as four years as a curriculum writer. This certainly oriented the way the sessions were conducted.
9 Ethnographic notes after informal meetings and conversation between Simon, Francis and the leading researcher.
10 In Figure 7.9, 100% represents the total of selected dialectical units of meaning in the verbatim.

References

Barma, S. (2008). *Un contexte de renouvellement de pratiques en éducation aux sciences et aux technologies: Une étude de cas réalisée sous l'angle de la théorie de l'activité* [Doctoral thesis]. Université Laval.

Barma, S. (2011). A sociocultural reading of reform in science teaching in a secondary biology class. *Cultural Studies of Science Education, 6*(3), 635–661. doi:10.1007/s11422-011-9315-9

Barma, S., Lacasse, M., & Massé-Morneau, J. (2015). Engaging discussion about climate change in a Quebec secondary school: A challenge for science teachers. *Learning, Culture and Social Interaction, 4*, 28–36. doi:10.1016/j.lcsi.2014.07.004

Barma, S., Power, T. M., & Daniel, S. (2010). *Réalité augmentée et jeu mobile pour une éducation aux sciences et à la technologie* [Paper]. Colloque scientifique Ludovia, Ariège, France.

Beijaard, D., Meijer, P. C., & Verloop, N. (2004). Reconsidering research on teachers' professional identity. *Teaching and Teacher Education, 20*(2), 107–128. doi:10.1016/j.tate.2003.07.001

Brandt-Pomares, P., Aravecchia, L., Buisson-Fenet, E., Bally, J., Conio, M., François, N., & Maironne, C. (2008). Comment former des enseignants pour une éducation à l'environnement et au développement durabl. *Aster, 46*, 205–229. doi:10.4267/2042/20036

Carlsen, W. S. (1998). Engineering design in the classroom: Is it good science education or is it revolting? *Research in Science Education, 28*(1), 51–63. doi:10.1007/BF02461641

Clarà, M. (2016). Vygotsky and Vasilyuk on Perezhivanie: Two notions and one word. *Mind, Culture, and Activity, 23*(4), 284–293. doi:10.1080/10749039.2016.1186194

Conseil supérieur de l'Éducation. (2013). *L'enseignement de la science et de la technologie au primaire et au premier cycle du secondaire*. Gouvernement du Québec. https://www.cse.gouv.qc.ca/fichiers/documents/publications/Avis/50-0481.pdf

Conseil supérieur de l'Éducation. (2014). *Le développement professionnel, un enrichissement pour toute la profession enseignante*. Gouvernement du Québec.

Edwards, A. (2010). *Being an expert professional practitioner: The relational turn in expertise*. Springer.

Engeström, Y. (1987/2015). *Learning by expanding: An activity theoretical approach to developmental research* (2nd ed.). Cambridge University Press.

Engeström, Y., & Sannino, A. (2011). Discursive manifestations of contradictions in organizational change efforts: A methodological framework. *Journal of Organizational Change Management, 24*(3), 368–387. doi:10.1108/09534811111132758

Engeström, Y., & Sannino, A. (2013). La volition et l'agentivité transformatrice : perspective théorique de l'activité. *Revue internationale du CRIRES : innover dans la tradition de Vygotsky, 1*(1), 4–19.

González Rey, F. (2016). Vygotsky's concept of perezhivanie in the psychology of art and at the final moment of his work: Advancing his legacy. *Mind, Culture, and Activity, 23*(4), 305–314. doi:10.1080/10749039.2016.1186196

Guo, C.-J. (2008). Issues in science earning: An international perspective. In S. K. Abell & N. J. Lederman (Eds.), *Handbook of research on science education* (pp. 227–256). Routledge.

Haapasaari, A., Engeström, Y., & Kerosuo, H. (2016). The emergence of learners' transformative agency in a change laboratory intervention. *Journal of Education and Work, 29*(2), 232–262. doi:10.1080/13639080.2014.900168

Hartley, D. (2009). Education policy, distributed leadership and socio-cultural theory. *Educational Review, 61*(2), 139–150. doi:10.1080/00131910902844721

Jornet, A., & Roth, W.-M. (2016). Perezhivanie—a monist concept for a monist theory. *Mind, Culture, and Activity, 23*(4), 353–355. doi:10.1080/10749039.2016.1199703

Konopasky, A. W., & Sheridan, K. M. (2016). Towards a diagnostic toolkit for the language of agency. *Mind, Culture, and Activity, 23*(2), 108–123. doi:10.1080/10749039.2015.1128952

Layton, D. (1994). *Innovations in science and technology education*. UNESCO.

Leontiev, A. N. (2005). Study of the environment in the pedological works of L.S. Vygotsky: A critical study. *Journal of Russian & East European Psychology, 43*(4), 8–28. doi:10.1080/10610405.2005.11059254

Ministère de l'Éducation du Loisir et du Sport. (2007). *Québec Education Program: Secondary cycle two*. Gouvernement du Québec.

Roth, W.-M. (2001). Learning science through technological design. *Journal of Research in Science Teaching, 38*(7), 768–790. doi:10.1002/tea.1031

Roth, W.-M. (2007). Emotion at work: A contribution to third-generation cultural-historical activity theory. *Mind, Culture, and Activity, 14*(1–2), 40–63. doi:10.1080/10749030701307705

Roth, W.-M., & Boyd, N. (1999). Coteaching, as colearning, is praxis. *Research in Science Education, 29*(1), 51–67. doi:10.1007/BF02461180

Roth, W.-M., Tobin, K., & Ritchie, S. (2001). *Re/constructing elementary science*. Peter Lang Publishing.

Sannino, A. (2015). The principle of double stimulation: A path to volitional action. *Learning, Culture and Social Interaction, 6*, 1–15. doi:10.1016/j.lcsi.2015.01.001

Sannino, A., Daniels, H., & Gutiérrez, K. D. (2009). *Learning and expanding with activity theory*. Cambridge University Press.

Sannino, A., & Laitinen, A. (2015). Double stimulation in the waiting experiment: Testing a Vygotskian model of the emergence of volitional action. *Learning, Culture and Social Interaction, 4*, 4–18. doi:10.1016/j.lcsi.2014.07.002

Sawyer, J. E., & Stetsenko, A. (2018). Revisiting Marx and problematizing Vygotsky: A transformative approach to language and speech internalization. *Language Sciences, 70*, 143–154. doi:10.1016/j.langsci.2018.05.003

Severance, S., Penuel, W. R., Sumner, T., & Leary, H. (2016). Organizing for teacher agency in curricular co-design. *Journal of the Learning Sciences, 25*(4), 531–564. doi:10.1080/10508406.2016.1207541

Stetsenko, A. (2016). *The transformative mind: Expanding Vygotsky's approach to development and education*. Cambridge University Press.

Vasilyuk, F. (1988). *The psychology of experiencing*. Progress Publishers.
Virkkunen, J., & Newnham, D. (2013). *The change laboratory. A tool for collaborative development of work and education*. Sense Publishers.
Vygotsky, L. S. (1986). *Thought and language*. MIT Press.
Vygotsky, L. S. (1987). *The collected works of L. S. Vygotsky: Vol. 1. Problems of general psychology*. Springer.
Vygotsky, L. S. (1997). *The collected works of L.S. Vygotsky: Vol. 4. The history of the development of higher mental functions*. Plenum Press.

CHAPTER 8

Problematizing Questions about Development in Adulthood and Freedom in Developmental Intervention

The Relevance of the Concept of Zone of Proximal Development

Frédéric Saussez and Philip Dupuis-Laflamme

Abstract

The latest developments in Vygotsky's theory of the historical development of specifically human capacities are intrinsically linked to a philosophy of education (Yvon & Zinchenko, 2011). *The Ethics* of Spinoza could be one of Vygotsky's sources of inspiration (Léopoldoff, 2014). In this chapter, we defend the idea that *The Ethics* provides Vygotsky with a normative orientation to define education and, in general, for any developmental intervention. These are then conceptualized as the source of the development of a person's power to act (agendi potentia) in and on the social world and his own subjective universe, and also as the process of intellectualizing the relation (rapport à) to the world (Brossard, 2008; Saussez, 2017).

Such a vision of developmental intervention raises the question of agency and freedom in reference to the idea that systematic concepts have a liberating power. The purpose of intervention is to create the conditions for the person to progress on the path of freedom, to free herself from the sadness linked to inappropriate ideas.

Thus, the transformative imperative addressed to a science of the human psyche (Vygotsky, 1927) is embodied in the development of people's power to act. For the researcher, transforming the social activities means to help people transform their own situations. This position raises different epistemological, ethical and methodological issues that we will discuss in connection with the idea that intervention is an artificial space-time, an intermediary living environment between theory and practice.

Keywords

developmental intervention – development – power to act – agency – freedom

> We teach people how to remember, we never teach them how to grow.
> OSCAR WILDE (1904)

∴

Vygotsky (1999) laid the foundations for a critical and transformative psychology. In his book *Historical Meaning of the Crisis in Psychology*, he argued that the essential function of human consciousness is to refract the world in such a way as to open up new possibilities for action to the individual, and therefore to transform the world in the desired direction. He also advocated that practice—in the sense of a material, concrete activity bent on transforming the world—is the ultimate epistemological criterion of truth.

In *The History of the development of higher mental functions*, Vygotsky (2014) sets forth an explanatory framework as well as groundbreaking analytical categories for a psychology whose subject is cultural development itself. As follows, this historical psychology's objective is to study the processes through which cultural development is functionally linked to the historical evolution of a given society. Vygotsky therefore postulates that development is at once the object and method of this new psychology.

Furthermore, there are clear grounds to conclude that throughout his work, Vygotsky was driven by a critical imperative: that transformation and explanation of distinctively human behaviors should never be separated. This monistic philosophy of method (*"philosophie de la méthode"*) embodies what Sève (2014) identified as the Marxian influence in Vygotsky's work. Yet, upon the conclusion of *The History of the development of higher mental functions* (HDHMF), Vygotsky (2014) stresses that his historical psychology of cultural development demands a brand-new philosophy of education (see Chapters 12 and 13).

In this chapter, we will argue that Spinoza's *Ethics* (1967) provided the normative groundwork from which Vygotsky delineated this practical philosophy and a vision for education which endeavours to sustain the human person as they strive to preserve their own—as well as *The Other's*—ability to be affected and to transform affects into free actions. More generally, Spinoza's ideas served as a frame of reference to conceptualize any intervention/research whose aim is developmental. In fact, Spinoza's work seems to have played a crucial role as Vygotsky—nearing the twilight of his life—revisited his lifework (Zavershneva, 2010; Zavershneva & Van der Veer, 2007). As a matter of fact, he refers to Spinoza quite extensively in the writings that immortalized this reorientation. For instance, in *Theory of emotions*, Vygotsky (1998) problematized the relationship between affect and intellect as the driving force of human development. Likewise, in *Thought and Language*, he conceptualized the relationship between everyday concepts and scientific concepts as the process through which one's relationship to the world (*"rapport au monde"*) is intellectualized (Vygotsky, 1997b). Moreover, Spinoza's influence is also noticeable in his pedological work related to the Zone of Proximal Development (ZPD), in which he problematized the relationships between learning and development in school activities.

Consequently, we believe that Vygotsky saw the development of agency as intrinsically linked with that of freedom in the Spinozian sense. Indeed, he conceptualized development as the growth of a person's power to act (*agendi potentia*) both among and within their own social world and subjective universe. Such a vision bears significant implications with regards to the conditions that must be met to support a person as they undergo and participate in this process. Principally, it approaches the issue of agency and freedom from the standpoint that consistent concepts are imbued with liberating force. Consequently, it postulates that the purpose of developmental interventions is the creation of conditions that will nurture a person's progress on the path to freedom. This is for us the Spinozian influence in Vygotsky's vision for education and any developmental intervention: striving to provide the person with means to free themselves from the sadness caused by inadequate ideas of what affects the course of their action.

Thus, the transformative imperative addressed to a science of the human psyche (Vygotsky, 1999) is restated in terms of what conditions may be conducive for the development of a person's power to act. Henceforth, for the researcher[1] transforming the social world means helping people transform their own situations. This position raises different methodological and ethical issues that we will address in relation with a discussion of the notion of *Zone of Proximal Development* (ZPD).

Indeed, in the first section of this essay, we will be defending the idea that the ZPD consists in a reorientation of the method of double stimulation that aims to study the reorganization and/or the construction of semantic relationships between different higher mental functions (HMF) at play in specific social situations of development. To us, this does indeed seem like the way Vygotsky (1997b) pointed at when he discussed the role of systematic concepts in the expansion of consciousness's area of action. It is important to be careful, however, when we consider the question of development in adulthood through the historical theory of cultural development since Vygotsky never really addressed it.

Nevertheless, we will still attempt to engage this question in the second section by examining the requirements associated with the fragmentation of social life into multiple spheres of activity, which then push towards the constructions of personal and collective capacities in order for them to cope with such a fragmentation of people's living spaces (*"milieux de vie"*).

In the third section, we will review several elements taken from a criticism of different *intervention-research* with developmental purposes that were conducted in the French tradition of ergonomic analysis of teaching activity (Saussez, 2017). If the development of individual and collective abilities to transform the social world is an intervention's central ambition, then research's transformative goal is materialized as the researcher's expertise is made available to serve the person's purposes engaged in a transformative project, through the help provided them so they can (re)gain control over their own lives and individually as well as collectively produce new conditions of existence. It is in fact a matter of seeing the development of a person's power to act as the ideal of betterment in adulthood and the normative reference of transformative research.

1 The Concept of ZPD: An Interpretation in Terms of Development of a Practical Philosophy

The notion of ZPD appears late in Vygotsky's writings (Chaiklin, 2003) and has undergone different modulations (Yvon & Zinchenko, 2012). This concept is contemporaneous with Vygotsky's project to re-found pedology as a science of child development (Schneuwly & Leopoldoff Martin, 2018) as well as the elaboration of the concept of psychological system to characterize the relationships between various HMF that are structuring the person's personality (Vygotsky, 2012d).

Even though this concept rests only on a few writings, it is part of a web of meaning that weaves together some of the concepts at the core of the historical psychology of cultural development, namely: the general law of development, the relationship between everyday concepts and scientific concepts, between thought and language, the role of meaning in mental life, etc. We therefore disagree with some authors who asserted that the ZPD holds only a minor position in Vygotsky's psychology (see Dafermos, 2017). On the contrary, we believe that it sheds light on the conditions to be met in order to be able to observe how semantic relationships are reconfigured and/or constructed between the different mental functions composing the personality at play in socially normed educational activities. More broadly, we are relying on this concept to articulate a reflection on adult development with regards to its relationships with particular forms of doubling experience.

1.1 A Re-emphasis of the General Law of Cultural Development in Formal Educational Contexts

One of the earliest references to the ZPD has for its background a radical critique of psychometrics and its application to the composition of homogeneous classrooms based on children's so-called intelligence quotient and the adjustment of the teacher's interventions to it (see Vygotsky, 2012b). In this text, he extends his criticism to various conceptions of the relationship between learning and development with regards to the psychological function of educational processes in school settings (Vygotsky, 2012c).

He firmly believed these processes should not be oriented backwards towards capacities that are already developed, but towards the future in order to decipher prospective capacities to act that involve the restructuring of pre-existing abilities. Seen this way, the ZPD constitutes an analytical category to problematize the sociogenesis of human capacities in formal educational contexts. Using this notion, Vygotsky (2012a) conceptualized the relationship between teaching and development in an original way: "teaching processes awaken internal development processes in children, that is, they bring them to life, are their source and stimulate them" (p. 166, authors' translation).[2]

It is on these grounds that Vygotsky (2012c) contested the idea that the teaching/learning activity must be adjusted to the child's actual level of development. Thus, we think the ZPD was for him an intellectual tool meant to provide another outlook on socially normed situations where the person is asked to engage in complex cultural activities that differ radically from their everyday life. These activities require, in fact, the redeployment and/or reconstruction of acquired capacities in a new form and/or the construction of new capabilities.

As Brossard (2004) points out, development is indeed about transformations produced within the person's psychological universe in relation to their engagement in new forms of activity that require the use of new cultural instruments. For example, the act of writing involves redeploying psychological operations initially related to oral language, perception or imagination, as well as the development of inner language on the part of the novice writer. It places him in an environment saturated with meanings with which he must deal to fulfill his significant intentions. It is instrumental in building the capacity to work on meanings and to control, at least partially, the psychological operations at play in the movements between inner language, which is oriented by *sense*, and externalized language, oriented by *meaning*. Thus, this complex cultural form of activity profoundly reorganizes the inter-functional relationships of the various HMF involved in the development of verbal thought and contribute indirectly to develop inner language.

This concept is part of the same mindset which pushed Vygotsky (2012d) to develop a systemic vision of the psyche. Development is then defined in terms of the reconfiguration of the inter-functional relationships between HMF and the intellectualization of these functions. This leads us to understand cultural development in terms of the intellectualization of the relationship to the world. We will come back to this later. For now, it is important to bear in mind that Vygotsky focuses on a structured process of teaching/learning of cultural heritage into specific social settings that arouses potential development.

As Schneuwly (2008) aptly indicates, the term *obuchenie*, which has unfortunately been simplistically translated into *learning*, refers in fact to the double-sided teaching/learning process. It is therefore important that the learning process not be detached from the teaching one since the latter is shaping the former. This is the meaning of various principles stated by (Vygotsky, 1997b, 2012a, 2012b, 2012c) concerning the need to conceptualize the relationships between the teaching/learning process and development. They must not be confused any more than they should be believed to coincide. Thus, for Vygotsky (2012c): "the theory of the zone of proximal development is expressed by a formula that stands in direct opposition to the traditional approach and which states that the only good teaching is the one that precedes development" (p. 242). From this point of view, the teaching/learning process is "a necessary and universal element for the development in children of these human, non-natural characteristics that have been acquired during the course of historical development" (Vygotsky, 2012c, p. 245). Using this concept, Vygotsky (2012a, 2012b, 2012c) invites us to consider the dialectical relationships between the processes of teaching/learning new cultural forms of activity and the development of the capacity to act voluntarily and consciously within these activities. These are the two faces of the same process of building specifically human capacities to act voluntarily in and on the world as well as in and on the person's psychic universe. The teaching/learning of new resources is therefore a source of potential development. It then awakens developmental processes which, without it, would not take form. The teaching/learning process foreshadows a potential development. As Vygotsky (2012c) points out:

> Concerning our hypothesis, its essential point is to state that the process of development does not correspond to that of learning but rather that the process of development follows the process of learning which creates the zone of proximal development. (p. 247)

The anteriority of the teaching/learning process over the developmental one is logically linked to the pre-existence of cultural forms and the need to mediate the person's encounter with them. In order to build their own world by means of these forms, the person must first acquire their mastery. Indeed, "to become conscious of something and to master it, you must first have it at your disposal" (Vygotsky, 1997b, p. 103). For Vygotsky (1994a), the emergence of human-specific capacities:

> owes nothing to the biological evolution of man as a living being, but rather to the historical development of man as a social being. It is only through the dynamics of collective social life that all higher forms of intellectual activity which are unique to humanity are built and developed. (pp. 156–157)

Specifically, this concept expands the general law of cultural development's meaning (Vygotsky, 2014) as an analysis of structured educational processes aimed at facilitating the development of new capacities of acting (Saussez, 2017). The subject's involvement in a teaching/learning activity on the inter-psychological plane thus constitutes a necessary moment for a reconfiguration of their own mental universe (intra-psychological plane). Indeed, for Vygotsky (2012c): this law applies to teaching/learning which has the function to generate the ZPD in the sense that this process produces in the person internal development dynamics that are only accessible to her through collaboration with others. For Vygotsky (2012c), teaching/learning is a process that is distinctive of cultural development, and without which the latter could not take place.

With respects to this relationship between the ZDP and the general development law, we would like to underline that affects are at stake in this context. Indeed, the genesis of HMF begins as part of a significant experience in a social relationship with another person (see Veresov, 2004, for a discussion on the meaning of the term category in the first formulation of the law).

This experience has such an emotional resonance that the person is literally worked from within and pushed to reconfigure their relationship to the world. It is perhaps in this possibility of being affected in a relationship with others that lays the driving force behind the development that Vygotsky (2014) describes in terms of self-movement or self-stimulation. Thus, the concept of ZPD clarifies the conditions necessary for the person to transform what affects her in the situation into an active search for the means to act voluntarily.

These first mentions of the ZPD were the basis for its most common interpretation. It is thus defined as the distance between a person's actual level of development and the threshold at which they need help to accomplish increasingly complex activities of the same kind. On the one hand, a person's actual level of development is assessed in terms of whether they are able to carry out on their own a task whose complexity exceeds their level of mastery. On the other hand, their potential level of development, recognized through the skillfulness they demonstrate in collaboration with another person that masters the means to fulfill the task (Vygotsky, 2012c). This prospective capacity to acquire new modes of conduct reflects a "proximal development potential" (Vygotsky, 2012c, p. 240).

Vygotsky (1997b) also discusses the ZPD in his work on the limits of Piagetian reasoning regarding the relationship between spontaneous and scientific concepts. It then allows him to specify the dynamics of the relationships between the daily concepts acquired in the fullness of experience and the scientific concepts transmitted in a structured way in school activities. As a matter of fact, these are not readily available in the course of everyday life. Consequently, the progressive mastery of these resources must be built through specific forms of activity. The ZPD then refers to such activities and, in particular, the cruxes to be arranged in order to put in tension a spontaneous and a systematic relation to the object of activity. It is a question of creating a situation in which the subject can raise himself a head above his own experience, double it (Vygotsky, 1994a), and free himself from the determination of his conduct by the situation and instead control it according to a principle of intelligibility that he could give to himself (Brossard, 2004). Thus, educational intervention is conceived as being in the service of the progressive construction of an intellectualized relationship to the world.

Knowledge is a key resource to develop one's capacity to act voluntarily and consciously, and the process of teaching/learning aims to make the person able to use new psychological tools to master their own intellectual operations involved in a conceptualization's activity and a transformation of their own conduct. It is therefore important to maintain the link between teaching, mastery and development, as suggested by (Vygotsky, 1994a):

> For the new higher mental functions are also and to the same extent intellectualized and voluntary. Knowledge and mastery go hand in hand [...]. The capacity of knowing opens up new possibilities for action. To know always means to some extent to master. (p. 228)

The concept of ZPD brings to light the way in which scientific concepts gradually permeate spontaneous conducts and contribute to the emergence of a new particular activity: an intellectualized one (Vygotsky, 1994a). It is therefore important not to confuse experience with knowledge. This requires thinking about their contradictory relationships as well as the conditions under which a doubling of the experience through language leads the subject to the formation of knowledge. Accordingly, we will later argue that systematic concepts are the person's instruments of free action in the sense that such tools structures a conscious and voluntary relationship between the person and a particular sphere of the world.

In fact, we maintain that this notion refers to systematic forms of knowledge in reference to what Spinoza (1967) called a *second kind of knowledge*. Thus, in this relationship with an *Other*, the challenge at stake for the person, with regards to knowledge, is to develop an adequate idea of what affects them. Systematic concepts are likely to enhance the person's power to act freely in and upon the world in the Spinozian sense, that is, in full knowledge of what is driving their activity and beingness, as suggested by the following quote:

> I explained how error consists in the privation of knowledge, but in order to throw more light on the subject I will give an example. For instance, men are mistaken in thinking themselves free; their opinion is made up of consciousness of their own actions, and ignorance of the causes by which they are conditioned. Their idea of freedom, therefore, is simply their ignorance of any cause for their actions. As for their saying that human actions depend on the will, this is a mere phrase without any idea to correspond thereto. What the will is, and how it moves the body, they none of them know; those who boast of such knowledge, and feign dwellings and habitations for the soul, are wont to provoke either laughter or disgust. (Spinoza, 1967, Part II, note to proposition XXXV)

From the point of view of dialectical logic, systematic concepts integrate singular experiences in the living network of its determinative relations. Thus, such doubling of the lived experience through the mediation of a systematic concept makes it richer and thicker because it opens up new relationships between the object of experience and other objects (Vygotsky, 1994a):

> If the object is not really discovered in direct experience, but in its variety of bonds and relationships that determine its place in the world and its connection with the rest of reality, its understanding will be more profound. It will correspond more closely to reality and be more accurate and comprehensive in its expression than the representation. (p. 185)

The experience takes on new meanings and is opened to new possibilities with regard to its inclusion in a system of determination relationships (necessities) that the concept makes accessible to consciousness. The subject thus becomes able to master a kind of reflective process directed at their acting in the world, and through self-observation, find out what is shaping their action as well as ways to deliberately alter its course by taking the appropriate action given the circumstances.

1.2 Reformulating the Method of Double Stimulation to Conceptualize Developmental Interventions Designed to Reconfigure Inter-functional Relationship

In the first case as in the second, the concept of ZPD refers to a socially ruled and normed activity of transmission/acquisition of a cultural heritage and a potential development of new capacities to act voluntarily and consciously. It is an invitation to question educational interventions designed to support a person's involvement in such activity. It problematizes a real social situation of development where a person tries to succeed in a complex task for which they have, in their present state of development, very little chance to achieve on their own. Such a task involves challenges and obstacles that are novel to the person. Hence, they find themselves lacking the means to address and fulfill it efficiently, and yet these abilities prove to be essential to their successful participation in new forms of collective activities where they must find their place and actively self-control the course of their actions.

As we have previously stated the concept of ZDP is introduced by Vygotsky to study developmental interventions involving conducts based on the construction or reconfiguration of a complex network of inter-functional relationships that shape personality at some point along its developmental trajectory. It is a way of redefining the *method of dual stimulation* which was designed to study the essence of the development of a specific HMF (e.g. memory). The researcher's function is therefore to work out a situation that will confront the person with a problem that they cannot overcome without the use of specific cultural resources and sustain potential development of new capacities to think, to act and to feel voluntarily. From this standpoint, the ZPD is indeed a reformulation of the methodology of double stimulation—which has been developed to artificially induce the process of development in an experimental realm and thus study its essence (Vygotsky, 2014)—into a methodology of the intervention structured in a social environment and the prerequisites for making the intentional teaching of cultural resources a genuine source of potential development.

In this situation, the researcher plays a developmental role (Rivière, 1990). Incidentally, Vygotsky has given almost no indications regarding this role. He did however sketch it out when he called for a reconsideration of the purpose of intellectual imitation in human development (Vygotsky, 2012c). This is not to be understood as a simple matter of reproducing new conduct. It corresponds to the moment of its mastery through the progressive understanding of its logic.[3] In more specific terms, it refers to a form of active experimentation, under the guidance of the researcher of a new relationship to experience and its gradual transformation into a new personal form of conduct (Valsiner & Van der Veer, 2014).

Intellectual imitation materializes the person's engagement in an activity that both tears them away from yesterday's possibilities and propels them towards a new horizon of possibilities for future action (Valsiner & Van der Veer, 2014). Thus, the researcher must allow the person to experience mental and emotional contradictions inherent to this relationship. His role is furthermore to keep active the contradictions at stake between appropriated and new modes of action involved in the transmission/acquisition process. To this end, he may have recourse to suggestive questions, examples and counter-examples, demonstrations, etc. (Vygotsky, 2012c, p. 239) and new forms of conceptualization (Vygotsky, 1997b).

We also need to keep in mind that an initial impulse is necessary to lead the person into a potential development, that is, to make them live, within social relationships such as those we have been describing, a meaningful experience that gives rise to positive affects.[4] The researcher ultimately acts as a representative of culture and social groups (Rivière, 1990, p. 93). Consequently, the transmitted cultural forms are embedded in a socio-political framework governing the imputed value of the capacities to be transmitted. The researcher must therefore be actively committed to transforming the person's ability to act according to an ideal form (Vygotsky, 1994b). He plays an essential role by making available, during the course of activity, resources that can give shape to new modes of conduct. On this point, we agree with Stetsenko's analysis (2016, p. 37) when she analyzes the consequences of her transformative activist stance on critical scholarship.

It is important to reiterate that, while the process of transmitting new cultural resources is indeed managed externally, it is nevertheless enabled by pre-existing, internalized capabilities. These, in turn, follow, foster and encourage the progressive mastery of the appropriate capacities. Subjectivity is thus at work, experimenting with new modes of action based on its current structures. Another of the key functions of the researcher (as well as the model or instructor) is therefore to generate contradictions between these two planes of activity. This is undoubtedly one of the possible sources of contradiction between the external and internal plans that are indispensable for development, since according to Vygotsky (1994a) internal contradictions steers development.

In this sense, under certain conditions, the developmental process is made possible by the gradual mastery of new forms of conduct built as part of a collaborative action. In other words, although development invites us to consider the person's becoming, it is crucial not to neglect analysis of processes that stimulate it in the here and now of the transmission/acquisition of new resources.

From this perspective, Vygotsky (1997b) urges caution and warns against confusing awareness (*"prises de conscience"*)—involved in establishing new relations to experience in collaboration with the researcher—with development. Instead, he invites us to see it as potential development. Thus, for Vygotski, it is indeed through their participation in a new activity that the person doubles their experience and actively experiments a new relationship to them which, through taking a different point of view, allows them to envision things in new ways and gradually consider new moves, as suggested by the chess metaphor employed by Vygotsky (1997b, see chapter 6).

Based on the above analysis, we defend the idea that the transmission/acquisition process is played out in the realm of collaboration with others. This process of building new capabilities to act operates at the inter-psychological level (the forefront of sociogenesis) and corresponds to the progressive control of one's conduct within new forms of cultural activities that require the use and control of cultural instruments and the rules that regulate their use in collaboration with others.

Development, on the other hand, is a matter of appropriation/internalization of this new mode of conduct (Wertsch, 1991). It operates at the intra-psychological plane (backdrop of sociogenesis) and consists in a reconstruction of the subject's mental universe as well as his ability to act, think and feel in novel ways, voluntarily and consciously. It corresponds to the various reconfigurations of the existing HMF and/or their relations. It refers also to the diversity of the materials on which existing functions carry out their work and to the reconfiguration of the personal relationship to the world. It could therefore be defined as a form of self-determination. We will come back to this topic later as we discuss more specifically development in adulthood.

Vygotsky (1994a, 2014) makes contradiction the driving force of development. This process can be conceived in terms of the reconfiguration of the person's relationship to the external and internal worlds, and also to oneself, acting in and on these worlds under the transformative effect of contradictions between possibilities of action linked to existing abilities and those that are opened by those under reconstruction in the subjective realm.

Hence, Potential development becomes the person's possession and takes the form of their capacity to deliberately mobilize and control new forms of conduct in different spheres of human activity. It is made visible through the reorganization of the person's worldview in relation to the reconfiguration of personality, understood as the system of semantic relationships between different HMF involved in such activity (Brossard, 2008).

2   The Problem of Cultural Development in Adulthood in Relation to Learning

It strikes us as relevant to point out that the use of the ZPD concept to problematize and conceptualize learning situations and their relationships to the possibility of developing power to act in adulthood—as we have just proposed—is debatable. In fact, Vygotsky forged this concept to study the relationships between instruction and development in school-age children. He has only made very brief remarks on the issue of the relationship between learning and development in adulthood.

2.1   *Is There Any Personality Development in Adulthood?*
Vygotsky seems, in some cases, reluctant to accept adult development when he argues that learning does not produce changes in human mental configuration at this age since it uses developmental cycles that have already been fully developed (Vygotsky, 2012a). Yet, in his discussion of Lewin's theory of volition, Vygotsky (1994a) opened the door to the possibility of development during adulthood and to the continuing stratification of consciousness in response to the growing distinction between spheres of everyday life, the problems one is able to fathom, and the means they mobilize to perform the tasks they must accomplish.[5]

This hypothesis is reminiscent of certain sociological analyses of the transformations of the social world. This one is characterized by a growing differentiation of socially regulated spheres of activity in which people are compelled to undertake.[6] The concept of *"acteur pluriel"* (literally "a plural actor") introduced by Lahire (1998) emphasizes the pluralization of human living milieux and the normative models of action in which they are socialized. It means that, in everyday life, men and women are nowadays subjected to positions, roles and responsibilities, norms or tasks, that are sometimes complementary, but most often contradictory according to their socialization with—and transitions between—different social spheres of activity[7] (labour, family, community, education, politics, sports, etc.). Consequently, we hypothesize that the development of personality in adulthood and the reconfiguration of the worldviews associated with it would be functionally linked to such requirements primarily by virtue of the norms and values that structure roles, responsibilities, and models of action in these various life *milieux* (Saussez, 2019).

This plurality of social situations through which people confront a multiplicity of social frames that give shape to the way they have to act, is believed to push the development of relevant personal and collective coping capabilities forward (Thevenot, 2006). Indeed, it is essential for people to be able to recognize themselves, and to be recognized, in their contribution to the transformation of their own living conditions and those of others with whom they are in solidarity (Stetsenko, 2016). In such a social situation of development, the individual must negotiate with contradictory norms (Schwartz, 2007), settle dilemmas, and address concerns of various kinds and magnitude (Clot, 1999).

More generally, this fragmentation entails the subjective creation of meaningful links between various activities through investigation and comprehension of these relationships and the necessities that organize the person's conduct as well as that of others. On this point, we agree with Clot's analysis (1999, see chapter 2) when he delineates what he means by the psychological function of work. For him, work is one of a variety of socially regulated activities and as such, he considers it important to understand the meaningful relationship that the person is able to construct between his different life milieux. Thus, working conditions would be only one of the systems governing the conduct of the person at work. These would also be shaped by the rationalities structuring the other spheres of activity. Thus, it may very well be that the significance of the relationships between various activities are central in building up the *humane within the human*. This construction would therefore develop or tear down in the meaningful links which the person is able or not to establish between these different spheres of activity, through conflicting values experienced as part of contradictory demands weighing on his activities, and the person's ability to build an enlightened vision of the world and of himself acting in and on this world.

Such fragmentation, and the psychological dynamics it may generate, then converge on the person's ability to behave ethically in the Spinozian sense of the term, that is, to form an adequate idea of what motivates them to act (Spinoza, 1967, see V.3). In other words, the developmental challenge for the adult in the working age is to access a worldview appropriate to their present situation by gaining a adequate understanding of what they are doing and why they are doing it.

However, it must be noted that social spaces where these relationships could be constructed and deconstructed are uncommon. Notably in the workplace, as a consequence of new methods of management in businesses and public services, opportunities for people to formally or informally put into words their experience of conflicting norms and values—and how such tensions disrupt their ability to act responsibly—are undermined (Clot & Gollac, 2014).

In a social world where intelligibility diminishes as people struggle with the ever-growing complexity of *interdependent relations* (Elias, 1993) between the various spheres of activity and a phenomenon of *social acceleration* (Rosa, 2010), lies, a political issue for the historical psychology of cultural development. It is concerned with the construction of tertiary space/time ("tiers milieux") that create conditions for helping people to gain an understanding of these interdependent relationships and the social systems of proximal or distal determining forces that organize them. Vygotsky's critical imperative addressed to this psychology could then be translated into the construction of such tertiary milieux whose normative reference is an ideal of human betterment in the Spinozian sense, that is, supporting the person as they struggle to preserve their ability—and that of others—to be affected and to transform their affects into free actions.

2.2 The Ideal of Betterment as a Normative Reference for Developmental Interventions in Adulthood?

The Spinozian orientation which inspired Vygotsky's practical philosophy is particularly visible in one of the few writings in which he explicitly addresses development in adulthood:

> Finally, from a differential and characterological perspective we must make a fundamental distinction between primary characterological connections, which yield certain proportions, for example, a schizoid or cycloid constitution, and connections that develop completely differently and which distinguish the honest person from the dishonest, the honest from the deceitful, the dreamer from the business person. These do not reside in the fact that I am less tidy than you, or more deceitful than you, but in the development of a system of relations between the different functions that develop in ontogenesis. Lewin correctly says that the formation of psychological systems coincides with the development of personality. In the highest cases of ethically very perfect human personalities with a very beautiful spiritual life we are dealing with the development of a system in which everything is connected to a single goal. In Spinoza you will find a theory (I am changing it somewhat) which says that the soul can achieve that all manifestations, all conditions relate to a single goal. A system with a single centre may develop with a maximal integrity of human behaviour. For Spinoza this single idea is the idea of God or nature. Psychologically this is not at all necessary. But a person can indeed not

only bring separate functions into a system, but also create a single centre for the whole system. Spinoza demonstrated this system in the philosophical plane. There are people whose life is a model of the subordination to a single goal and who proved in practice that this is possible. Psychology has the task of demonstrating that the development of such a unified system is scientifically possible. (Vygotsky, 1997a, pp. 106–107)

As mentioned above, we consider that affects are the driving force of cultural development and construction of personality. This leads us to think that, perhaps through a relation to a fragmented social world subjected to some sort of social acceleration, certain conditions may be deciphered that could bring about circumstances conducive to the development of a distinctive adult personality in which ethical conflicts would be of particular importance. Whereas the ability to think systematically occupies a central place in the personality being established during the age of transition, we believe that in adulthood, this neo-formation is reworked from the inside by the ethical issues that arise at the crossroads of these worlds through the person's activity. These issues pertain to matters related to the right conduct, the appropriate action, and finding out how to conduct a just and good life (Rosa, 2010) in a fragmented social world (Thevenot, 2006). They require the person's capacity to fully assume responsibility for their actions.

On this basis, we expand on Vygotsky's discussion about the intellectualization of the relationship to the world, to oneself, and to others, that is presented the sixth chapter of *Thinking and Language*. We do so by drawing on Spinoza's idea of passage from knowledge based on effects to knowledge based on causes, which he postulates to be necessary to carry out a free action. This inspires us to understand the potential development of a person's power to act during a developmental intervention in terms of the resources they found so that they would be able to move from the first type of knowledge to the second one (Spinoza, 1967).

The purpose of such an intervention is to create the conditions that will allow people (1) to retake their experiences (doubling their experience) in a meaningful relationship with an Other, (2) to take ownership of the intellectual means of explaining the manner in which their unique experience weaves together their own power to act and that which hinders it, in such a way that (3) they may be empowered to take action on the real causes of their passions and self-determine their engagement in the transformation of their conditions of existence enlightened by an adequate idea of what they desire.

Developmental intervention should therefore focus on eliciting the potential development of a person's capability to understand the logic of effects—what is really, effectively at work in each situation—and to trace the effects they incur to causes for which they would progressively become contributing subjects (Saussez, 2019). In this perspective, the notion of ZPD provides us with a means of thinking about developmental intervention as a way to replace the person within a new social relation and to conceptualize the resources to be mobilized so as to involve this person in a process of doubling and resignifying their own experience.

Thus, such intervention, as it raises the possibility of seeking further (Spinoza, 1967, see propositions 31 to 41) as well it introduces intellectual means of systematizing the experience, may provide a way to delineate *a way to freedom* (Zavershneva, 2010) for people involved. We will be discussing this idea in the following section in relation to research-intervention carried out in the field of francophone research on teachers' education and professional development.

3 The Problem of Development in Activity Analysis

In the world of francophone research on teachers' education and teacher's work, the French school of ergonomic analysis applied to the study of teaching has contributed to a new perspective grounded in the analysis of concrete materials that capture teaching activity at it happens (Saussez & Yvon, 2014). This school has also inspired and encouraged research pertaining to the impact of teaching activity analysis on professional development (Saussez, 2014). In *la francophonie*, numerous research programs postulate that the involvement of a person in the analysis of their own activity is indeed a source of development. That said, empirical evidence supporting this postulate lacks vigour (Saussez, 2017).

In this section, we investigate some of the conditions that must be met to foster a process of potential development in activity where the person is actively involved in the analysis of her own teaching activity. As stated before, our thesis is that any potential development of a person's power to act requires a structured process of transmission/acquisition of new cultural forms of systematization of one's relation to teaching activity, and the understanding of its relationship to other activities in which the person is involved.

We believe that the analytical category of the ZDP is an intellectual means that is highly helpful to problematize the relationship between transmission/acquisition of new ways to reflect about the person's activity and conceptualize it and the potential development of new capacities to act upon, to think about, to feel, to assess, and to control one's own activity.

3.1 Of Modes of Operation and Meaning

As far as we are concerned, we understand activity analysis in reference to two dimensions that are inextricably linked in their relations with different socio-historical horizons: (1) an operational dimension (the concrete, tangible material activity) which refers to the act of doing (knowing that not doing is by definition an act) which is productive in the sense of that it is finalized on the transformation of an object, (2) and a significant dimension (the various meanings attached to it and the rationalities shaping them).[8]

Therefore, activity analysis relies inevitably on the production and recording of traces of actual, concrete material activity as it occurred in its living environment, in order to reconstruct its modes of operation, and also on utterances and statements generated under different conditions by the person (or persons) involved in the activity, for the purpose of reconstructing its possible meanings. It thereby claims day-to-day activity as a laboratory, and common sense as essential resources for research.

Such an approach seeks to articulate an external and internal stance with respect to activity. Indeed, it is not about cutting off the activity of its inclusion within an explanatory framework in which social, biological, psychological forces, etc., are active, but is also important to explain how this interplay of forces is singularized through the particular relationship structured by the activity between the biographical and social experiences of the persons involved, their concerns and intentions in the here and now, and what they seek to make happen in their daily life. Moreover, it also requires the concrete material activity to be rendered intelligible other than through the lens of idiosyncratic experience.

Most of the designs employed in research-intervention for the co-analysis of teaching activity rely on the use of audiovisual records to conduct self-confrontations—a procedure in which the person confronts recorded images of their own activity—in order to obtain traces of actual, concrete material activity. Its main function is to lead the subject into a critical reflection and to engage them in a methodical investigation of their own activity. Confronted with its footage, the person is questioned by the researcher and assisted through a process in which the person question what they have or have not done. This procedure seeks to foster conditions conducive to a doubling of experience. To paraphrase Vygotsky (1994a), it arranges the necessary conditions for the activity experienced to be shifted through consciousness so as to transform it into a new kind of activity: a reflective one.

In the course of this investigation, the person explores ways to signify how they view themselves acting by acting with the help of the recorded traces of their own activity and the researcher's questions. Under certain conditions—

that have yet to be formally defined—the person becomes aware of unsuspected logic at work in her activity. Self-confrontation therefore aims to pursue a developmental intention and seeks to produce *awareness* about what settles, but also what disrupts the person's activity. In some research-intervention inspired by the clinic of activity, self-confrontation is part of a more general approach where a form of social conflictuality is orchestrated through crossed or collective self-confrontation processes and critical reflection with an extended collective of workers.

We believe that these research-interventions highlight what could be at stake ine the creation of a tertiary milieu. These correspond to a socially normed activity in which the researcher instrumentalizes the confrontation between the subject and himself. He encourages him to question what he *sees himself do as he is doing it*, to question its biographical and social resonance and depth, to discover and debate possibilities of action that may seem unsuspected at first glance.

It is then a question of outfitting the person with instruments so that they can foresee new possibilities for action in order to influence the course of the necessities that weigh on their activity. These possibilities are not predefined. They are co-constructed with the person according to the analysis of their activity. From this perspective, such an approach is consistent with a critical and transformative stance. It includes a clinical dimension in that it questions the subject about what they have done and what they could have done without taking a normative look at the modes of operation and tools they have used. Indeed, these allow them, in spite of everything, to do what they must in this situation, and the object of the approach is to help the person to explore new possibilities for action created by the co-analysis and not to judge the conformity of their past action with a form of rationality that would be foreign to them.

3.2 *Returning to the Issue of the Development of the Power to Act in Research-Intervention*

Despite the explicit developmental objectives of this research, it is necessary to question their developmental effects and the conditions under which the co-analysis of one's—and others'—own activity is able to contribute to the development of the power to act (Saussez, 2017; Saussez & Yvon, 2014). It is a matter of exploring, theoretically and methodologically, a question that is relevant to us: how to conceive and act on the learning and development potential concealed by the co-analysis of activity?

More specifically, it is a matter of establishing some guidelines to initiate a debate on the developmental intents of co-activity analysis: how to problematize under what terms interventions may be able to awaken a process of potential development when a person is involved in the analysis of their own activity, or that of others?

As stated before, our thesis is that potential development of the power to act requires a structured transmission/acquisition process of new cultural forms of systematization, understanding, and judgment of the logic that explicate the analyzed activity. Without this, the analytic primacy given to development could be detrimental to the understanding of the components that generate it in the here and now of activity co-analysis (Saussez, 2017).

One of us (Saussez, 2017) showed in a critical analysis of different research programs that in data analysis, some researchers either overlapped or confused the processes of transmission/acquisition of new cultural resources and development. As stated before, the co-analysis of activity discussed in this section is concerned with concrete work operations carried out by a person. Under the scope of the ZPD, it involves taking the person out of the usual constraints of laborious activity and immersing them in the analysis of their own activity according to different material records (audiovisual content, accounts of critical incidents, observation notes, etc.). It is a matter of getting the person involved using different instruments and of questioning the researcher in an investigation of their own activity, in the sense of *self in activity* ("*soi en activité*"). In collaboration with the researcher, the person questions the executive techniques, modes of operation, and their relationship to the goals being pursued; they revisit their preoccupations and the relationship they have with their conduct, or they question their choices in the face of other possibilities for action that emerge from their own ways of doing things. It is indeed a situation where a person tries, through collaboration with others, to build a particular relationship to their experience of labour.

Admittedly, it can be considered that within the frame of such activity, specific analytical capacities are being built and that the instruments and questions of the researcher contribute to the person's detachment from his experience and to the possibility for them to see themselves as they are engaged in deed. The awareness that emerges during co-analysis clearly indicates that it is part of a learning process. However, it appears that the concept of ZPD invites us to go further as it problematizes the issue of understanding the logic and principles of intelligibility that are brought into play by the researcher in the process of investigating the activity. These research-interventions are therefore concerned with helping the person to gain access to a system of ideas about work activities, and also about them in their work situations.

The doubling of experience does not simply proceed through a repetition of the experience in another form. For Vygotsky (1994a), this entails an activity of conceptualization of the experience of the lived activity in which its components, their arrangement, and the way in which the person contributes to them, are the object of the reflective method. Therefore, the function of these researches is indeed to render visible and discernible to oneself and to others what organizes the lived activity, to transform it into a reflective activity (Vygotsky, 1994a), but also to provide means to help the person seeks after *another future* (Stetsenko, 2016). Through such a doubling, the activity experienced is made available to the person so that they are able, under certain conditions, to handle it differently.

What can the person then do with what she becomes aware of as she sees herself acting, as she is asked to explain what she understands seeing herself acting, and as she is invited to explain to herself with her own vision of the world? The function of the researcher here is to gradually provide the person with means to control how they are affected by the situation and to inflect the necessity of the choices available to them in order to make happen what they desire in a responsible and free way. Here again, the issue is to enable them to construct an adequate idea of what impedes their power to act.

In a way, it is a question of tensioning a conceptualization of the situation directed by the pursuit of the "reasons for," and a conceptualization oriented by the pursuit of "how can it work" (Brossard, 2004). Such a perspective raises ethical issues related to the researcher's decision to introduce, at some point and in collaboration with the person, a form of conceptualization based on what he understands about what the person needs at that time, so that they can move further along the path towards free action. Indeed, it is a question of helping the person to "re-signify" their experience, understand its underlying causes, in order to develop an adequate idea of what is affecting them. In these circumstances, there is a great risk that the researcher will explain what is happening pouring into a form of explanation that would keep the person in a state of passivity (Spinoza, 1967) or in a servile attitude (*"attitude servile"*) (Rancière, 2010).

This issue was raised by Vygotsky (1925) as early as the publication of his book *Psychology of Art* (2005) where he questioned the psychological function of art and discussed the role of criticism as a social pedagogy whose function is to open art to life. Hence, critics provide people with an explanation of how the work of art operates and of the processes through which it triggers an emotional reaction. Vygotsky then emphasizes that this explanation must be carefully delivered, so as not to prevent the persons' intellectual/emotional movement of its understanding. Indeed, this personal understanding is the only possible key to the development of new capacities to control their own emotional processes. It is therefore important not to submerge the person in the explanatory activity with passivity that could lead to a diminishment of their power to act. For us, this is a possible path for future research because research with developmental agendas are seldom discussed when it comes to the issues surrounding power, which are the hallmarks of collaboration between the researcher and the persons involved in research-intervention.

In the end, it seems to us that by reemphasizing the Spinozian inspiration of Vygotsky's practical philosophy, that he conceptualizes, using the notion of ZPD (Vygotsky, 1997b), the conditions to be met so that the person may involve themselves in building an enlightened relationship to their own experience of the world. This rests on the acquisition of systematic concepts and the experimentation by the person of a new relationship to their lived experience within specific social activity. These new forms of thought gradually penetrate the subjective space of the person and contribute to the emergence of an intellectualized relationship to the world (Vygotsky, 1994a, 1997b). This leads us to hypothesize that co-analysis requires a process of transmission/acquisition, not only of a mode of inquiry, but also of new intellectual means to signify it. Henceforth, their mastery leads to a new understanding of the experience. These means of systematizing of the experience by allowing it to be included in different explanatory networks and in the living history of work and its analysis then opens up the experienced activity to an emancipatory potential.

4 This Is Not a Conclusion

Based on the premise that Spinoza's Ethics provides Vygotsky with normative orientations to any developmental intervention, we have argued that its purpose is to develop the person's capability to explain their conditions and explain themselves with themselves, to relate the effects of which they are the objects to causes of which they could gradually become the subjects by reworking what determines their actions, by seeking to influence the necessity of the choices available to them. To this end, we have sought to demonstrate that the concept of ZPD, since it constitutes a reformulation of the method of dual stimulation for activities involving a complex set of HMF and the reorganization of their relationship, invites us to (1) problematize, with regards to developmental interventions, the means to replace the person in a meaningful social relation in which they would be able to double and actively develop their experience and (2) seek means to inflect the course of their actions and thus achieve a form of self-determination.

On this basis, we have tried to show that this normative orientation allows for the possibility to question adult development in reference to the ethical requirements that weigh on the activity of people torn between different normative and axiological references to which they are subjected in a fragmented social world (Lahire, 1998) subjected to social acceleration (Rosa, 2010). We also called into question the absence in such a social world of favourable conditions for human persons to exercise a form of practical wisdom and to find resources to act knowingly in an ethically responsible manner with reference to an adequate knowledge of what is at stake in their situations. It is a matter of create a third milieu where they may learn and develop the way they are affected. This normative orientation therefore makes the development of the power to act an issue concerning the construction of personality in adulthood. For us, it is indeed a question of setting the development of the power to act as an ideal for the betterment of concrete human persons (Roche, 2016) and for any developmental intervention in adulthood.

In this perspective, research-intervention based on activity co-analysis constitute socially normed activity designed to develop the participants' power to act. Under the scope of the ZPD, it is important not to sever it, neither from the significant social relationship at its source, nor from the means of doubling and re-signifying the lived experience put into play in the co-analysis of the activity. By creating the conditions conducive to a meaningful experience, the ZPD then becomes an indirect means both to generate a potential development of the action radius of consciousness, as well as to produce knowledge about the development of the power to act.

This transformative approach to development in adulthood has an impact on the way scientific activity is conceived. Indeed, here the researcher is also involved in a project of transforming the social world. However, the latter operates indirectly by helping people involved in research to (re)gain control over their own lives and to produce new living conditions, individually and collectively. Drawing on our understanding of the concept of ZPD, we have also sought to problematize certain conditions needed for persons to develop their power to act in a situation of activity co-analysis.

So, we have questioned the person's involvement in an activity in which they make their own activity visible and analyzable for themselves and others. This doubling of experience makes available for themselves their lived experience of the situation. It then becomes possible for the person to dispose of it differently and, under certain conditions, to further reflect on the various necessities affecting them. Developmental intervention therefore orchestrates a possible transition from the lived experience to its doubling such that the person is gradually able to transform it into a reflective activity.

More specifically, it strikes us as important to consider different questions, linked to this developmental aim.
– What can the person do with the awareness they reach during the course of co-analysis? How can they be supported in exploring new perspectives for action and also reflections over which action is appropriate (or not)?

- What are the intellectual and emotional resources available to the person to approach the situation from a different perspective?
- What does the person need to move forward in the transformation/explanation of the situation?
- How can they generate new ideas about that which affects them and the forces that hinder their power to act?
- What means of re-signifying their experience and of explaining what affects them in the situation could be introduced during the co-analysis process? At what time? In what way?
- How can we make sure that the person preserves their capability to be affected and engages in a struggle to create the future they desire (Stetsenko, 2017)?

These various questions all revolve around the issue of power relations at stake in activity co-analysis with respect to the different forms of knowledge it brings into play and the interrelationships it seeks to establish between them. They also shed light on a clinical matter related to the possibility for the person to authorize themselves to take a position and engage, in full knowledge of cause, in an activity participating in their construction as a person.

Finally, as we have tried to illustrate, while we are aware of the many problems it leaves unresolved, that our position raises some difficult questions that are worthy of being revisited. These involve in particular:

1. the participating persons' awareness of the unsuspected forces which are shaping their activity and the verbal re-elaboration of their experience,
2. the development of the power to act and the emancipation of the persons involved by instrumenting a reflective activity so that they may understand the determinisms that weigh on their action and find ways to inflect them,
3. the role of the researcher as an agent of development and transformation.

5 How Does the Chapter Address the Challenges of a Non-Dualist Methodology?

In this chapter, the authors discuss CHAT methodology and epistemology by focusing, first, on the fundamental dialectical relation of the relevance of knowledge and its use in practice to transform the world. They underline Vygotsky's monistic philosophy of method in which the transformation and explanation of human behaviors or society should never be separated. By deeply discussing the concept of Zone of proximal development, and criticizing some of its widespread usages, they reflect on the aim of the developmental and dialectical research. They discuss how CHAT research can create conditions to generate the development of individual and the collective abilities to transform the social world (both of which are conceived in a dialectical relation). They also discuss how during adulthood the pluralization of human "living milieux" and the normative models of action in which adults are socialized create a contradiction in terms of their involvement in different social spheres of activity, which may cause them to suffer if they do not master the conceptual instruments to understand them. In this context, the transformative goal(s) of research-intervention are to create a social process of transmission/acquisition—through the help of the researcher or other participants who are involved in a co-analysis activity—by drawing on new cultural resources to support the person's engagement in a transformative project. In line with Vygotsky's work, the authors approach issues of agency and freedom in considering that for the individual, the processes of progressively mastering purposeful concepts to understand their action and situation in their different living milieux is linked with a liberating force. They discuss their proposition based on research on activity analysis involving teachers in educational contexts where some teachers express powerlessness about their "work milieu."

The authors also discuss, from a Spinozian perspective, how this transformative project and the development of participants' power to act connects with the restoration—during the research-intervention and by opening a ZDP—of the participants' own ability to be affected, to affect others and to transform affects into free actions. They reaffirm Vygotsky's proposition "to consider the dialectical relations between the processes of teaching/learning new cultural forms of activity and the development of the capacity to act voluntarily and consciously within these activities." The authors emphasize the relation between affect and intellect in analysis of participant development during research-intervention. As the authors note, during a research-intervention the purpose is to create the conditions to open a ZPD that will allow people, in collaboration with others, to analyze their activity and doubling their experience within a significant relationship. By doing so, and with the help of intellectual and affective instruments, they can gradually master and gain power over their own lives and be individually and collectively engaged in the production of new conditions of existence and in the development of prospective capacities.

Notes

1 Throughout this text, we will use the word researcher to refer to different types of actors in the fields of education, teacher education, counselling and work analysis.
2 Throughout this text, we have chosen to translate into English the quotations from Vygotsky when we worked on the French version of the text. Indeed, there are translation gaps between English and French, as for example in the formulation of the General Development law.
3 To support our argumentation, it seems important to emphasize that at the end of the 4th chapter of HDFPS, Vygotsky (2014) already introduced the question of intellectual imitation, linked to the double stimulation methodology, and a first formulation of the rapports between already mastered capacities and development. It seems to us that it foreshadowed the notion of ZPD.
4 Unfortunately, in this text, we cannot elaborate further on the emotional component at stake in this social relationship. It seems to us that there is an interesting avenue of research on the question of how to take care of others in such a situation.
5 We are tempted to further add, with reference to Vygotsky (2012a), the objects that the person encounters as they enroll in different fields of activity, the materials on which they exercise their abilities, etc. (see p. 103).
6 See Beck's hypothesis (1992) on a new modernity characterized by a destructuring of the traditional instances of socialization of people and of their relationships in the shaping of the biographical trajectory of individuals.
7 This question echoes, but is not limited to, the work initiated by Star and Griesemer (1989) on boundary objects and, subsequently, the work on boundary crossing (see Akkerman & Bakker, 2011, for a synthesis of research in education) or the work on transitions in management (see Ashforth et al., 2000) or in developmental psychology (see Zittoun, 2008). Although a critical discussion of these researches would be relevant, it is not the object of this text.
8 We will not discuss here the three related components in any ergonomic analysis of the activity: work organization, task and, of course, activity.

References

Akkerman, S. F., & Bakker, A. (2011). Boundary crossing and boundary objects. *Review of Educational Research, 81*(2), 132–169.

Ashforth, B. E., Kreiner, G. E., & Fugate, M. (2000). All in a day's work: Boundaries and micro role transitions. *Academy of Management Review, 25*, 472–491.

Beck, U. (1992). *Risk society towards a new modernity*. Sage Publications.

Brossard, M. (2004). *Vygotski. Lectures et perspectives de recherche en éducation*. Septentrion.

Brossard, M. (2008). Concepts quotidiens/concepts scientifiques: Réflexions sur une hypothèse de travail. *Carrefours de l'Education, 26*(2), 67–82. doi:10.3917/cdle.026.0067

Chaiklin, S. (2003). The zone of proximal development in Vygotsky's analysis of learning and instruction. In A. Kozulin, B. Gindis, V. S. Ageyev, & S. M. Miller (Eds.),

Vygotsky's educational theory and practice in cultural context (pp. 39–64). Cambridge University Pres.

Clot, Y. (1999). *La fonction psychologique du travail*. Presses Universitaires de France.

Clot, Y., & Gollac, M. (2014). *Le travail peut-il devenir supportable?* Armand Colin.

Dafermos, M. (2018). *Rethinking cultural-historical theory: A dialectical perspective to Vygotsky*. Springer.

Elias, N. (1993). *Engagement et distanciation*. Presses Universitaires de France.

Lahire, B. (1998). *L'homme pluriel. Les ressorts de l'action*. Nathan.

Rancière, J. (2010). *Le philosophe et ses pauvres*. Flammarion.

Rivière, A. (1990). *La psychologie de Vygotski*. Mardaga.

Rosa, H. (2010). *Accélération une critique sociale du temps*. La Découverte.

Saussez, F. (2014). Une entrée activité dans la conception d'environnements de formation pour sortir d'une vision fonctionnaliste de la formation, un essai de conclusion. *Activités, 11*(2), 188–200. doi:10.4000/activites.969

Saussez, F. (2017). Les visées développementales de la co-analyse de l'activité: une lecture critique à l'aide de la notion de Zone de Développement le plus Proche. *Travail et Apprentissage, 17*(1), 121–148.

Saussez, F. (2019). Lev Vygotski et la théorie du développement culturel. In P. Carré & P. Mayen (Eds.), *Psychologies pour la formation* (pp. 55–70). Dunod.

Saussez, F., & Yvon, F. (2014). Problématiser l'usage de la co analyse de l'activité en formation initiale à l'enseignement. In L. Paquay, P. Perrenoud, M. Altet, J. Desjardins, & R. Etienne (Eds.), *Travail réel des enseignants et formation. Quelle référence au travail des enseignants dans les objectifs, les dispositifs et les pratiques?* (pp. 113–126). De Boeck.

Schneuwly, B. (2008). *Vygotski, l'école et l'écriture*. Université de Genève.

Schneuwly, B., & Leopoldoff Martin, I. (2018). Introduction. In B. Schneuwly (Ed.), *La science du développement de l'enfant. Textes Pédologiques (1931–1934)*. Peter Lang.

Schwartz, Y. (2007). Un bref aperçu de l'histoire culturelle du concept d'activité. *Activités, 4*(2). doi:10.4000/activites.1728

Sève, L. (2014). Introduction. In L. Sève (Ed.), *Histoire du développement des fonctions psychiques supérieures*. La Dispute.

Spinoza, B. (1967). *Ethics and on the correction of the understanding*. Button.

Star, S. L., & Griesemer, J. R. (1989). Institutional ecology, "translations" and boundary objects: Amateurs and professionals in Berkeley's museum of vertebrate zoology 1907–1939. *Social Studies of Science, 19*(3), 387–420.

Stetsenko, A. (2016). *The transformative mind: Expanding Vygotsky's approach to development and education*. Cambridge University Press.

Thevenot, L. (2006). *L'action au pluriel : une sociologie des régimes d'engagement*. La Découverte.

Valsiner, J., & Van der Veer, R. (2014). Encountering the border: Vygotsky's zona blizhaishego razvitia and its implications for theories of development. In R. Yasnitsky, R. Van der Veer, & M. Ferrari (Eds.), *The Cambridge handbook of cultural-historical psychology* (pp. 148–174). Cambridge University Press.

Veresov, N. (2004). Zone of proximal development (ZPD): The hidden dimension? In A.-L. Ostern & R. Heil-Ylikallio (Eds.), *Language as culture—tensions in time and space* (pp. 13–30). Abo Akademi.

Vygotsky, L. S. (1994a). *Défectologie et déficience mentale*. Delachaux et Nietslé.

Vygotsky, L. S. (1994b). The problem of environment. In R. Van der Veer & J. Valsiner (Eds.), *The Vygotsky reader* (pp. 338–354). Blackwell Press.

Vygotsky, L. S. (1997a). *The collected works of L.S. Vygotsky: Vol. 3. Problems of the theory and history of psychology*. Plenum Press.

Vygotsky, L. S. (1997b). *Pensée et Langage*. La Dispute.

Vygotsky, L. S. (1998). *Théorie des émotions*. L'Harmattan.

Vygotsky, L. S. (1999). *La signification historique de la crise en psychologie*. Delachaux et Nietslé.

Vygotsky, L. S. (2005). *Psychologie de l'art*. La Dispute.

Vygotsky, L. S. (2012a). Analyse paidologique du processus pédagogique. In F. Yvon & Y. Zinchenko (Eds.), *Vygotsky. Une théorie du développement et de l'éducation*. Presses de l'Université d'État de Moscou Lomonossov.

Vygotsky, L. S. (2012b). La dynamique du développement intellectuel de l'élève en lien avec l'enseignement. In F. Yvon & Y. Zinchenko (Eds.), *Vygotsky. Une théorie du développement et de l'éducation*. Presses de l'Université d'État de Moscou Lomonossov.

Vygotsky, L. S. (2012c). Le problème de l'apprentissage et du développement intellectuel à l'âge scolaire. In F. Yvon & Y. Zinchenko (Eds.), *Vygotsky. Une théorie du développement et de l'éducation* (pp. 223–249). Presses de l'Université d'État de Moscou Lomonossov.

Vygotsky, L. S. (2012d). *Six leçons de psychologie*. La Dispute.

Vygotsky, L. S. (2014). *Histoire du développement des fonctions psychiques supérieures*. La Dispute.

Wertsch, J. V. (1991). *Voices of the mind: A sociocultural approach to mediated action*. Harvester Wheatsheaf.

Yvon, F., & Zinchenko, Y. (2012). Introduction. In F. Yvon & Y. Zinchenko (Eds.), *Vygotsky. Une théorie du développement et de l'éducation. Recueils de textes et commentaires* (pp. 16–20). Presses de l'Université d'État de Moscou Lomonossov.

Zavershneva, E. (2010). "The way to freedom." *Journal of Russian & East European Psychology, 48*(1), 61–90. doi:10.2753/RPO1061-0405480103

Zavershneva, E., & Van der Veer, R. (2007). *Vygotsky's notebook. A selection*. Springer.

Zittoun, T. (2008). Learning through transitions: The role of institutions. *Culture and Psychology, 14*(4), 431–441.

CHAPTER 9

Studying with/out an Object

Participant Observation in CHAT

Alfredo Jornet

Abstract

Traditionally, the 'object' of study has been conceptualized in terms of an opposition between subject and object, where the purpose of study is for the former to render an accurate as possible representation or account of the latter. CHAT methodologies, however, overcome the opposition between subject and object, instead postulating their unity (identity) within the dialectical category of *object-oriented* (*sensuous practical*) *activity*. As an implication, the classical opposition between subjectivity and objectivity is supplanted for a process of mutual transformation in which both subjects and objects change through inquiry. In this chapter, I do explore such a process of mutual transformation as it concerns a one-year *participant observation* at an arts-based elementary school. Drawing from video recordings, field notes, and other ethnographic materials from that project, I analyze and describe the change process by means of which the participant researcher becomes a legitimate member (teacher assistant) of the school as the process by means of which the school practice, as object, also changes. I describe how an inherent tension that characterizes the school's everyday praxis, namely the tension between the need to give space to (artistic) emergence and the need of achieving curricular content objectives, becomes a lived, experienced tension, opening up opportunities for change in praxis. The chapter concludes with a discussion on the notion of object as lived praxis and its significance in CHAT methodology.

Keywords

subject-object unity – object-oriented activity – participant observation – arts-based education

1. Introduction: Meeting CHAT as an Outsider

Approaching CHAT for the first time as a student is, in most cases, not a straightforward task. Having only recently become popular among Western scholars and practitioners, coming to terms with CHAT requires some cognitive (intellectual) and—as I will argue—also affective bending. By the time students come into contact with CHAT, they most often have already been familiarized with and accustomed to a majority of research approaches and discourses that rely on ontological and epistemological premises that are not just different, but *radically* different from those at the core of CHAT. Yet, introductory textbooks on research in psychology and education tend to present CHAT as a theory that differs from the other approaches only superficially, in its emphasis on the social aspects of thinking and learning. In this way, as we note elsewhere, "Vygotskian concepts are often presented as [if they were] part of classical psychological frameworks and paradigms that Vygotsky himself strongly rejected and attempted to overcome" (Roth & Jornet, 2017, p. 1), while the deeper premises and historical lines of inquiry that make CHAT a unique approach remain obscured. As a result, students using CHAT concepts in their research tend to either assimilate those concepts into frameworks that are indeed incommensurable, often leading to critique and rejection in peer review, or else struggle to make use of the theory in actual research practice.

I have seen these confusions happening in numerous occasions among colleagues, and I have experienced them myself as student. Trained in cognitive psychology, and having mostly worked with psychometrics and statistical analyses of variance as a means to investigate learning and education, I did very much struggle coming to terms with CHAT during my PhD studies. Through the years since, I have come to understand the process of learning CHAT as a process of deep conceptual change, where some fundamental premises need to be questioned about what such things as learning and thinking are (ontology), and how one can go about investigating them (epistemology). As I document in an auto-ethnography study on this process (Jornet, 2019), this is a change that involves a shift in our *professional vision* as scholars—in the ways in which intellectually, pragmatically, and also affectively we come to relate to the world of objects that make up our professional field. In fact—as I hope I show throughout this chapter—from a CHAT perspective, the very production of scientific knowledge in the social and the learning sciences can be conceived as a process of personal change, as a process of *subjectification* as part of which we scholars and research participants alike become subjects of and are subjected the new material conditions that the research brings about.

In this chapter, my aim is to provide a first-hand account of what this process of coming to terms with a CHAT perspective involves as a matter of praxis of method, that is, as the *lived work* of perceiving and acting upon an emerging (CHAT) research object. I certainly do not mean to address this question through a set of statements about what it "means" to do CHAT research, as a sort of hermeneutic exercise; nor do I intend to present a step-by-step set of purely practical procedures that should be followed to achieve a CHAT research object in all and any instances. In line with the dialectical premises upon which CHAT emerged as a research program, my aim is to present an account of the way a research thing, or more precisely a research *object*, emerges as an object of CHAT research in the course of actual, lived and living concrete praxis. To do so demands reporting on a concrete case of actual research, not as a succession of purely (random) empirical facts, and not as a succession of only rationally connected interpretations, but as the movement from the abstract to the concrete through the actual study of a given phenomenon. In the current chapter, this involves reporting on a participant ethnography I conducted during my postdoctoral studies at an arts-based primary school, and the process by means of which I came to know my object.

Discussing how a research *object* emerges as a course of lived praxis involves, first, acknowledging the use of the notion "object." I do therefore begin by discussing how CHAT conceives the notion of object generally and more specifically as it relates to the notion of *subject*. The connection between these two notions, subject and object, is often discussed in terms of another important concept in research literature, *reflexivity*, which I take up in this chapter in terms of yet another important concept: object-oriented activity. I then proceed to provide an account of a participatory ethnography as a case to illustrate the emergence of a research object and the dialectically connected movement it entails in generating a subjectivity as well.

2   Objectivity, Subjectivity, and Object-Oriented Activity

2.1   *The Separation of the Subject and the Object in Classical Literature*

The problem of objectivity is foundational to the very idea of scientific research and is the crux of any discussion on philosophy of science. In such discussions, objectivity has often been framed as a means to address the question of certainty, the key to what differentiates scientific knowledge from non-scientific (e.g., everyday) knowledge. An intellectual lineage of this idea can be traced back to the *Cartesian doubt*, often cited as the origin of all sins of dualism in

Western thought (e.g., Rorty, 1979). This is the doubt that raises when one questions his or her own senses to the point of wondering, how do I know that what I think I know is actually true? The original sin of this debility? Subjectivity. It is because we think of and experience the world from our subjective perspective that we cannot be certain about it. What if I got it wrong? What if what I experience is not what I think I am experiencing? From our perspective as (social) scientists—which is likely the future or current profession of the reader—these questions seem particularly relevant. How do I know that the knowledge I am generating is not just my invention but actually an accurate "representation" of what exists out there? And of course, the reader must understand, these are questions that I am posing in the key that determines the way of thinking that I am exposing through this section: a classical Cartesian perspective. When we will shift to a different key, that of non-dualist perspectives and CHAT, then these questions will make no sense, or, rather, these will not be the kind of questions that will interest us. We will see how the assumptions underlying these questions, including that knowing is about "representing," are at odds with the non-dualist premises at the core of CHAT.

The quest for certainty that the Cartesian doubt inaugurated was critically addressed by a modern thinker, John Dewey, who saw in it the genesis of the infamous division between theory and practice that so much literature still aims at remediating. As Dewey (1929) writes, "man's (sic) distrust of himself has caused him to desire to get beyond and above himself; in pure knowledge he has thought he could attain this self-transcendence" (p. 7). The paradox is that, at the origin of the doubt, there is the premise that our subjectivity exists as inherently removed or disconnected from the world. It is only connected to it through some "mediators," whether the pineal gland in Descartes, in the information-processing that characterizes much of recent scholarship in psychology and the cognitive sciences (Roth & Jornet, 2013), or even in attempts to position culture (language, socialization, practice, activity) as mediating between the objective world and the subjective experience of the person (Mikhailov, 2001).

This premise of a subjectivity that is—by definition—opposite to objectivity, has important implications to current conceptions on the role of observation in the social sciences. It leads to an "spectator theory of knowledge" (Dewey, 1929, p. 23), according to which,

> knowing is modeled after what was supposed to take place in the act of vision. The object refracts light to the eye and is seen; it makes a difference to the eye and to the person having an optical apparatus, but none to the thing seen. (p. 23)

The spectator theory of knowledge is definitely not unlike the one I had before I encountered CHAT during my PhD studies. Up to that point, for me, the craft of doing research in psychology had revolved around questions of how to best render measurable and amenable to (statistical) analysis otherwise unobservable 'psychological' phenomena. This work had been firmly anchored on the assumptions that psychological phenomena (including learning) are most primarily subjective phenomena that concern individuals' mental (private, internal) sphere, requiring of special methods to make those phenomena public and amenable to study, methods which should in turn be tested for their validity as means to render objective knowledge about those subjective phenomena. Thus, for example, to investigate psychological dimensions of mobile phone use, I would contribute generating, testing, and refining so-called psycho-metrics, adequate questionnaires capable of capturing measuring those otherwise unobservable dimensions that underly mobile phone use. Through factor analyses and analyses of variance I would transform the students' responses into as-objective-as-possible data concerning relations between psychological aspects of mobile phone (ab)use (Jornet et al., 2009). The objectivity of my observations resided, precisely, in the guarantee that the measuring instrument had as little as possible to do with the measurement.

Hence, according to the spectator theory of knowledge that has reigned in scientific discourse and practice during decades, observing something is an exercise of removal, of disconnecting from the thing to be known, and getting personally or otherwise involved or engaged in it may invalidate any observation, for it may be the result of subjective creation and not the recording of objective fact. As anthropologist Tim Ingold (2018b) presents it,

> for the scientist even to admit to a relationship of give and take with the things in the world with which he deals would be enough to disqualify the inquiry and any insights arising from it. Ideally, he (sic) should leave it all to his recording equipment and exit the scene, only to return to register the outcomes once the job is done and to transfer them to a databank or storage facility for safe keeping. That this is impossible in practice ... is often considered a shortcoming, a weak point in the methodological armoury that could compromise the objectivity of the results. (pp. 100–101)

In its depiction of this archetypical way of thinking, the quotation presents the challenge of scientific practice generally, and of methodology more specifically, as consisting on protecting data from the influence of the subject of observation. To achieve objective knowledge, then, involves excruciating the object of observation from the fullness of life experience in which the observer originally finds it. Objectivity is in this regard defined as that which is not subjectivity, the opposite of experience. During my undergraduate studies, mine, as that of many others working in cognitive science and/or (educational) psychology, was a view of objectivity as the stamp of things which exist out there, independently of our subjective experience of them; that which "really" exists and which, therefore, is not the product of "fantasy" or of the "imagination."

Vygotsky (1997a) indeed wrote about the term "objective" as being "often vulgarized and equated with 'truthful,' while the term 'subjective' is equated with 'false'" (p. 339), a dichotomic perspective that Vygotsky rejected in pro of a dialectical conception in which the proper question was not whether knowledge was subjective or objective but rather what *scientific knowledge* implied as something other, over and above every day, common-sense knowledge. For Vygotsky it is not the objectivity of the facts in and of themselves, but the embedding of these empirical facts into larger conceptual wholes that would reveal the nature of phenomena. This nature, while of course to be explored through means of human perception and experience, cannot and should not be reduced to experience. The problems of psychology need therefore to be solved by overcoming these simplistic dichotomizations and require of a conceptual exploration of what the object of psychology, as scientific discipline, actually is.

2.2 *From Object-Subject Divide, to Sensuous, Object-Oriented Activity*

> The chief defect of all previous materialism … is that things [Gegenstand], reality, sensuousness are conceived only in the form of the object, or of contemplation, but not as sensuous human activity, practice, not subjectively. (Marx, 1924/1998, Theses on Feuerbach, thesis one)

The crucial aspect that sets apart CHAT from most other approaches in education and psychology is the one that tends to be most absent or only mentioned but seldom elaborated on when CHAT is introduced in educational (psychology) textbooks: CHAT's Marxist, dialectical materialist basis. Foundational to this basis is the thesis that knowing is not about contemplation, not even about "sensuous contemplation," but about "actual, practical, human-sensuous activity" (thesis 5). Here sensuousness, the sensorial engagement with the world through which we may generate anything like a (scientific) observation is active, purposeful engagement with it. The point of science, of philosophy, and of the human intellect more generally, is not to "interpret" the world, but to *change* it. From this view, knowing, and thinking more generally, is not *about* but *of*, *in* and *for* the world.

CHAT's foundational basis represents thus an approach to knowledge that is radically different to that of the spectator theory described in the previous section. Knowing here is not about removing oneself from the world, from our object of observation, to become a mere spectator. It rather is about *participating* in the world; knowing is about getting involved. Observation is not modelled on the act of vision as one where a subject sees or perceives, through the senses, an objective world out there that then appears in subjective experience as an image. Of course, the world can be perceived, but if we are to know about it, objectively, then we are to engage with it in and through objective *sensuous activity*. This sensuous activity, then, is not to be abolished from the scientific record as condition to preserve the objectivity of the observation or data to be "extracted" (as per Ingold's quotation above). In fact, the operation can no longer be reduced to one of "extraction," but rather must be understood as one of production—or to be more correct, of the production of the means of livelihood, which in turn concerns not just productive activity but also the needs and satisfaction of needs that complete the livelihood cycle. By contrast to the spectator theory, data are not observed but *produced* through objective activity. The intellectual orientation towards the world is not one of passive contemplation, but one of active, purposeful transformation (Stetsenko, 2009).

Interestingly, though, in Marx's quotation above, sensuous human activity is referred to as knowing *subjectively*. Is this a contradiction? May this mean, as Surmava (2018) recently wrote in ironic tone, that "Marx was not a materialist but secretly professed a subjective method, and in fact was a subjective idealist?" (p. 372). The answer is to be found in the way dialectical materialism changes the meaning of the terms object, subject, and most importantly, of the relation between the two. From a dialectical materialist perspective, we can no longer define subjectivity as that which is "opposite" to objectivity; at least not in the classical (non-dialectical) sense. The question, cultural-historical psychologist Feliks R. Mikhailov (2001) reminds us, "is how to understand the nature of *opposite*" (p. 14).

In the classical view, subject and object are depicted as "opposites" in the sense that subjectivity is that which objectivity is not; the essence of the relation is mutually exclusive. From the Spinozist perspective that is the forbearer of Marx's dialectical materialism, however, the relation is not mutually exclusive, but rather *mutually constituting*. It is a relationship in which the "opposed" elements constitute an identity, "as the mutual generation of the antithesis by the thesis and of the thesis by the antitethis. One without the other is unthinkable" (Mikhailov, 2001, p. 16). Two forms of expressions of one single substance; not two ontological distinct, somehow to-be-bridged realms. Not two realms at all, indeed, but one: the realm of the history of objective, subjective human activity. We've have previously used the nomenclature {subjectivity | objectivity} to refer to this dialectical unity or identity (Roth & Jornet, 2017).

Leont'ev (1978), thus, does not speak of psychological analysis in the classical sense, but in the sense of the *psychological analysis of activity*, which,

> consists ... not in isolating from it its internal, psychological elements for further isolated study but in bringing into psychology such units of analysis as carry in themselves psychological reflection in its inseparability from the moments that give rise to it and mediate it in human activity. (p. 7)

Here, objectivity and subjectivity form an *identity* in that they are but two ways in which a single substance, objective human conscious life, exits. Leontiev does indeed explicitly contrapose this view to the mentioned spectator theory of knowledge, as, according to the Soviet psychologist, "consciousness must be considered not as a field contemplated by the subject on which his images and conceptions are projected but as a specific internal movement generated by the movement of man's [sic] activity" (p. 7). Consciousness, thus, is not something that predates activity, but is generated in and through activity.

In the context of this non-dualist approach, the category of *object-oriented activity* emerges as a means to address the agentic nature of being alive in general, and of being human more specifically. In object-oriented activity, we are not simply "effected" by external "objects" that impact our senses but sense the objective world in and through being actively engaged in purposeful activities that transform it. And these activities are societal in nature. Individual "subjectivities," thus, are not primary; rather, society, culture, are primary, and contain both subjectivity and objectivity. The way in which the world presents itself to us, thus, is shaped through and through by the activities by means of which we come to both sense and shape it. This developing unit in which both psyche (subject) and world (object) mutually shape each other is object-oriented activity.

Does the negation of the formal opposition between objectivity and subjectivity mean that scientific knowledge, from a CHAT perspective, is to be grounded on subjectivity alone, because it is objective subjectivity we are referring to? Not exactly, because the point is not to choose a side of the dichotomy, but to understand objectivity and subjectivity *dialectically*. And, if we follow the premise that observation is not disengaged of activity, does that then mean that we cannot gain objective knowledge at all, or that we need to embrace subjectivity as our source of knowing and learning about human activity? Nothing farther from the truth. Vygotsky (1997a) was quite clear on that matter: "scientific knowledge and immediate perception do not coincide at all" (p. 250). In fact, for Vygotsky, "the need to fundamentally transcend the boundaries of immediate experience is a matter of life and death" (p. 274). This imperative had to do with the condition, for psychology to become a scientific discipline, to reject empiricist assumptions on the primacy of immediate experience and instead strive towards a conceptual and methodological formulation of psychology's premises as a science that, as such, seeks objective truth.

The key to a CHAT perspective is thus the rejection of a dichotomic (because of partial, incomplete) understanding of objectivity as opposite to subjectivity, and instead consider, as our object of study, the unity of objectivity and subjectivity that psychological phenomena must exhibit to be considered (to be observable, indeed) as such from a CHAT perspective. This, again, brings us back to the notion of object-oriented activity: studying psychological phenomena from a CHAT perspective consists in examining the emergence and development of psychological categories that are irreducible to a given persons' internal "mental" structures. It needs to consider how psychological functions indeed emerge as social relations, where affective and cognitive dimensions are but expressions of these larger (supra-)organic unit that includes individuals and social practices. This is in line with Vygotsky's most foundational principle, the genetic law of development according to which, "every function appears on the scene twice in the child's cultural development, i.e., on two levels, first the social, and then the psychological, first between people as an interpsychological category, and then within the child" (Vygotsky, 1989, p. 58). Here, the interpsychological is primary, it is part of the process/phenomenon that is the object of study, not simply an external factor or input to the core psyche that belongs to the individual. Without an understanding of the dynamics and structure of the social relation, there cannot be understanding of the individual. The objective is not so because it is external, and the subjective is so because being internal, for, according to Vygotsky, psychological functions indeed are both organic and instrumental, they include both the persons and the cultural means by means of which they meaningful establish social relations, that is, object-oriented activities.

3   CHAT as a Methodology

According to the premises laid out so far in this chapter, research from a CHAT perspective rejects the classical dichotomy that considers subjectivity and objectivity as opposites, and instead conceives object-oriented activities, which are social in nature and include the pursual of meaningful goals by the transformation of objective reality, as leading to the development of anything that can be observed or claimed to be "psychological." Affects, attention, memory, ways of thinking, concepts ... all of these categories can be approached as varied expressions that together constitute given fields of practice, cultures, or *communities of practice* as Lave and Wegner (1991) famously coined them. The requirement is that these psychological categories are studied in their intrinsically genetic relation to situated, material human activities, the collective activities that constitute the politics of human life organization.

Does this imply that there are only a limited set of methods that would allow us to document and understand object-oriented activity? If the focus is on wholistic, meaningful practices, do we need to restrict ourselves to so-called qualitative approaches and avoid quantitative ones, or is it still OK to "count" things as part of my CHAT research?[1] Are interviews enough to describe object-oriented activities, or should I use video-based ethnography and perform detailed analyses of interaction, as many scholars in CHAT research do? As I hope it will become evident, there is no particular method that is, in itself, better or worst suited for conducting CHAT research. But first, a key distinction needs to be made between methods and *methodology*. It is in fact methodology that concerns us in this chapter, and the entire book for that matter.

Vygotsky was indeed concerned with methodology, as he made clear in his Historical Meaning of the Crisis of Psychology, where he elaborated on how "anyone who attempts to skip this problem, to jump over methodology in order to build some special psychological science right away, will inevitably jump over his horse while trying to sit on it" (1997a, p. 329). Here, we understand methodology in the sense of a system of methods that is consistent with a particular set of ontological and epistemological premises or cosmovision, and not as a particular method. Note that Vygotsky himself (or at least an English translations thereof) seems to have referred to these two notions in the opposite meaning, at least in an posthumously published chapter titled "The Instrumental Method in Psychology" (Vygotsky, 1997a), where Vygotsky writes, "[the instrumental] method can make use of any methodology i.e., technical methods of investigation: the experiment, observation, etc." (p. 89). Be as it may, the two main points being made are that, (a) as logic of method (methodology), Vygotsky envisioned what he referred to as *instrumental method*, and (b) that this approach was not dependent on any given or specific method or technique. What is important is understanding what the key moments or elements of the instrumental method are that may guide our selection of methods.

Vygotsky's instrumental method is consistent with a (psychological) science that takes object-oriented activity as its most general object of study. For it takes the active, purposeful transformation of the "natural" conditions of a situation as its core, minimal unit of analysis. Psychological acts, accordingly, are seen as acts of labor. Unlike is the case in classical psychology, where psychological phenomena's formation is taken as premise, in Vygotsky's approach, the focus of analysis is on the process of cultural formation of the mental functions, which emerge in and through the purposeful transformation of the environment. A CHAT inquiry is an inquiry into the genesis of psychological formations. And this process is not one of biological maturation, but involves the transformation of biological, naturally endowed functions as they become embedded in social relationships of labor. This is, for Vygotsky, a creative process, a process of artificial, instrumental mediation: a situation that is transformed by the insertion, in it, of cultural means: artificial tools and/or techniques that change the way we meet our otherwise biologically anchored needs.

The most basic unit of interest here is thus not the mental act, as the individual and primarily internal phenomenon that is of interest to classical psychology, but the *instrumental act*, which is cultural in its constitution. "Psychological tools are artificial formations. By their nature they are social and not organic or individual devices" (Vygotsky, 1997a, p. 85). Psychological categories are here treated as irreducibly connected to the instrumental (and hence societal, not just individual) act. They are hence not a mere enaction of a biologically endowed function. Psychological tools are to be conceived as part and parcel of the broader, transformative, life-forming human activities: the tool-mediated activities by mens of which we transform our own life conditions. As examples of psychological tools, Vygotsky (1997a) mentions the following: "language, different forms of numeration and counting, mnemotechnic techniques, algebraic symbolism, works of art, writing, schemes, diagrams, maps, blueprints, all sorts of conventional signs, etc." (p. 85). Psychological tools are not given, but emerge in practice-contexts, as a response to emerging practical needs. And when they do, they transform what otherwise would have been some naturally given psychological function.

> By being included in the process of behaviour, the psychological tool modifies the entire course and structure of mental functions by determining the structure of the new instrumental act, just as the technical tool modifies the process of natural adaptation by determining the form of labour operations. (Vygotsky 1997a, p. 85)

Thus, for example, mnemotechnic devices fundamentally transform the function of memory: remembering itself is accomplished through a ritual that embeds an artificial and societal element (a technique) into the cognitive function, thereby transforming the very nature of that function—and what it is possible to achieve with it. Psychological tools, however, are not some super- or supranatural force, "Artificial acts are natural as well" (p. 85).

What makes the instrumental act to be at the center of Vygotsky's cultural-historical theory (and by extension also the notion of psychological tool) is the fact that such an act implies the purposeful mastery of one's own biological means. For, in the instrumental act, psychological tools "are directed toward the mastery of [mental] processes—one's own or someone else's—just as technical devices are directed toward the mastery of processes of nature" (Vygotsky 1997a, p. 85). It is thus not that humans have developed a super-natural power. The "power" lies in the perfectly natural fact that, in human activity, our nervous system, though still organized according to biological laws, becomes itself a means in the pursual of collectively organized, culturally mediated activities. Thus, the same conditional connections that characterize any other nervous system are at play: "What is new is the artificial direction which the instrument gives to the natural process of establishing a conditional connection, i.e., the active utilization of the natural properties of brain tissue" (p. 86).

There are at least two important aspects to the above. First, the instrumental act, as a primary unit of analysis in the study of human psychology, cannot be reduced to the individual. Psychological tools, as quoted above, are "social devices." They are social because they emerge and develop as part of larger culturally and historically situated activities. The second point is this: instrumental acts are transformative and emancipatory; they are about will and volition, about gaining control and mastery over oneself through the mastery of one's own life conditions. Vygotksy (1997b) puts it this way:

> The person, using the power of things or stimuli, controls his own behavior through them, grouping them, putting them together, sorting them. In other words, the great uniqueness of the will consists of man having no power over his own behavior other than the power that things have over his behavior. But man [sic] subjects to himself the power of things over behavior, makes them serve his own purposes and controls that power as he wants. He changes the environment with the external activity and in this way affects his own behavior, subjecting it to his own authority. (p. 212)

To study the process by means of which individuals "subject to themselves the power of things over behavior," Vygotsky devised an experimental method, the method of "double stimulation," where the subject is presented with a first stimulus: a problem to be solved. The subject is then allowed to use a (given or spontaneously emerging) set of additional stimuli, which in the problem-solving become *auxiliary means* for solving the first problem. The experimental interest is in fact on the emergence of these auxiliary means, the way they transform the cognitive task by virtue of becoming psychological tools as part of the problem-solving instrumental act. The experimental set up is one in which emerging needs are met with emerging means of addressing these needs. And the methodology is one that is interested in the *genesis* of tools and operational devices that subjects deploy or appropriate in order to address historically emerging needs, mastering our own (organic and inorganic) life conditions.

4 The Case of Participant Observation/Ethnography

In the previous section, the instrumental method or method of double stimulation is discussed to operationalize the logic of the CHAT approach—its method(o)-logy. But, as Vygotsky noted, the approach does not have to rely on a given technique of data collection and analysis; multiple methods may be applied. However, some core aspects must be present in any methodological approach that is to be considered CHAT: it shall considers psychological categories as irreducibly social (that is, psychological categories cannot be reduced to the individual as ultimate unit or cause but need to consider individuals as embedded in cultural-historical practices). Psychological functions are not organically endowed but developed in and through sociocultural practices that involve the mastery of one's own life conditions through the appropriation and developmen of (cultural) instrumental acts and devices. A CHAT methodology focuses thus on the emergence—the *genesis*—and the subject's appropriation of psychological and technological tools, which are mobilized as means to satisfy human needs or problems that emerge as activity's motives.

Understood as object-oriented activities, psychological phenomena are both individual and social simultaneously, and they always are an integration of cognitive and affective, as well as of organic and inorganic aspects of activities. And, when it comes to higher order, conscious phenomena, they always involve the purposeful orientation towards the meeting of needs that emerge in historically situated, cultural activities. To study psychological phenomena from a CHAT perspective involves approaching human activities as fields of human pursual, which also always means such things as struggle, passion, joy.

To exemplify this perspective, in this chapter I have chosen to focus on *participant observation* or *ethnography*. Now, by using this term I am not trying to encapsulate a particular technique that can be deployed across diverse research settings independently of both the particularities of the research goals and settings, and of the theoretical inclinations that inform its application. In general, it may be agreed that participant observation or ethnography is an approach in which (a) the aim is to record the cultural customs and practices of different nations, societies or peoples—as the term ethno-grapy literally states—and, (b) a specific position of the researcher as someone who becomes a member of the culture being studied as the means of analysis. However, this is only an approximation, as the very notion of ethnography is under continued discussion and revision (see for example Forsey, 2010), and is quite dependent on the specific field and even the nature of the particular problem being investigated within any given field. In this line, a widely cited primer on ethnography concludes,

> Across the spectrum of the social sciences, the use and justification of ethnography is marked by diversity rather than consensus. On that basis, it is arguable that it is futile to try to identify different types of "qualitative research." Rather, one has to recognize different theoretical or epistemological positions-, each of which may endorse a version of ethnographic work. (Atkinson & Hammersley, 1994, p. 257)

Being so widely and diversely applied, the very notion of ethnography runs the risk of becoming too general and diffuse, for, it has been argued, "ethnography has become a term so overused, both in anthropology and in contingent disciplines, that it has lost much of its meaning" (Ingold, 2014, p. 383). It is definitely not my intention to add to this overuse. Yet, I choose to focus on participant observation for two reasons. First, despite diverse definitions and applications, ethnography continues to be a distinctive research method in the social sciences that both students and seasoned scholars resort to when doing research on social and cultural practices/phenomena. Considering what the significance and very shape that this method takes when considered from a CHAT perspective should be of relevance to many. Second, participant ethnography—because it implies a form of immersion or embeddedness of the researcher into the research field—the approach is particularly well suited for discussing and making salient aspects of the unity of subjectivity-objectivity in the (instrumental) act of observation that are discussed throughout this chapter.

In the following, I narrate the process by means of which a research object—the arts-based teaching and learning practices at a small but growing primary school in the British Columbia (Canada)[2]—emerges in and through ethnographic observation, from the perspective of the participant observer. This, we shall see, involves not just "observing" in the "spectator" sense that

Dewey critiqued (see discussion above), but as a mutually transforming process of cognitive and affective participation that leads to being able to see and become response-able with respect to a field's objects/objectivity. The narration and ensuing reflections, which exemplify how a CHAT perspective takes shape in and through a concrete ethnography, serves as conclusion section for the chapter.

5 Encountering a Research Object as a Subjective-Objective Process in Participant Observation

I first encounter the arts-based primary school during the 2016–2017 school year, as I was searching for a school for my own daughter. Having just moved to British Columbia from Norway, we were interested in a smaller and hands-on oriented school that could make the transition to the new language and country easier for our daughter. As a Spanish and Catalan speaker raised in Norway (and proficient in Norwegian), our daughter faced the challenge of starting primary school in yet a fourth new language (English), and in a new country. We thought that finding a school that would de-emphasize verbal proficiency and encourage non-verbal forms of participation would be beneficial. We learned about several options and felt particularly compelled by an arts-based primary school that was quite young, still in expansion. We signed our daughter up, and three months later, she was speaking English quite proficiently, and learning to read and write just as everyone else in her class.

In approaching the school as a researcher, I was not so much interested in understanding how come my daughter had been able to integrate and seamlessly develop into the new literacy culture of British Columbia,[3] as I was in understanding the very notion of arts-based education more generally. What was it indeed? How does integrating arts across other curricular tasks work, and how does it look in actual situated practice? Arts-based education as a genre was my "object of study," but I did not yet know how it would look like. What was an "observation" of that sort of object?

To find out, I offered my help as a part-time teacher assistant. I would then, of mutual agreement, be able to document the school's practices from within—with the adequate approval from all parents, students, and staff. I would also and at the same time be able to share my insights and findings with the school for their own benefit/use, hence entering in what is broadly referred to as a participatory research approach (Cornwall & Jewkes, 1995), where the production of knowledge is directly tied to the contexts of action and use that are being addressed.

5.1 Learning to "See" a Research Object as "Meeting" a Need

My premise was quite straightforward: by immersing myself in the school's practices, I would be able to capture my research object, to experience it and document it. I was in this way taking as starting point the quite widely extended idea that ethnography (or participant observation) is about "render[ing] an account—in writing, film or other graphic media—of life as it is actually lived, thought and experienced by a people, somewhere, sometime" (Ingold, 2018a, p. 63). But how would I be able to render such an account without first learning how to see what I was supposed to see?

Yes, I did see teachers performing specific actions in classrooms and elsewhere. I did follow teachers and students across subjects and activities, both within and outside the school's building, and I did part take in organizing those activities. But the focus was unclear, erratic. Different teachers acted differently and seemed to follow very different teaching styles, not to mention differences across subjects as well as with regards to the nature and extent to which art was part of all of it. In fact, based on observations and interviews, I discovered that I was not alone in having trouble to nail down what the core of arts-based teaching practice was. The research object was fuzzy and slippery for me, and it was so also for several other teachers in the school. My problem of research was a problem of learning to orient myself in meaningful ways within a living practice.

Of course, one could see many things just by "looking" around, as an external observer who throws a gaze on a given space and gathers some materials to reflect upon and inspect. One could for example have developed an observation protocol based on prior literature on arts-based educational practices (although the literature is scarce, and it most often remains at a programmatic rather than actual pragmatic level). In that case, one could have checked for the presence or absence of some pre-established categories in this school. However, two important shortcomings of this approach are the following. First, by having pre-established what to look for, the protocol already has defined for you what your research object is. The remainder of the inquiry amounts to a mostly quantitative investigation concerning how much or how little this school is like the ones that had been studied or theorized before. This is of course a valuable approach, but one that misses any qualitative difference or insight on what arts-based education is or can be. Secondly, as is well known from sociological and ethnomethodological studies of science and technology, there is a fundamental difference between plans and actions (Suchman, 1987), that is, between formal representations and actual courses of situated action.

Perhaps the most important thing that I was learning about my research object during the first weeks working in the school was that, just as Dewey's critique to the "spectator theory of knowledge" described above has it, I could not just arrive at the school and gather (document) an observation of it without enduring a process of personal change and investment into the object. I could not disentangle my data collection from the learning process in which I was invested in trying to competently take part in the schools' activities. In other words, my data collection and analysis was not so much about intellectually grasping my object as it was learning to *attend to it* (see Ingold, 2018, for a discussion on learning as an "education of attention"). The process was not one in which I would come to intellectually "understand" the research object per se, but one in which I would become able to *correspond* with it, so that my participation, my situated actions, would be response-able and adequate to this phenomenon.

In line with CHAT premises, the situated process of corresponding with and becoming response-able to an object of social inquiry (a social practice, here the practice of teaching and learning disciplinary competences through the arts) is not simply one of cognitively understanding something in the abstract; but it is neither something primarily perceptual either. It is both cognitive and perceptual, and also affective and motivational. For one always becomes aware of the world in the context of object-oriented activities, that is, as part of activities that have given orientations, that are for-the-purpose-of. Thus, from a CHAT perspective, the first contact that I made with my research object was when I first came in touch with a *need* that emerged from within the target practice.

The need was of course personal: it was felt and experienced subjectively by me as an existential phenomenon. It first came as a sense of confusion and frustration. It emerged in the midst of my own attempts to fit into a teaching and learning practice that I could not yet master and contribute to seamlessly. I remember being invested in assisting 6 to 9 years old students—the class groups were organized by shared interests and affinities rather than age—trying to help them be creative during a science class in which they were preparing materials for a later presentation on different habitats. One of the groups was however not focusing on the task and my approach was characterized by a resort to coercive authority as well as by re-organizing the task in a way that the creative component no longer was on focus. Now, my frustration and confusion was not the result of a naïve believe that one can go about teaching without ever resorting to more directive modes of teaching. My frustration emerged because I finally had begun to develop some form of image or orientation (a goal) that did not match with what was being experienced and achieved. This dissonance, this tension, was indeed symptomatic of my emerging *purposeful commitment* to something; that something was my object of analysis.

5.2 The Socio-Material and Affective Nature of the Object

Most often, CHAT perspectives are discussed in terms of their emphasis on relational, social nature of human psychology. But the core of CHAT, which makes it different from other perspectives, is precisely its focus on activities as purposeful and as object-oriented. As Anna Stetsenko (2012) has argued across several works,

> The next step in theorizing personhood and human development after establishing their relational character is, in my view, to dialectically expand relationality through the notion that human development is an activist project that is not only imbued with dialogism, ethics, and inter-relatedness but also, and more originary, is grounded in collaborative, purposeful, and answerable deeds ineluctably colored by visions of and commitments to a particular project of social transformation. (p. 147)

In this sense, psychological and/or learning phenomena are to be understood in their inherent connection to issues of will and freedom, which—as Vygotsky's instrumental method has it—are as much about mastering one's own psyche and personality as they are about socio-political struggle for controlling the instrumental, material conditions of one's own life. Accordingly, and in the case of my investigation, I was not just experiencing something individual. Rather, my feelings and subjective experiences as I was attempting to become a member in a community were expressions of the collective work that was invested in running a small, growing, and innovative arts-based primary school. I was both actively involved (agent) and passively subjected to the broader social practice phenomenon that I was trying to understand.[4]

Testifying to the collective, instrumental, multifaceted, and objective-subjective nature of the phenomenon of teaching arts-based education, I could document, through encounters and interviews, how the same "situation" or practice was experienced differently by different members.[5] Indeed, many of my feelings of frustration were shared by several other teachers, particularly those who were new in the school. It was making sense of these experiences that I came then to understand that a core aspect in the school's current practices was the fact that the school had recently moved to a new, larger building, as part of the school's continued expansion.

The prior school year had taken place in another building, which had been home for the school for the last few years. In that smaller building, a few large areas were used by several class groups. The set up allowed for flexible organization of activities and quick uptake of spontaneous initiatives, as teachers could catch up with each other on the spot. If a spontaneous idea came up from a group's activity, this could be communicated quite seamlessly to others in the school and scale up activities, or coordinate to support each other. There was no need for formal training either, as teachers could learn from each other by proximity, and the division of roles was not very defined (teachers could address emerging administrative issues and administrative staff could also step in on pedagogical tasks. But as the school grew bigger (one class per year), the need for a larger building grew too.

The larger building had provided more rooms, allowing for more group classes to have their own spaces. It also had made it more difficult to be flexible and spontaneous, and required of more formal ways of communicating across teachers. Administrative tasks were more numerous and required further specialization and division of labor. Most importantly, all of these changes had taken place without a purposeful development process and/or training involved. New teachers hired responding to new teaching and administrative demand had been enrolled based on pedagogical affinities and interviews and meetings had taken place, but without prior habits or experiences with regards to practicing arts-based education in this particular new socio-material configuration, such measures were little effective.

New teachers described being frustrated over lack of understanding of the school's overall vision as it translates in concrete praxis (just as I was!), but also about what they experienced as tension between their way of teaching and the students' ways of being in classroom. Having grown into particular ways of being in the smaller school, students were struggling too, especially when encountering new teachers who had different habits and expectations than those they were used to. More experienced staff who had been working in the school longer, in turn, yearned for the spontaneous and fluid way of working they had before, and expressed concerns and need for changes to address the new situation.

Here we see clearly how the subjective experiences of all those who worked and learned at the school were intrinsically tied to the instrumental, historical, cultural organization of the teaching and learning activities. These activities exist across material and organizational dimensions as much as they do exist across personal and interpersonal dimensions. Psychological phenomena here appear as socio-historical, political and collective processes that involve— again, as Vygotsky had it—the purposeful mastery of one's own life conditions. Research objects from this perspective are therefore as much subjective as they are objective, as much personal as they are political.

5.3 *Knowing Your Research Object as the Power to Transform Reality*

In the spectator theory of knowledge that Dewey was critiquing, and to which CHAT offers an alternative framework, knowing is conceived in terms of intellectual grasping, where the researcher's gaze is supposed to examine its object without somehow "contaminating" the object's "objectivity." The aim is to "understand" without necessarily engaging with the object in any personal way. However, in my own process of coming to see and grasp or understand my object of study, the process of caring and actually being invested—both emotionally and intellectually—was key. Thus, coming to terms and understanding my research object—arts-based education through participant observation—was inherently tied with my developing the will and commitment to actually pursue the object—the praxis of teaching and learning through the arts—as a goal, as an envisioned end that had psychological but also and at the same time material, ethical and normative dimensions. In participating in the practice, I realized that I was immersed, as my colleagues and learners were, in the task of making that very same practice I wanted to understand. It is that will that allowed me to feel frustration, excitement, and to start discerning between what was relevant and what was not relevant. A field of significance emerged before my eyes not because the practice I wanted to study was out there for me to observe it, but because I begun participating in the task of making it, and could then be caught up, see and understand, the cultural, affective, social and cognitive currents of being with which one starts to correspond to as one starts to become a knowledgeable participant. For practices do not simply happen upon subjects; they also engage them, albeit with diverse degrees of agency.

Once understanding is considered as inherently tied to will, the division between knowledge and action that classical approaches to learning inherit is erased, and with this erasure, the political and material nature of knowing comes together. Knowing, as others have put it, is an *activist* task (Stetsenko, 2009). In Vygotsky's original terms, and when it comes to my ethnography, the process of understanding was one of instrumental method, of transforming the tools (practical and psychological) by means of which the schools' activities (and by extension, the participants' experiences thereof) were organized. Understanding the "teaching and learning through the arts" grew in the form of a reflective process in which I, together with schoolteachers, administration and school leaders, started exploring new ways of conceiving and of making the socio-material conditions that allowed for the school's everyday activities. This was a process of re-instrumentalization and where, most importantly, we came to (re-)define what was that we were doing (the object!). We did this not just in words but also through changing the material conditions of our activities. We did change the way the school spaces were used, the time and division of roles, as well as the pedagogical concepts and ideas being used. We did re-organize the conditions upon which each one of us participated in the collective object of sustaining teaching and learning so that the arts-based practices that had been successful in prior years could go on in the new circumstances. This was a process of changing the instruments that allowed us to master our own relations and ways of being in the school. Through the CHAT lenses that inform my work, the research project became thus, at the same time, an emancipatory project: a project of understanding as the project of purposeful transformation of reality.

6   How Does the Chapter Address the Challenges of a Non-Dualist Methodology?

This chapter discusses a participant ethnography conducted in arts-based primary school from a non-dualist perspective that elaborates and illustrates how the research involves overcoming the subjective-objective dichotomy otherwise assumed in classical approaches. Throughout the case, Jornet describes how the research object—the object of "participant observation," emerges and evolves in and through the researcher's evolving participation in the school setting. The chapter starts by narrating the gradual but radical epistemological transformation process that the author underwent as he moved from his initial education in cognitive psychology to the development of a research practice consistent with a CHAT epistemology, describing the personal challenges he—as student and later as scholar—experienced through this transformation. Weaving a criticism of dualist perspectives in the narrative, Jornet discusses the dialectic relation between object and subject as this is conceived in CHAT, and the ensuing implications for researchers interested in ethnographic methods. Rather than a "spectator" aiming at observing some external and hence "objective" knowledge object, research itself consists in the sensuous, subjective but equally objective material activity that the researcher gets involved into and aims at capturing. Here, the acts of describing and of analyzing become acts of mutual transformation, where both research object and research subject change. The chapter restates the importance and illustrates the significance of the concept of object-oriented activity with regards to concrete methodological considerations. It grounds the discussion on Vygotsky's notion of instrumental method, and elaborates on how psychological instruments, as language and art, emerge in and through object-oriented activities as means to transform the participants' own life conditions so as to meet emerging needs and the resolving of historical contradictions. These contradictions, far from only being abstract concepts, are described through the arts-based school case as emerging both affectively and practically. In this way, the chapter also illustrates how, in and through CHAT informed research, the classical dichotomy of thinking on the one hand, and of feeling and acting on the other, is overcome, leading to enhanced opportunities for research to have import to social and lived practices.

Notes

1 For a discussion on quantitative—qualitative dichotomies in social science research, see Ercikan and Roth (2006).
2 See Jornet and Damsa (2021), for a more detailed description of the case study.
3 This is not (only) a proud's parent perspective. It is the feedback we got from teachers too. Among them, a remark by a new teacher, who had joined the school in the middle of the school year, stood out: At first, she had not realized that our daughter had just moved into Canada just a few months back. She had noticed she was not native, but was convinced and had assumed—based on her language competence—that our daughter had lived in the country for years.
4 On agentive and subjective moments of experiencing, see Roth and Jornet (2014).
5 In a lecture titled "The problem of the environment," Vygotsky (1994) discusses precisely this issue of a shared situation being experienced by different individuals in different ways, arguing that a proper category of "experience" must be understood as the unity of person and environment, where environments are refracted differently through experience, while being intrinsically connected to those experiences.

References

Atkinson, P., & Hammersley, M. (1994). Ethnography and participant observation. In N. K. Denzin & Y. S. Lincoln (Eds.), *Handbook of qualitative research* (pp. 248–261). Sage Publications

Cornwall, A., & Jewkes, R. (1995). What is participatory research? *Social Science & Medicine, 41,* 1667–1676.

Dewey, J. (1929). *The quest for certainty: A study of the relation of knowledge and action.* Minton, Balch & Company.

Ercikan, K., & Roth, W.-M. (2006). What good is polarizing research into qualitative and quantitative? *Educational Researcher, 35,* 14–23.

Forsey, M. (2010). Ethnography as participant listening. *Ethnography, 11*(4), 558–572.

Ingold, T. (2014). That's enough about ethnography! *HAU: Journal of Ethnographic Theory, 4*(1), 383–395.

Ingold, T. (2018). Between science and art: An anthropological odyssey. In S. Bergmann & F. Clingerman (Eds.), *Arts, religion, and the environment: Exploring nature's texture* (pp. 96–114). Brill.

Jornet, A. (2019). Living the praxis of method, or how I learned letting worldly practices organize my professional gaze as scholar. In J. C. Richards & Roth, W.-M. (Eds.), *Empowering students as self-directed learners of qualitative research methods: Transformational practices for instructors and students.* Brill.

Jornet, A., & Damsa, C. (2021). Unit of analysis from an ecological perspective: Beyond the individual/social dichotomy. *Learning, Culture, and Social Interaction.* doi:10.1016/j.lcsi.2019.100329

Jornet, A., Eisemann, M., & Chóliz, M. (2009, July). *Pattern of use of mobile phone in Norwegian adolescents: A crosscultural comparison between Spanish and Norwegian teenagers* [Poster presentation]. 11th European Congress of Psychology, Oslo, Norway.

Lave, J., & Wegner, E. (1991). *Situated learning: Legitimate peripheral participation.* Cambridge University Press.

Leontiev, A. N. (1978). *Activity, consciousness, and personality.* Prentice Hall.

Marx, K., & Engels, F. (1998). *The German ideology.* Prometheus Books.

Mikhailov, F. T. (2001). The 'other within' for the psychologist. *Journal of Russian & East European Psychology, 39*(1), 6–31.

Rorty, R. (1979). *Philosophy and the mirror of nature.* Princeton University Press.

Roth, W.-M., & Jornet, A. (2013). Situated cognition. *WIREs Cognitive Science, 4,* 463–478.

Roth, W.-M., & Jornet, A. (2014). Towards a theory of experience. *Science Education, 98,* 106–126.

Roth, W.-M., & Jornet, A. (2017). *Understanding educational psychology: A late Vygotskian, Spinozist approach.* Springer.

Stetsenko, A. (2009). Teaching-learning and development as activist projects of hjistorical becoming: Expanding Vygotsky's approach to pedagogy. *Pedagogies: An International Journal, 5,* 6–16.

Stetsenko, A. (2012). Personhood: An activist project of historical becoming through collaborative pursuits of social transformation. *New Ideas in Psychology, 30,* 144–153.

Suchman, L. (1987). *Plans and situated actions. The problem of human machine communication.* Cambridge University Press.

Surmava, A. (2018). Spinoza in the science of object-oriented activity. *Mind, Culture, and Activity, 25*(4), 365–377.

Vygotsky, L. S. (1989). Concrete human psychology. *Soviet Psychology, 27*(2), 53–77.

Vygotsky, L. S. (1997a). *The collected works of L. S. Vygotsky. Vol. 3: Problems of the theory and history of psychology.* Plenum.

Vygotsky, L. S. (1997b). *The collected works of L. S. Vygotsky. Vol. 4. The history of the development of higher mental functions.* Plenum.

CHAPTER 10

A Reflection on CHAT's History and Direction
Interview with Michael Cole

Patricia Dionne and Alfredo Jornet

To conclude our book, we decided to conduct an interview with a scholar whose work has profoundly shaped the field of CHAT and whose contributions were key to making this approach known outside of the Soviet Union and relevant to international issues of cultural and cross-cultural research: Professor Michael Cole.[1] His seminal work with the Fifth Dimension involving after-schooling programs for diversity has served as models and inspiration for many on how to do "CHAT in the wild" research (Cole & The Distributed Literacy Consortium, 2006). Through the interview, Cole shares his experience as a long-established researcher, with specific and rich historical experience of relevance to the methodological and epistemological challenges and opportunities of CHAT practice that have been covered throughout the chapters in this volume.

We conducted this interview with the idea that the initial questions that we asked at the outset of this book (see Chapter 1, Introduction) should be posed here anew:
– How can we make visible, for outsiders and novices as well as for colleagues and practitioners, the lived world of doing CHAT research, the approach's living praxis of method?
– What are the concrete challenges faced in the pursuit of a non-dualist approach in actual inquiry?
– How can we apprehend theoretical notions such as the unity of theory and practice in methodological terms?
– What are the "real life" stakes and implications involved in confronting deeply ingrained and long-standing beliefs and attitudes concerning the dualism between person and society, and between a "subjective" soul and an objective "body"?
– How do these otherwise theoretical and abstract problems exist in, and as, practical matters of living inquiry and method?

The interview has been transcribed and edited, in collaboration with Mike, and using a thematic analysis that assisted us in re-grouping central themes around the epistemological and methodological questions that are discussed throughout the book. We add titles to structure the text and inserted clarifying comments in brackets.

1 On the Roots of CHAT as a Unifying Approach

Editor's note: We began the conversation by thanking Professor Cole for having accepted our invitation to participate in a chat about CHAT's history and development, and by asking how he would describe the foundations of historical cultural theory to a newcomer; a prominent insider's account of the early days of CHAT as an international approach followed.

Editors: Perhaps the first question to ask is about the origins of CHAT in relation to the broad field of cultural-historically oriented research inspired by Vygotsky?

Michael: The term, CHAT, is an acronym for Cultural-Historical Activity Theory. It brings together two interconnected lineages of research: Cultural-historical is the term currently used by those who claim Vygotsky as their inspiration. It combines two different terms: cultural-historical and activity theory. The central concept in Vygotsky's cultural-historical theory was sign/semiotic/cultural mediation. The term, Activity is the central concept used by A. N. Leontiev, Vygotsky's junior colleague, as their inspiration. Bringing the two terms together is a commitment to the idea that mediation and activity are complementary aspects of a single life process.

Editors: What are the sources of your own experience that brought you to the idea of CHAT?

Michael: For many years, stemming from my cross-cultural on the cognitive consequences of schooling in Liberia and Mexico, I took it for granted that human learning and development have to be studied in their cultural context. Our research began with the question of why rural Liberian children found mathematics taught in school especially difficult to learn. The work began with ethnographic observation of both classrooms and a variety of everyday indigenous activities involving mathematical knowledge (farming, building houses, measuring cloth). Our reasoning was motivated by nothing more than the commonsense notion that if you want to teach someone how to carry out culturally valued activities, you need to begin by understanding the learner's current state of knowledge about those activities in addition to your own experience and expertise.

This work was carried out before I had begun seriously to study either Vygotsky's ideas or Leontiev's, so our notion of activity was a common sense one. When we were first exposed to Leontiev's ideas by James Wertsch (1981), we were attracted to his focus on activities of weavers at a spinning wheel as an example of an activity because we were in fact interested in weaving as one of the community's valued activities.

From our prior readings of Vygotsky we found it perfectly relevant to include mediated action as a central constituent of the activities we were studying. A decade later, when we first began to develop the idea of designing and implementing new forms of educational activity as a research strategy, my colleagues and I drew liberally from Vygotsky, Leontiev, and Luria as well as a variety of American and Western European social scientists for theoretical inspiration and appropriate methods of research (LCHC, 1982; Newman et al., 1989).

The origin of the acronym, CHAT, and its use in cultural-historical discourse can be traced back to a conference in Utrecht in 1985 where I first met Yrjo Engeström. My talk adopted a "cultural context theory" to study the relationships between learning, culture and education in post-colonial countries. I illustrated this approach using a typical Vygotskian triangle to represent "culturally mediated action in social context." Yrjo and Marianne Hedegaard gave a paper on the use of models in the teaching of history. They employed the "expanded triangle" to represent mediated classroom activity (Engeström & Hedegaard, 1985).

I immediately recognized my habitual representation of a "mediational triangle" as a subset of their more inclusive approach. It included mediated action that I was interested in as part of a systemic whole in a principled and plausible way. It linked the concepts of activity and context in a manner that allowed Yrjo several years later (Engeström, 1993) to declare that "the activity is the context." Yrjo's formulation of a convergent cultural historical (Vygotskian) activity theory (Leontievian) way of thinking promised a way to synthesize the two poles of a binary, stimulus-response formulation, a common goal for both Vygotsky and Leontiev. Fortunately, the following year we were both attended

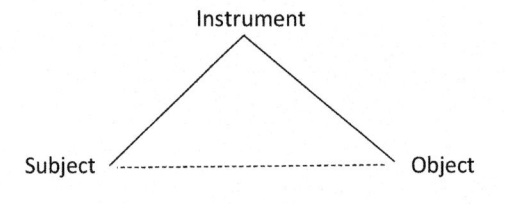

FIGURE 10.1
Model of the structure of learning activity, inspired by Engeström and Hedegaard (1985, p. 189)

the international conference in Berlin where the International Society of Cultural Research and activity (ISCRAT) was formed where we had the opportunity to explore the overlap between our approaches.

As luck would have it, during this period I was engaged with Russian psychologists and educationalists on the design of computer-mediated instructional activities for elementary school children, which allowed me to visit Yrjo in Finland in route. These visits permitted us to work on the many questions that needed resolution if we were to successfully articulate the relationship between these competing approaches.

Yrjo joined the faculty at UCSD; not long after that, we initiated the first international journal addressing these issues, Mind, Culture, and Activity. Over the decades, we have each developed our different "flavors" of CHAT. Both rely on the method of dual stimulation which we elaborate upon differently in ways appropriate to research questions we focus on and the populations and institutions we study. Yrjo and his colleagues in Finland developed the idea of developmental work research via the Change Laboratory focused on the work practices of adults. I focused on the general question of culture's role in development and the influence of formal education during ontogeny and social history. In this work, carried out as part of the overall LCHC remit to study the social causes of social inequality, issues of cultural diversity and educational equity have always been a focus of concern. It has been a long and productive professional collaboration.

2   Questions of Methodology

2.1   *On Dualisms and Overcoming Them*
Editors: One shared concern of CHAT's scholars is the problem of dualism and the importance of overcoming them in our methodological practices.

Michael: At the most general level I believe it is fair to say that all of those who engage in some form of Vygotskian-inspired approach to learning and development anti-dualist in general, and anti-Cartesian. This is certainly true of Vygotsky who is famous for his ideas about the fusion of language and thought as well as thought and emotion.

The dualism that gave rise to the division between Vygotsky and Leontiev is an apt example of how difficult the problem can become. Both worked within a tradition that drew upon Marx and Engels, Hegel and Spinoza, yet they and their intellectual progeny parted ways in their interpretations of the role of the environment in human development.

Shortly before his death, Vygotsky (1933–34/1998) characterized the issue as follows:

> We admit in words that it is necessary to study the personality and the environment of the child as a unit, but we must not think that the influence of the personality is on one side and the influence of the environment on the other side, that the one and the other act the way external forces do. However, exactly this is actually done frequently: wishing to study the unity, preliminarily investigators break it down, then try to unite one thing with another. (p. 292)

He found his own answer to this problem by arguing that experience (*perezhivanie*)[2] is the unity of person and environment, a unit of analysis in which emotion and thought, thinking and speaking are united as constituents of "the actual dynamics of the unity of consciousness." Some idea of the complexity of these dynamics is indicated in his summary of the process he is referring to:

> To state a certain, general, formal position, it would be correct to state that the environment determines the development of the child through the child's perezhivanie of the environment. (Vygotsky, 1933–34/1998, p. 294)

This formulation placed *perezhivanie* at the center of a variety of hot button ideological issues, not the least was the relationship of the ideal and the material, central to any cultural-historical theory. Stalin had strong views about the politically correct understanding of this issue, consistent with his own form of totalitarianism. One cannot understand the arguments among academics that ensued without taking seriously into consideration the historical moment in which they occurred.

Six months after Vygotsky died, Stalin used the excuse of the murder of a popular Party leader from Leningrad to consolidate his power initiating the Great Purges. In 1936, the Central Committee of the Communist Party issued a decree abolishing Pedology, Vygotsky's home discipline, as a recognized science. Leontiev's critique of Vygotsky's paper was written in 1937 when terror was at its height (in Russian the purges are often referred to simply as 37 (The Year of "37"). This historical context, which brought terror to the entire society makes it's difficult to interpret and evaluate Leontiev's criticisms. As his son noted many decades later, it was an existential necessity for Leontiev to offer some form of criticism of Vygotsky using the offensive language of Stalinist politics—not only his job, but his life was at stake (Asmolov, 2000; Leontiev, 2005). The article did not vilify Vygotsky, despite its critical tone regarding Pedology as a whole. After an extended discussion of the key theoretical concepts in dispute, Leontiev (2005) ends with the following summary of Vygotsky's work. Note its internal incoherence. In the first half of the final paragraph, he writes:

> Of course, we are far from believing that the concept of perezhivanie is an empty concept. On the contrary, we believe that this concept, along with the concept of meaning, as well as numerous other concepts introduced into Soviet psychology by Vygotsky, truly enrich it and bring an essential vitality and concreteness to our psychological analysis. It would be crude nihilism to simply discard the beneficial content that they represent ... (p. 27)

He then undercuts these sympathetic evaluations with the caveat that

> These concepts must be introduced into psychology, but they absolutely must be introduced differently from the way that Vygotsky did. Each concrete proposition, each fact lying at their basis, must first be critically refined and interpreted from the position of a coherent materialistic psychological theory. (Leontiev, 2005, p. 27)

The contradictory messages within the final paragraph illustrate the problem of separating legitimate (if eventually incorrect) criticism from ideologically driven character assassination. Under other circumstances (the Oxford debating society, for example), Leontiev's essay might be interpreted as normal, even mild, academic argumentation. (e.g., *You have almost the right parts, but you are organizing them according to the proper whole*). In its historical context of the Great Terror, however, the essay signaled publicly that he was separating himself from Vygotsky and all of his colleagues who adhered to their Vygotskian roots (which he had already done, de facto, several years earlier on similar philosophical, not political, grounds).

For our present purposes, its sufficient to comment that the serious points in dispute between Leontiev and Vygotsky about the dynamics of development exist to this day, more or less stripped of their Soviet ideological and historical context (Zavershneva, 2014, p. 90).[3] Superseding the dualism between Vygotsky's "sign-o-centricism" and Leontiev's "activity-o-centric" theory remains a just-out-of-reach goal, worthy, perhaps even, an essential motive, for developing a coherent science of human development.

2.2 Dualisms in Cross-Cultural Research

Editors: Could you reflect whether and how, more concretely, you have encountered dichotomies in your own research work?

Michael: From the moment I began to conduct research on education and development in rural Liberia in the 1960's, I have understood that the analysis of cultural diversity in human development must begin with a deep understanding of the modes of life of the people involved. But my professional toolkit as a psychologist did not include the methods for acquiring such knowledge. The study of the social contexts within which our tasks were presented was the domain of the anthropologists, sociologists, and linguists. Fortunately for me, the project I was assigned to work on cobbled together sufficient disciplinary breadth to launch a series of studies with adequate inter-disciplinary support.

For the rest of my career, I have worked in teams, sometimes as leader, sometimes as part of a group that included as many relevant disciplinary and social backgrounds as possible. One good example is the project on literacy on literacy among the Vai of Liberia headed by Sylvia Scribner (Scribner & Cole, 1981). The fact that the Vai had invented and were using a writing system but did not teach the use of the system in a formal system offered a rare opportunity to test several hypotheses about the cognitive consequences of literacy.

We used a combination of methods that included ethnographic observation of the uses of written Vai, a sociological questionnaire to ascertain the social correlates of Vai literacy, commonly used experimental tasks that had previously demonstrated that schooling enhances a variety of forms of cognitive performance, and specially designed cognitive tasks modeled on the uses of written Vai observed in the ethnographic research. We found that the cognitive consequences of acquiring Vai literacy were closely tied to the functions of the specific activities that such literacy enabled. Vai literates were superior to non-literates of those who acquired English literacy in school when asked to analyze oral Vai in terms of syllables. They were superior to non-literate Vai when carrying out tasks that mimicked the practice of letter writing. But they showed no general changes in cognitive performance.

These overall findings support the conclusion that the cognitive consequences of literacy (and by extension of any form of mediated activity) are a function of the range of practices that require the ability to use written language in particular practice in a given society; as the practices become more general, so do the cognitive consequences. Vai literacy, restricted in use as it was, produced correspondingly restricted cognitive consequences.

In terms of the concern about binaries, this research provides an example of how widespread binaries associated with the concept of literacy can be the starting point for systematic research that takes seriously into account both mediational means and the activity systems they mediate. Unfortunately, at this point in our research, we hit an insuperable barrier. As outsiders to Vai society-rich white non-Vai speaking people and their rich Americo-Liberian sponsors, we were totally unprepared to study the "cognitive ecology" as a foundation for discovering a representative sample of everyday practices and circumstances associated with improved, experimentally controlled performance and school success. Knowledge of mundane problem-solving activities of a particular group of people presupposes a detailed description of the language and culture of these people at a level which few ethnographers (let alone cross-cultural psychologists) have achieved. Finding little in either the ethnographic or the cross-cultural psychology literature to encourage us, we decided to study the representativeness of experimental, cognitive tasks in the everyday life of a culture we knew well—our own.

3 The Problem of Ecological Validity

Editors: This seems to relate to the question of ecological validity. You often emphasize the need for researchers to consider carefully the ecological validity of the tasks that they use to gain evidence about children's development. Ecological validity is not term one associates with either Vygotsky or Leontiev. Why do you find it so important?

Michael: For me, the most accessible discussion of ecological validity comes from the work of Urie Bronfenbrenner. Bronfenbrenner (1979) insisted that in order to be ecologically valid, research must fulfill three conditions. First, it must maintain the integrity of the real-life situations it is designed to investigate. Second, it must be faithful to the larger social and cultural context from which the subjects. Third the analysis must be consistent with the participant's definition of the situation, by which he means that the experimental manipulations and outcomes must be shown to be quotes perceived by the participants in a manner consistent with the conceptual definitions explicit and implicit in the research design.

The fact of the matter, as Bronfenbrenner and many others have pointed out, is that these requirements are often overlooked and when they are not, they can be very difficult to satisfy in practice.[4] The first and second mean that the experimental task must representative of the same task occurring in a variety of identifiable situations elsewhere in people's lives. In Bronfenbrenner's memorable admonition, the study of learning and development should not be more than the "the science of strange behavior of children in strange situations." The third requirement means that researchers have to be certain that the people they study interpret the task in the same way that the researcher does. When this condition is not met, it is impossible to distinguish between poor performance and failure to interpret the task as required ("properly").

Fifty years ago, Jerome Bruner and I summarized the implications of these requirements for educational research:

> (a) Formal experimental equivalence of operations does not insure de facto equivalence of experimental treatments; (b) different subcultural groups are predisposed to interpret the experimental stimuli (situations) differently; I different subcultural groups are motivated by different concerns relevant to the experimental task; (d) in view of the inadequacies of experimentation, inferences about lack of competence among black children are unwarranted. (Cole & Bruner, 1971, p. 869)

When differences are invalidly evaluated as deficits, the deficiency is created by the assessment and the subsequent treatment. Importantly, the subsequent pedagogical interventions often exacerbate the problem. In a sense, our strategy in the early cross-cultural research of creating experiments as models of cultural practices in context was an exercise in the study of ecological validity.

In the fall of 1976, we undertook a study with 17 children 8–10 years of age who attended a small, racially, and economically diverse private school in mid Manhattan, New York City. Our approach was as direct as it was simple-minded. We video and audio tape-recorded activities of the children in a range of settings: their classroom activities, and an afterschool club where they engaged a variety of tasks involving reading, writing, problem solving such as baking cakes or building elementary electrical circuits. We also recorded hour-long testing sessions during which each child individually was presented a variety of laboratory-derived cognitive tasks. We were fully aware that we were sampling a limited set of situations, but we hoped that our observations would allow us to identify cognitive tasks and how children performances change depending on the setting.

The series of cognitive tests we selected was meant to be representative of tests used to predict and evaluate scholastic aptitude or cognitive development. Additionally, we sought, insofar as possible, test instruments that made visible what the child was doing. We also tried to sample widely from the spectrum of task demands that we imagined might be encountered in school and various non-school environments.

Our test battery included modified versions of the word similarities subtest of the Wechsler Intelligence Scale for Children (WISC), a mediated memory test first developed by A. N. Leontiev in 1929, a figure-matching task of the sort used to assess impulsivity, a syllogistic reasoning task, and a classification task employing common household objects. These tests were administered by a professional tester who did not know the purpose of the study. We suffered from no illusion that this set of tasks exhausted the possible list of intellectual demands that children encounter daily. But we were confident that they were relevant to at least the classroom.

We began observing in the children's classroom to see if: (a) we could specify the ways in which the children responded to intellectual tasks there, and (b) we could observe the occurrence of any task that could be administered to the children in a later test session. Ultimately, we wanted to determine if children responded to a given task similarly or differently in the classroom, afterschool and test situations, but we wanted first simply to establish that we could identify cognitive tasks and the children's responses to them in the classroom. We videotaped samples of many kinds of classroom activities: directed lessons (such as an exercise in division or classification of the animal kingdom), individual study time (during which the teacher passed from student to student, checking on and assisting in a variety of assignments), group discussion of social interactional problems that arise in the classroom, and individual "free time" during which children could elect to engage in any one of a number of activities including drawing, playing board games, reading, keeping a diary, etc.

Initially we were encouraged because we seemed to be able to identify the occurrence of various cognitive tasks in the course of our classroom observations. Activities resembling classification, free recall, paired associate learning and a number of other well-studied experimental tasks could be found as a natural part of the children's activities, particularly during formally organized lessons.

To be certain, the tasks as encountered in the classroom were not isomorphic with the laboratory tasks. Nor were they constantly occurring; a good deal of time it appeared that "nothing was happening." But our initial results suggested that something like laboratory-style cognitive tasks in the test setting could be identified in actual school settings, so we had a starting point for making inter-situational comparisons with the less structured afterschool activities.

Midway into the fall, we also began to observe these same children in afterschool clubs. Half the children attended a club that emphasized nature activities while the remainder constituted a cooking club. These club sessions, which lasted one and one half to two hours, were conducted in a specially prepared playroom at The Rockefeller University where audio and visual recording equipment allowed us to obtain a relatively complete record of what the children said and did during their activities. These activities included preparing various dishes (cakes, breads, entire meals), training animals, growing plants, experimenting with electricity, and a variety of similar "constructing" tasks. The children's behavior was not rigidly controlled, but we did attempt to structure the activities by varying the extent to which successful completion depended on information available from written instructions, the club leader, and other children.

The most striking feature of these club sessions was the extreme rarity of identifiable cognitive tasks. If the classroom could be characterized as an environment where cognitive tasks were observable with intervals "doing nothing" interspersed, the club sessions could be characterized as an environment of chaotic activity with identifiable tasks interspersed at rare intervals for fleeting moments. It was certainly not the case that the children were sitting quietly, lost in thought. They were active, argumentative, and constantly busy. But classification, inference, and other tasks we had hoped to discover weren't easily detectable, even after several repeated viewings of our videotaped record. The recipes got read, the cakes baked, and the animals trained.

We found ourselves in the somewhat absurd situation where activities that clearly required the cognitive processes we were interested in studying have been operating, but we could not identify how these goals were accomplished in a way that was directly related to the intellectual tasks that are the backbone of process-oriented, cognitive psychology. Our initial assumption that we could identify cognitive tasks outside the laboratory and classroom and answer these questions was clearly wrongheaded. But the correct resolution to the difficulty of identifying and analyzing cognitive behavior across settings was not at all obvious.

Two years of analyzing video recordings made clear the difficulties. When working in pairs and small groups the children swiftly, often seamlessly, created a division of labor, shared (and sometimes withheld) information as they attended simultaneously to the task specified by the recipe (how many cups of flower do we need?) and to their social relations, which were often of more interest than whether the cake would get baked in time to eat before the bus came to take the children home. Use case studies of individual children proved possible, as well as group-level descriptions of social problem solving, but by and large, the idea that the cognitive tasks that were the focus of our interest psychological could be considered ecologically valid outside of tests and classroom led us to the conclusion that standardized tests remove features of everyday life settings which renders its laws fundamentally restricted and unrepresentative of the testing environment. It was as if, in creating a vacuum tube, physicists created an environment in which gravity was also inoperative. In such a case, the theory being evaluated will be applicable only to settings which share its restrictions. Our data urged on us the conclusion that many existing cognitive experiments represent the analogue of a gravity-less vacuum tube; they systematically suppress or exclude the interactional influence of individuals on their environments (including other people) that transforms the nature of the task environment in the course of responding to it. Several studies were subsequently designed to explore the consequences of misjudging the invalidity of standardized tests. I will illustrate this logic of measurement and how it can (mis)represent children's competences through two examples.

1. *Oral Language Experience and the Construction of Basel Readers*
My first example is taken from research by William Hall and his associates in the early 1970's (Hall, Nagy, & Linn, 1987). They studied the language experience of poor black children at home and school. The second is taken from the work of Luis Moll and Estaban Diaz on the organization of English language literacy acquisition for English Language Learners in a school with a bilingual teaching program (Moll & Diaz, 1987).

During the 1960's, research initiated in connection with Project Head Start and the War on Poverty sought explanations for ethnic/social class differences in academic performance in the children's environment, particularly the communicative environment of children's homes. These studies found that the amount and qualitative structure of parents' verbal engagement with their young children varied among families differing in education and income; lower economic status was associated with lower performance.

This research subsequently became embroiled in psychometric research on individual and group differences measured by standardized IQ tests (Jensen, 1969). As part of LCHC's work on the study of the social origins of social inequality, William Hall and his research team collected a substantial corpus of everyday speech from 40 pre-school children. Those children were fitted out with little vests, into which were sewn transmitting microphones, so that all of the speech in the child's environment was recorded as well as the child's own speech. Twenty of the families were White and 20 were Black. In each racial group one-half of the families were middle-class and the other half were lower class. The children were between 4½-5 years. Half were male and half female. Recordings were made in 10 different situations spanning a normal day, from home (getting dressed, preparing for school, having breakfast), the transition to school, and several different settings within the classroom. The basic data were 15-minute samples of naturally occurring conversations which were transcribed and then put into a database.

Two results stand out in overall word counts. Firstly, there is a lot more total talk, or at least a lot more words recorded, in homes than in the school, regardless of SES and ethnicity. Secondly, among the four different groups is that the poor Black children hear less total talk not only at home, but at school. A combination of being Black and being poor reduces the overall level of talk experienced.

The issue of ecological validity arose when Hall and his colleagues pursued the implications of this work in relation to assessment instruments such as IQ tests and the formulas used in constructing basal readers. In both cases they found the vocabulary used in the assessment instruments was disproportionately unfamiliar to the poor, black, children. Focusing here just on the implications of the readability formula analysis, it is clear that poor/Black children are confronted with a more difficult task because they are asked to read words that are not in their vocabulary. As Hall and his colleagues noted (p. 479), "If curricula are not changed, we must at least be aware that we are demanding much more of those children whose lives are not represented in the materials they use in school." To date, despite parallel arguments and engagement of pioneers such as Bill Labov in creating appropriate, locally normed reading materials, the misappropriate use of norms continues in many countries.

2. *Phonics before Comprehension Meets the Organization of Bilingual Reading Instruction*

My second example comes from research in which Luis Moll and Estaban Diaz (1987) studied how literacy instruction was organized for Latinx children in a Southern California city. The children had acquired sufficient oral English proficiency to qualify for a program in which they received two reading lessons per day. In one they were taught by a monolingual Anglophone teacher how to read in English. In the other they were taught by a bilingual Latina to read in Spanish.

In each class the children were grouped into a low-, medium-, and high-reading group in a manner still typical of such classrooms. However, the meaning of those labels differed depending upon which lesson, Spanish, or English, they observed. The predominant activity for all of the children in the English language classroom focused on accurate decoding the text phonetically. The teacher paid special attention to providing the children with practice in producing correct word sounds. In fact, all of the lessons emphasized pronunciation skills. For the highest reading group, when issues of comprehension did arise, the teacher provided simplified, structured, question frames that required only one- or two-word answers.

When these same children were observed in the Spanish language program, the results were dramatically different. Here even the low group was involved in comprehension-directed activities while decoding and phonetic drill were virtually absent. For the higher groups, the teacher demanded, and the children provided, inferences and generalizations that went far beyond simple information contained in the text. The very same children who were judged incompetent readers, "stuck on decoding" when instructed in English turned out to be reading for comprehension in their native language. I have always wondered what, theoretically, it could mean for children to be able to speak and comprehend spoken English (according to test results that placed them in the program), to read with comprehension in Spanish, but to be at the very beginnings of "learning how to read" in English? How is such a result produced?

First, there is the ideologically generated standard of correctly pronouncing in English and the stigma attached to language mixing. Its "common sense" that the child needs to pronounce a word correctly before s/he can recognize spell it and therefore read it correctly.

Second, there is the standard theory, then and now, that one begins to teach reading by teaching letter-sound correspondences. Third, there is standardization of the institutional arrangements whereby the Spanish-language and English-language teachers worked on mutually exclusive schedules so that could not compare experiences and where it is acceptable to have a non-bilingual teacher is placed in the English-language half of a bilingual program.

The result of these distortions is to put an interactional glass ceiling over the learning environment of the children in the English-only classroom. They could not even gain access to the language practices that were designed to build their already-considerable literacy skills.

Based on these findings, Moll and Diaz then conducted a very simple intervention to demonstrate that the children's comprehension of English text was far greater than their English-language teacher could imagine, let alone encourage. They arranged to be allowed to teach reading to the children. During the lessons, they asked the students to read the English texts silently, after which they spent time discussing the meaning of the text either in English or Spanish or any combination the two. Under these conditions, the measure of reading levels of the children in English shot up by several grade levels. The misuse of standardized assessments combined with the institutional organization of instruction based on a theory of reading that places decoding before comprehension was causing the achievement gap that they were supposed to be closing.

Unfortunately, to this day the problems revealed by this and other research at LCHC almost half a century ago remain part of the standard practices of educational researchers. At the same time, it has become abundantly clear that cultural differences in the role of literacy in the home and community are intimately tied up with an ecocultural niche of economic precarity and social marginalization of the communities involved. It remains the case that society has created the conditions it laments, blaming the victims for their own circumstances and that education is a major institution for continuing to sort people into those who suffer the outcome and those who are assigned to change it.

4 Lessons Learned

Editors: The only thing we miss that could be a great way to conclude it would be a reflection, from your experienced perspective, on what would be 5 main things you wished less experienced/starting scholars know as they move on into CHAT oriented research? It could be three, perhaps four? main realizations/insights that you think are crucial for today's starting CHAT scholars. As we envisioned, each insight would not need to go longer than a few sentences or a paragraph.

Michael: Whoa! That is a difficult task.

As described elsewhere, for the past forty years I have focused my empirical research on the problem of designing, implementing, and seeking to sustain new forms education of educational activity within the broad, CHAT framework briefly described above (LCHC, 1982). My closely coupled theoretical work has focused on elaborating on the fundamental CHAT principle that development takes place simultaneously at many scales of time and size (Cole, 2006; Packer & Cole, 2020).

As a consequence of my experience it has become clear that a commitment to using CHAT as a theoretical lens entails a variety of special burdens for developmentalists and educators, particularly those who engage in the design and implementation of new forms activity, putatively better than those they replace

1. CHAT research has long been associated progressive political commitments. This is most conspicuously true in the creators of Soviet psychology but it is equally true in the case of scholars from many parts of the world involved in the national liberation movements and academic supporters of the Civil Rights movement in the US, for example. In so far as the implications of your research threaten existing structures of power, do not be surprised if you find it especially difficult to find acceptance of your work. Such research is grounded in a political/ethical commitment that requires both additional labor to enact and even more labor to sustain against the pressure of institutionalized practices and political hostility. That sounds like a hard task, but it also means that you, through your research, get to engage in work that is not only very relevant to society and science, but also quite fulfilling for yourself as individual and as a citizen.

2. Because you are combining theory and practice and because you are advocating for the kinds of changes you hope to see realized (e.g., you are not an "objective" narrator), there is a special need for self-criticism. Research practices such as those employed by the CRADLE collective and my own suggestions for a mesogenetic methodology contain a phase "after the end" in which the mistakes of the past are analyzed in preparation for a re-envisioned new beginning. But they do not fit easily with social science research founded upon the standard laboratory and classroom-level experiment where the analyst defines the context and evaluates the outcome. On the positive side, this implies that research work is also creative work, and so you don't just apply theory, but also generate it through practices and community work in collaboration with others.

3. Because of a commitment to the testing of theory in meaningful social practices, the implementation of CHAT research routinely involves inter-institutional collaborations that reach beyond university settings in ways that require new forms of social organization. Such arrangements are difficult to achieve and difficult to sustain, particularly when one's research runs counter to the institutional practices that one is trying to change. Any scholar entering this line of scholarship should start preparing as early as possible, to obtain the inter-disciplinary, inter-institutional, and intersegmental resources that successful research requires. Engaging in such collaborations, though, is full of opportunities to enrich your research as you engage with the perspectives and resources of others you collaborate with. Interdisciplinary work is both a challenging task, and a precious resource.

4. Many additional difficulties associated with conducting CHAT-inspired research also merit attention, such as the impediments to knowledge growth associated with the fact that it has always been an international undertaking where ignorance of non-native languages and culture have been a major obstacle. Here modern students and practitioners have the enormous advantage of digital communication and translation technologies compared to people of my generation. From my experience, using native language in our research make visible, many competencies that children and adults can mobilize, which remains difficult to trace by using other languages.

Editors: We would like to express our immense gratitude to Professor Michael Cole for these very generous and inspiring reflections, which we believe will be of great relevance to anyone interested in CHAT's history and epistemological premises as a transformational research paradigm.

Notes

1 Distinguished Professor of Communication, Psychology & Human Development, Director Emeritus of the Laboratory of Comparative Human Cognition, University of California, San Diego.
2 For one of many discussions of the Russian term, perezhivanie see Cole and Gajdamaschko (2016).
3 From archival notes (Leontiev, 2005) it is clear that Leontiev was a lot closer to Vygotsky than he publicly admitted to. Leontiev never published this essay. It was discovered in archival files years later.
4 In an important sense, our research on the consequences of schooling and literacy were all directed at the issue of ecological validity.

References

Asmolov, A. G. (2000). LS Vygotsky and modern cultural-historical psychology. *Voprosy psikhologii*, 2, 117.

Bronfenbrenner, U. (1979). *The ecology of human development*. Harvard University Press.

Cole, M. (2006). Culture and cognitive development in phylogenetic, historical development in phylogenetic, historical, and ontogenetic perspective. In D. Kuhn & R. Siegler (Eds.), *Handbook of child psychology, Vol. 2: Cognition, perception and language* (6th ed., pp. 636–685). Wiley.

Cole, M., & Bruner, J. S. (1971). Cultural differences and inferences about psychological processes. *American Psychologist*, 26(10), 867–876. doi:10.1037/h0032240

Cole, M., & Gajdamschko, N. (2016). The growing pervasiveness of perezhivanie. *Mind, Culture, and Activity*, 23(4), 271. doi:10.1080/10749039.2016.1201515

Cole, M., & The Distributed Literacy Consortium. (2006). *The fifth dimension: An after-school program built on diversity*. Russell Sage.

Engeström, Y. (1993). Developmental studies on work as a test bench of activity theory. In S. Chaiklin & J. Lave (Eds.), *Understanding practice: Perspectives on activity and context* (pp. 64–103). Cambridge University Press.

Engeström, Y., & Hedegaard, M. (1985). Teaching theoretical thinking in elementary school: The use of models in history and biology. In E. Bol, J. Haenen, & M. Wolters (Eds.), *Education for cognitive development* (pp. 170–193). S.V.O.

Hall, W. S., Nagy, W. E., & Linn, R. L. (1984). *Spoken words: Effects of situation and social group on oral word usage and frequency*. Erlbaum.

Jensen, A. R. (1969). How much can we boost iq and scholastic achievement? *Harvard Educational Review*, 39(1), 1–23.

Laboratory of Comparative Human Cognition (LCHC). (1982). A model system for the study of learning disabilities. *Quarterly Newsletter of the Laboratory of Comparative Human Cognition*, 4, 39–66.

Leontiev, A. A. (2005). The life and creative path of A.N. Leontiev. *Journal of Russian and East European Psychology, 43*(3), 8–69.

Moll, L. C., & Diaz, S. (1987). Change as the goal of educational research. *Anthropology and Education Quarterly, 18*, 300–311.

Newman, D., Griffin, P., & Cole, M. (1989). *The construction zone*. Cambridge University Press.

Packer, M. J., & Cole, M. (2019). Evolution and ontogenesis: The deontic niche of human development. *Human Development, 62*(2), 175–211.

Scribner, S., & Cole, M. (1981). *The psychology of literacy*. Harvard University Press.

Vygotsky, L. S. (1998). *The collected works of L. S. Vygotsky: Vol. 5. Child psychology*. Plenum Press. (Original work published 1933–34)

Wertsch, J. V. (1981). *The concept of activity in Soviet psychology*. Sharpe.

Zavershneva, E. Y. (2014). The problem of consciousness in Vygotsky's cultural-historical psychology. In A. Yasnitsky, R. van der Veer, & M. Ferrari (Eds.), *The Cambridge handbook of cultural-historical psychology* (pp. 63–97). Cambridge University Press.